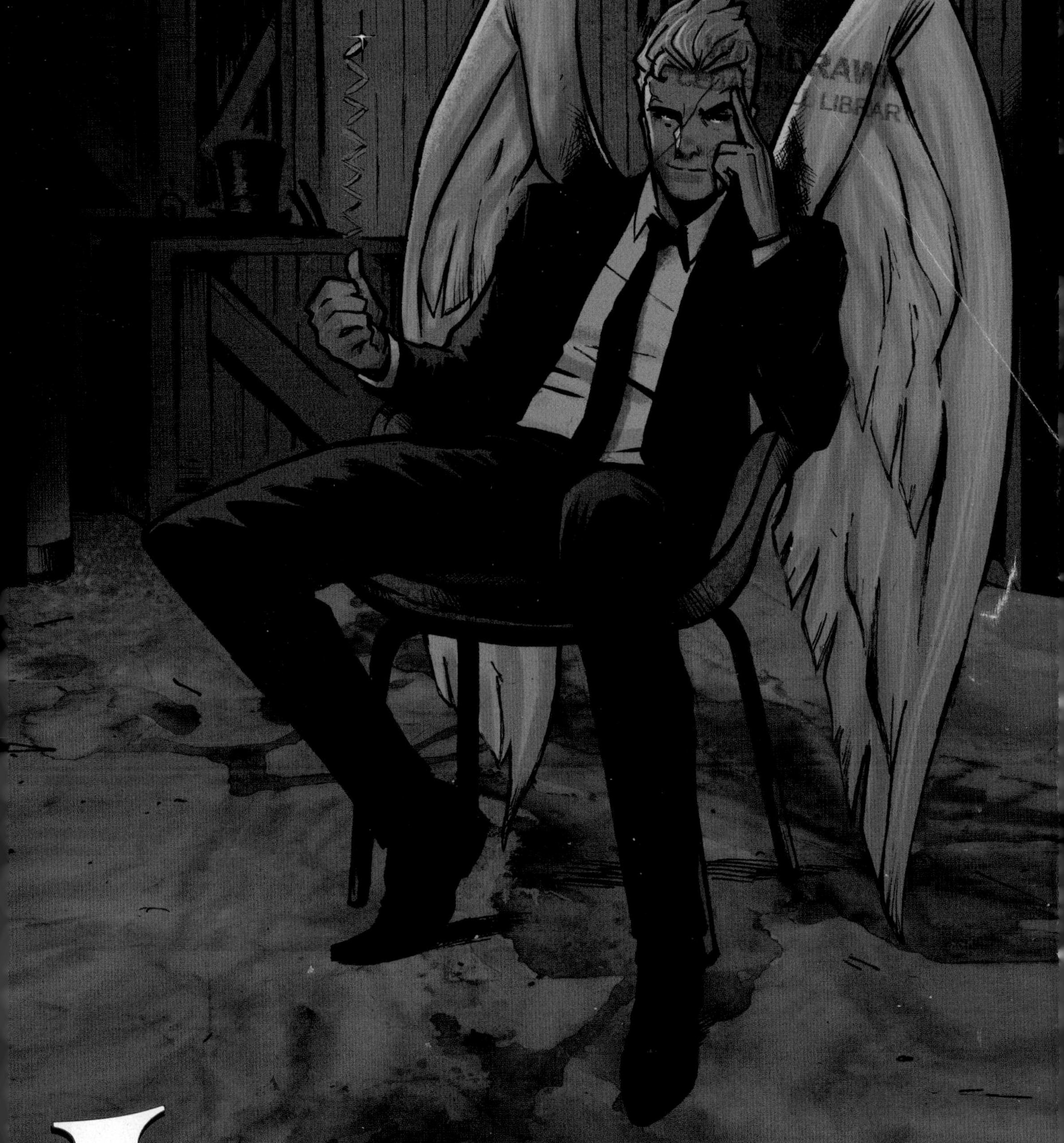

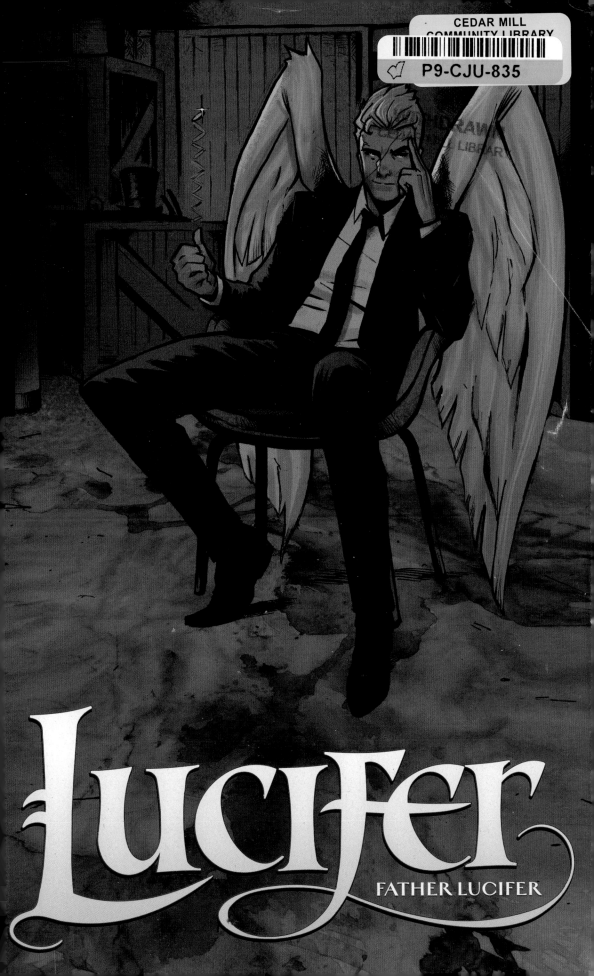

Lucifer

FATHER LUCIFER

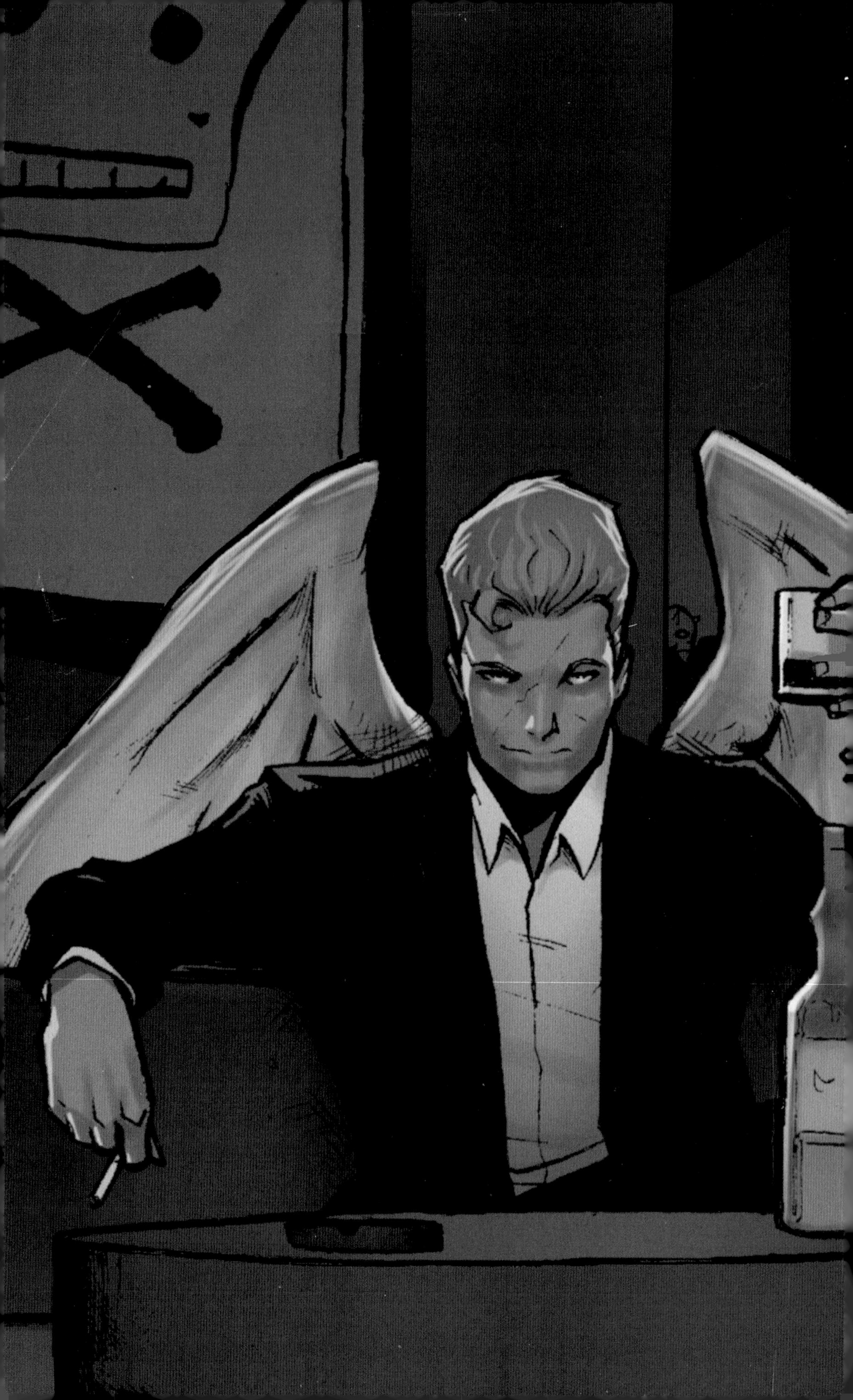

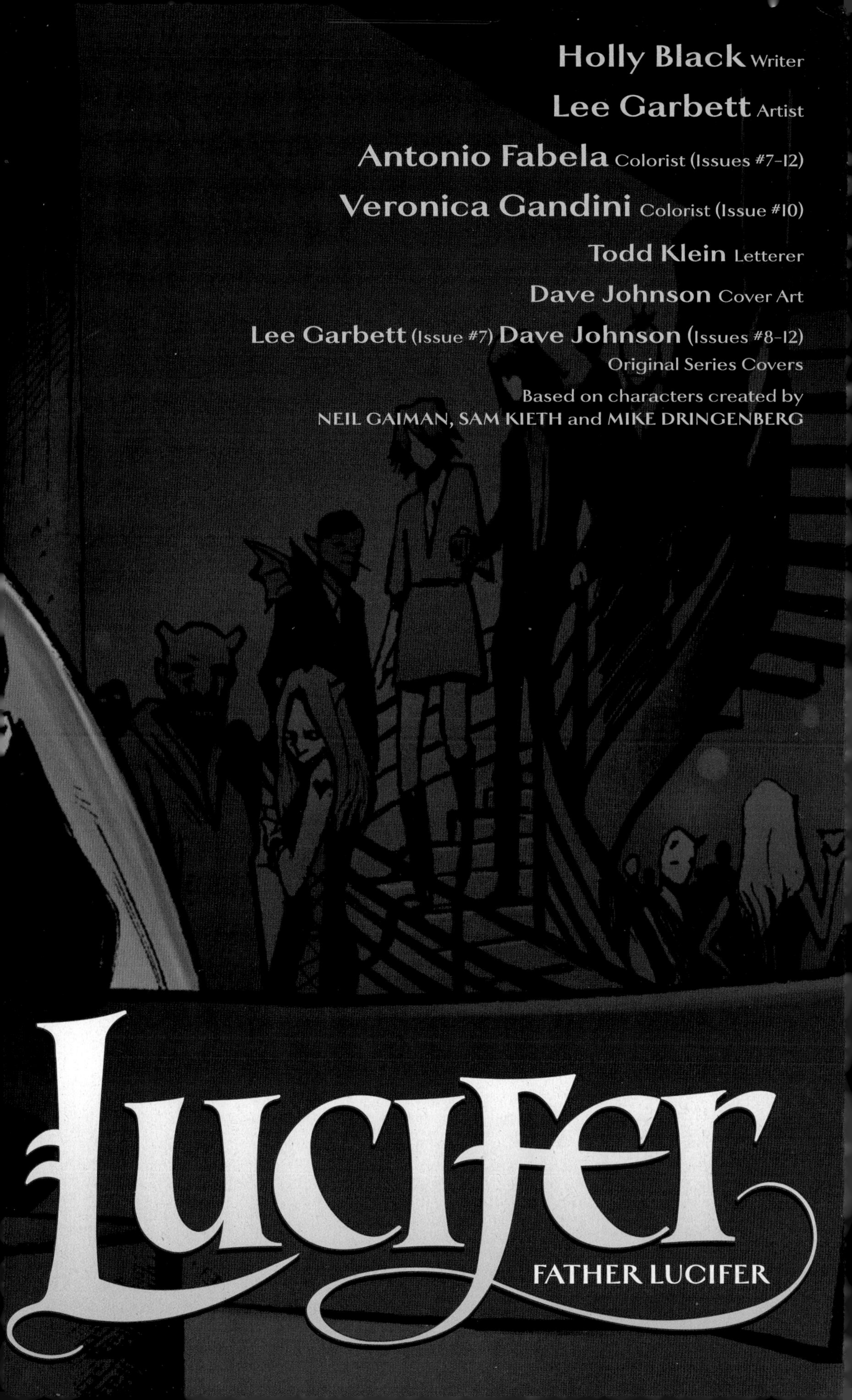

Holly Black Writer

Lee Garbett Artist

Antonio Fabela Colorist (Issues #7–12)

Veronica Gandini Colorist (Issue #10)

Todd Klein Letterer

Dave Johnson Cover Art

Lee Garbett (Issue #7) **Dave Johnson** (Issues #8–12)
Original Series Covers

Based on characters created by
NEIL GAIMAN, SAM KIETH and MIKE DRINGENBERG

Lucifer

FATHER LUCIFER

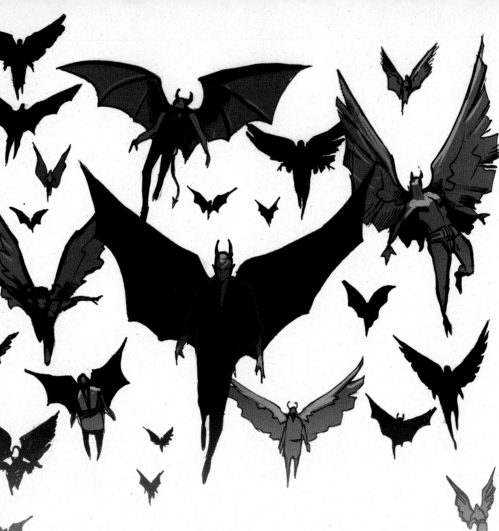

ELLIE PYLE Editor – Original Series
MAGGIE HOWELL Assistant Editor – Original Series
JAMIE S. RICH Group Editor – Vertigo Comics
JEB WOODARD Group Editor – Collected Editions
SCOTT NYBAKKEN Editor – Collected Edition
STEVE COOK Design Director – Books
AMIE BROCKWAY–METCALF Publication Design

DIANE NELSON President
DAN DiDIO Publisher
JIM LEE Publisher
GEOFF JOHNS President & Chief Creative Officer
AMIT DESAI Executive VP – Business & Marketing Strategy,
Direct to Consumer & Global Franchise Management
SAM ADES Senior VP – Direct to Consumer
BOBBIE CHASE VP – Talent Development
MARK CHIARELLO Senior VP – Art, Design & Collected Editions
JOHN CUNNINGHAM Senior VP – Sales & Trade Marketing
ANNE DePIES Senior VP – Business Strategy, Finance &
Administration
DON FALLETTI VP – Manufacturing Operations
LAWRENCE GANEM VP – Editorial Administration &
Talent Relations
ALISON GILL Senior VP – Manufacturing & Operations
HANK KANALZ Senior VP – Editorial Strategy & Administration
JAY KOGAN VP – Legal Affairs
THOMAS LOFTUS VP – Business Affairs
JACK MAHAN VP – Business Affairs
NICK J. NAPOLITANO VP – Manufacturing Administration
EDDIE SCANNELL VP – Consumer Marketing
COURTNEY SIMMONS Senior VP – Publicity & Communications
JIM (SKI) SOKOLOWSKI VP – Comic Book Specialty Sales &
Trade Marketing
NANCY SPEARS VP – Mass, Book, Digital Sales & Trade Marketing

LUCIFER VOL. 2: FATHER LUCIFER

Published by DC Comics. Compilation and all new material
Copyright © 2017 DC Comics. All Rights Reserved.

Originally published in single magazine form as LUCIFER 7–12.
Copyright © 2016 DC Comics. All Rights Reserved. All characters,
their distinctive likenesses and related elements featured in this
publication are trademarks of DC Comics. VERTIGO is a trademark
of DC Comics. The stories, characters and incidents featured in
this publication are entirely fictional. DC Comics does not read or
accept unsolicited submissions of ideas, stories or artwork.

DC Comics
2900 West Alameda Avenue, Burbank, CA 91505
Printed in Canada. First Printing.
ISBN: 978-1-4012-6541-0

Library of Congress Cataloging-in-Publication Data is available.

PEFC Certified

This product is from
sustainably managed
forests, recycled and
controlled sources

PEFC/26-31-02   www.pefc.org

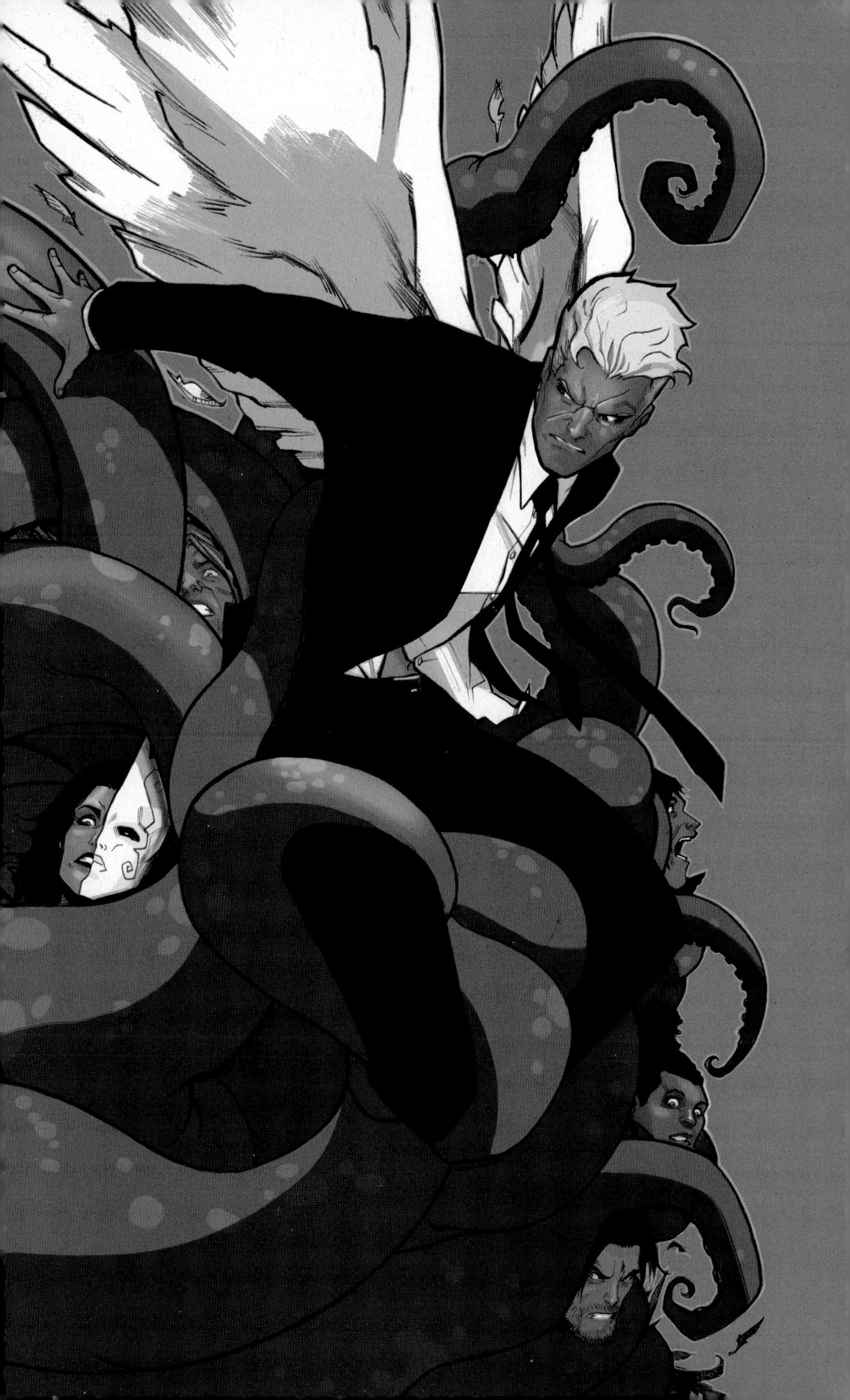

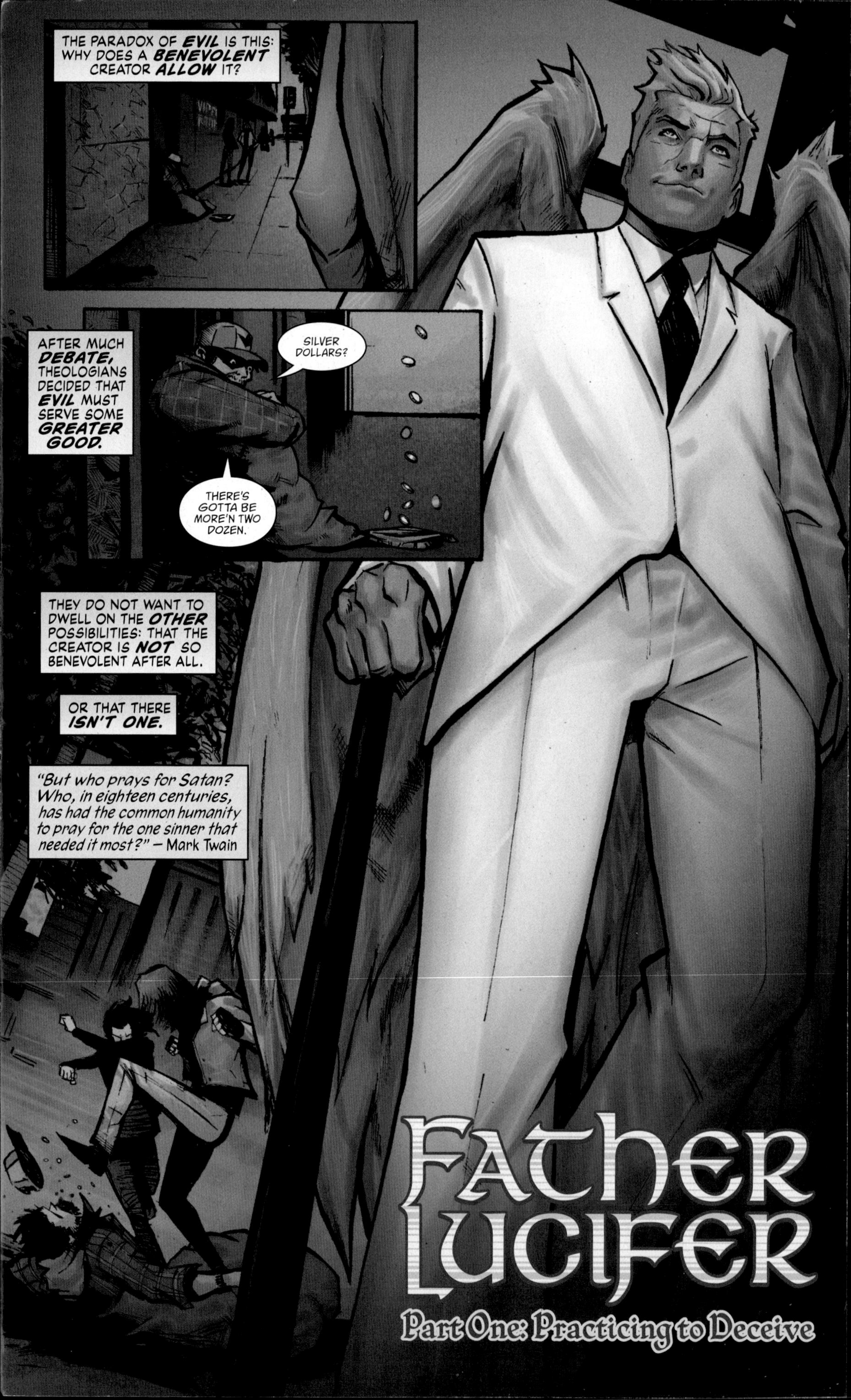
THE PARADOX OF EVIL IS THIS: WHY DOES A BENEVOLENT CREATOR ALLOW IT?
AFTER MUCH DEBATE, THEOLOGIANS DECIDED THAT EVIL MUST SERVE SOME GREATER GOOD.
SILVER DOLLARS?
THERE'S GOTTA BE MORE'N TWO DOZEN.
THEY DO NOT WANT TO DWELL ON THE OTHER POSSIBILITIES: THAT THE CREATOR IS NOT SO BENEVOLENT AFTER ALL.
OR THAT THERE ISN'T ONE.
"But who prays for Satan? Who, in eighteen centuries, has had the common humanity to pray for the one sinner that needed it most?" — Mark Twain
FATHER LUCIFER
Part One: Practicing to Deceive

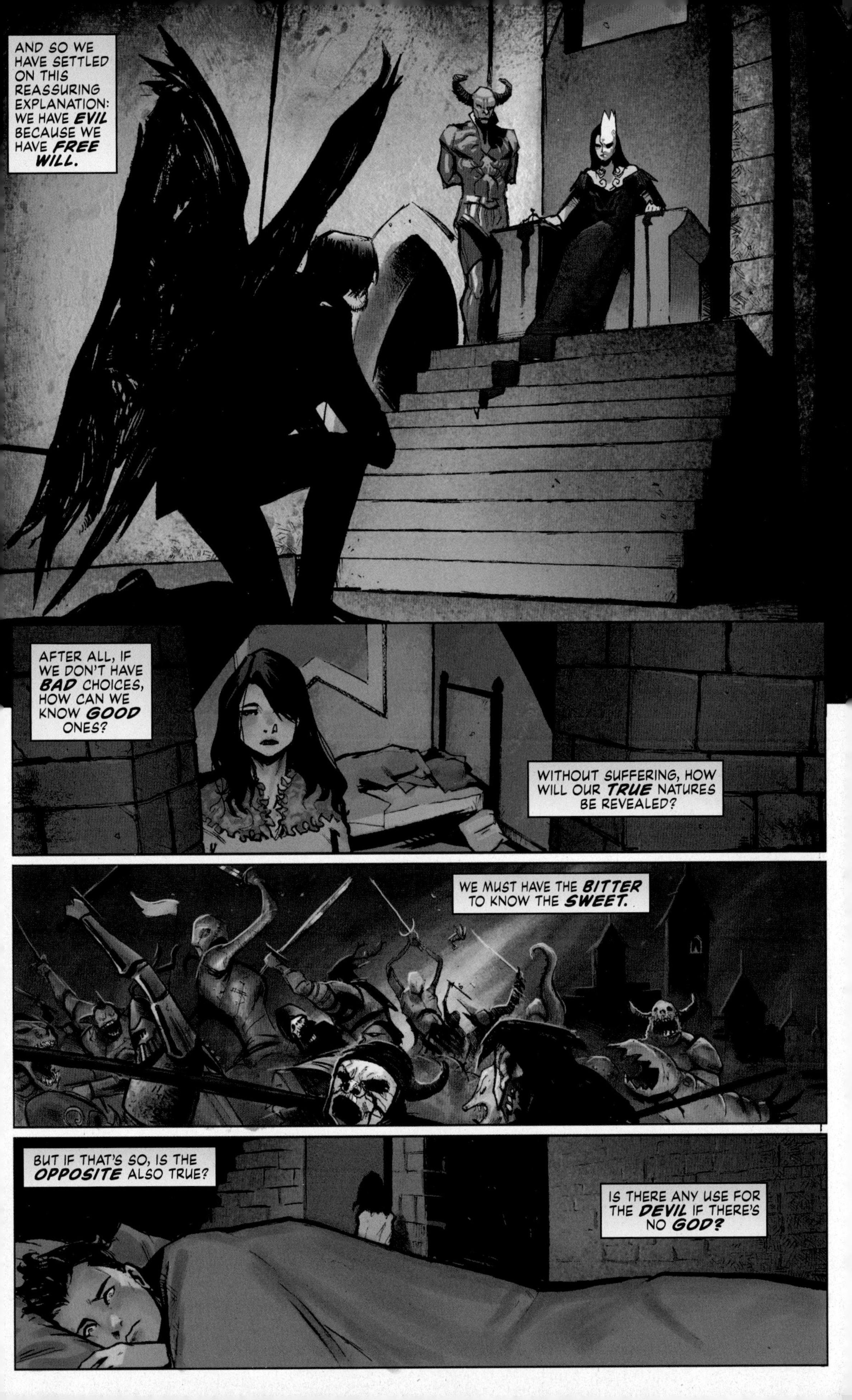
AND SO WE HAVE SETTLED ON THIS REASSURING EXPLANATION: WE HAVE EVIL BECAUSE WE HAVE FREE WILL.
AFTER ALL, IF WE DON'T HAVE BAD CHOICES, HOW CAN WE KNOW GOOD ONES?
WITHOUT SUFFERING, HOW WILL OUR TRUE NATURES BE REVEALED?
WE MUST HAVE THE BITTER TO KNOW THE SWEET.
BUT IF THAT'S SO, IS THE OPPOSITE ALSO TRUE?
IS THERE ANY USE FOR THE DEVIL IF THERE'S NO GOD?

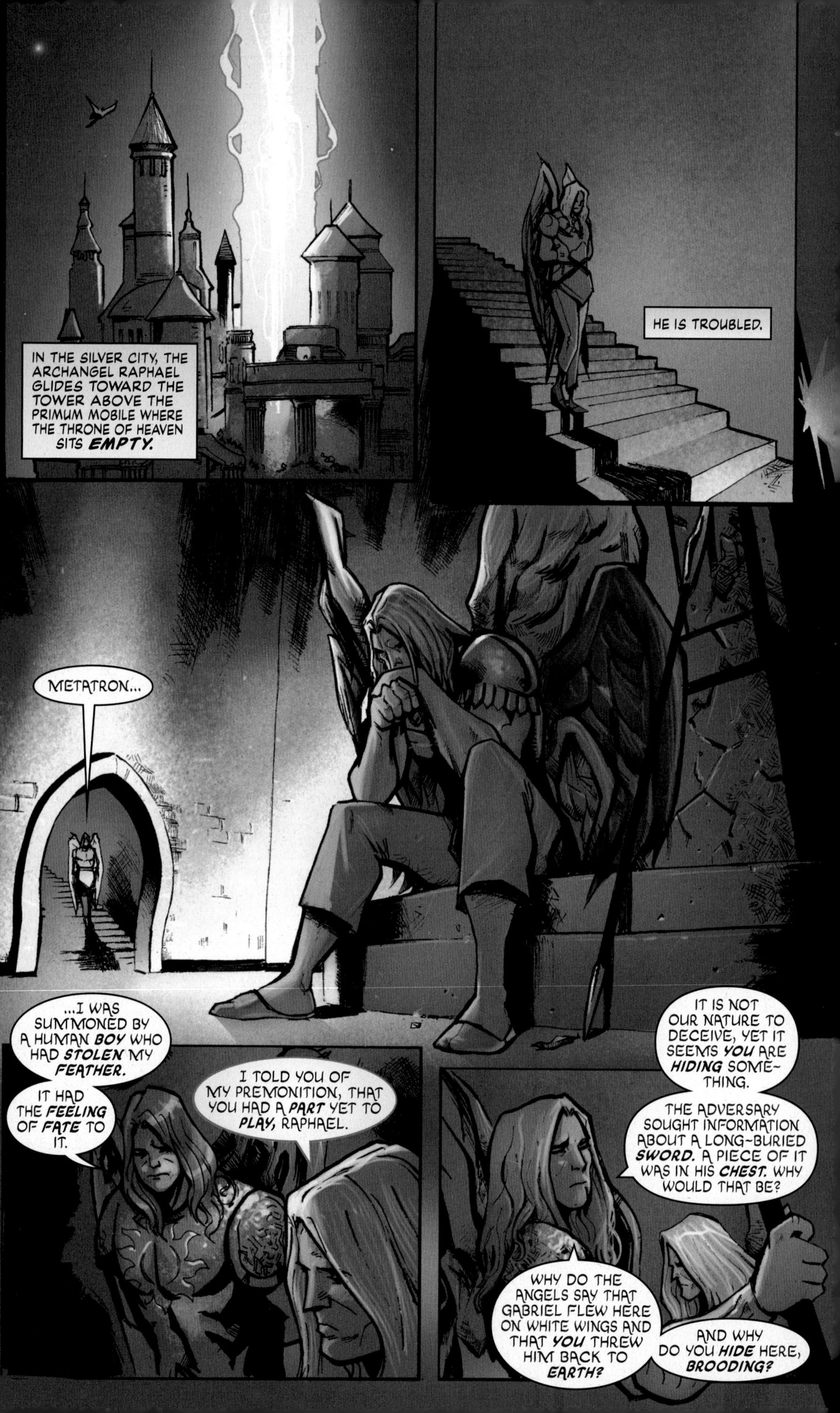

IN THE SILVER CITY, THE ARCHANGEL RAPHAEL GLIDES TOWARD THE TOWER ABOVE THE PRIMUM MOBILE WHERE THE THRONE OF HEAVEN SITS EMPTY.
HE IS TROUBLED.
METATRON...
...I WAS SUMMONED BY A HUMAN BOY WHO HAD STOLEN MY FEATHER.
IT HAD THE FEELING OF FATE TO IT.
I TOLD YOU OF MY PREMONITION, THAT YOU HAD A PART YET TO PLAY, RAPHAEL.
IT IS NOT OUR NATURE TO DECEIVE, YET IT SEEMS YOU ARE HIDING SOME-THING.
THE ADVERSARY SOUGHT INFORMATION ABOUT A LONG-BURIED SWORD. A PIECE OF IT WAS IN HIS CHEST. WHY WOULD THAT BE?
WHY DO THE ANGELS SAY THAT GABRIEL FLEW HERE ON WHITE WINGS AND THAT YOU THREW HIM BACK TO EARTH?
AND WHY DO YOU HIDE HERE, BROODING?

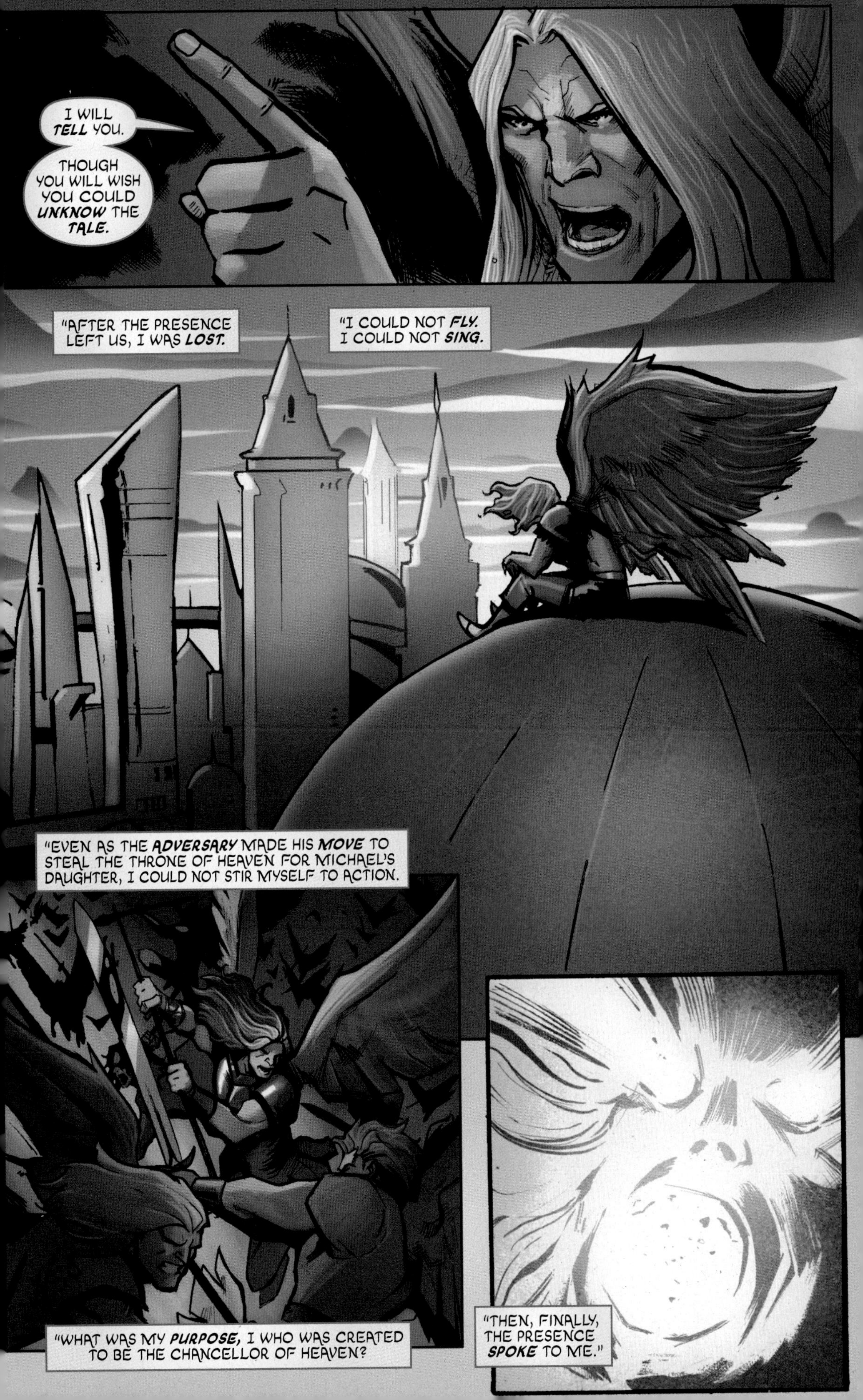

I WILL TELL YOU.
THOUGH YOU WILL WISH YOU COULD UNKNOW THE TALE.
"AFTER THE PRESENCE LEFT US, I WAS LOST.
"I COULD NOT FLY. I COULD NOT SING.
"EVEN AS THE ADVERSARY MADE HIS MOVE TO STEAL THE THRONE OF HEAVEN FOR MICHAEL'S DAUGHTER, I COULD NOT STIR MYSELF TO ACTION.
"WHAT WAS MY PURPOSE, I WHO WAS CREATED TO BE THE CHANCELLOR OF HEAVEN?
"THEN, FINALLY, THE PRESENCE SPOKE TO ME."

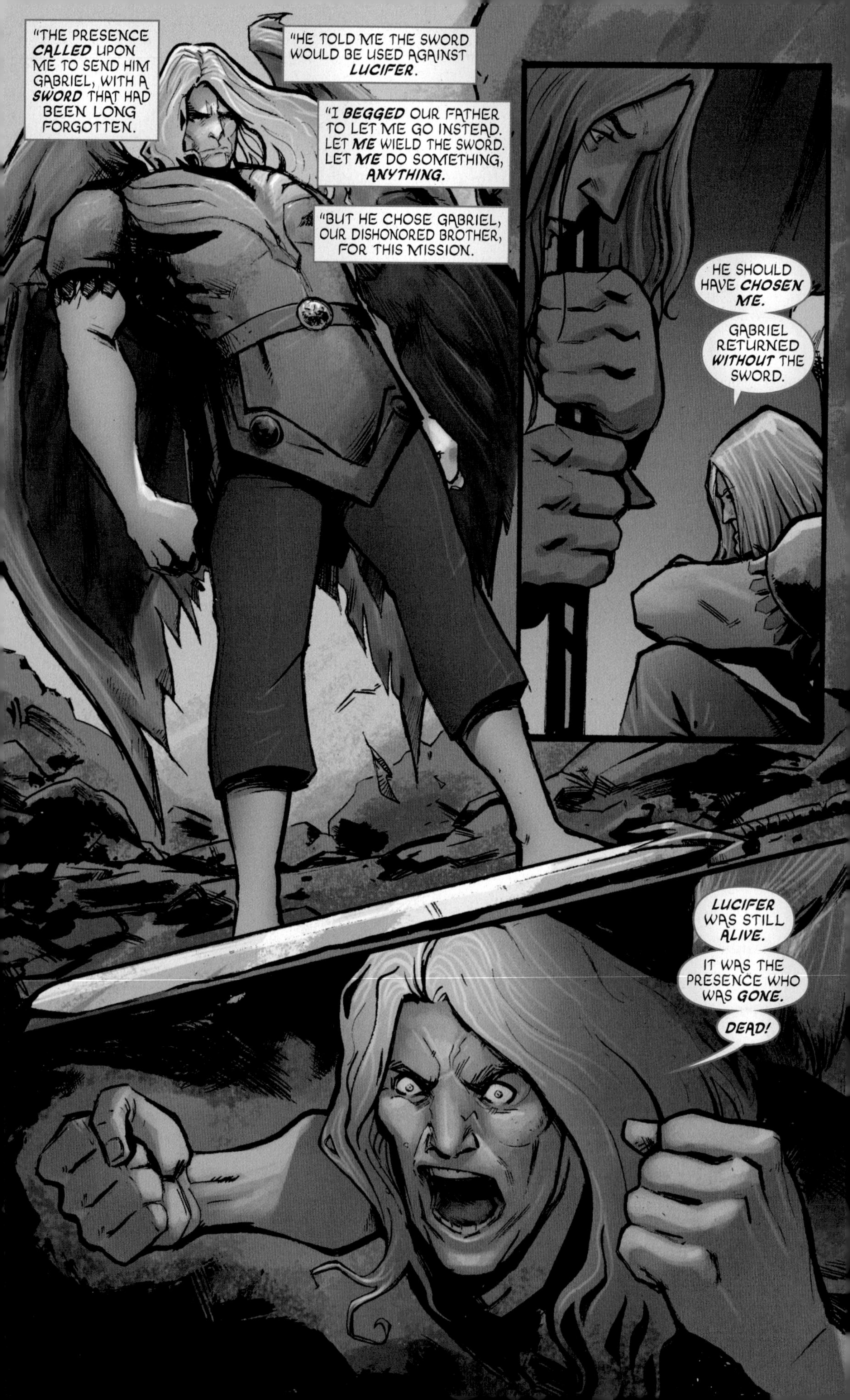

"THE PRESENCE CALLED UPON ME TO SEND HIM GABRIEL, WITH A SWORD THAT HAD BEEN LONG FORGOTTEN.
"HE TOLD ME THE SWORD WOULD BE USED AGAINST LUCIFER.
"I BEGGED OUR FATHER TO LET ME GO INSTEAD. LET ME WIELD THE SWORD. LET ME DO SOMETHING, ANYTHING.
"BUT HE CHOSE GABRIEL, OUR DISHONORED BROTHER, FOR THIS MISSION.
HE SHOULD HAVE CHOSEN ME.
GABRIEL RETURNED WITHOUT THE SWORD.
LUCIFER WAS STILL ALIVE.
IT WAS THE PRESENCE WHO WAS GONE.
DEAD!

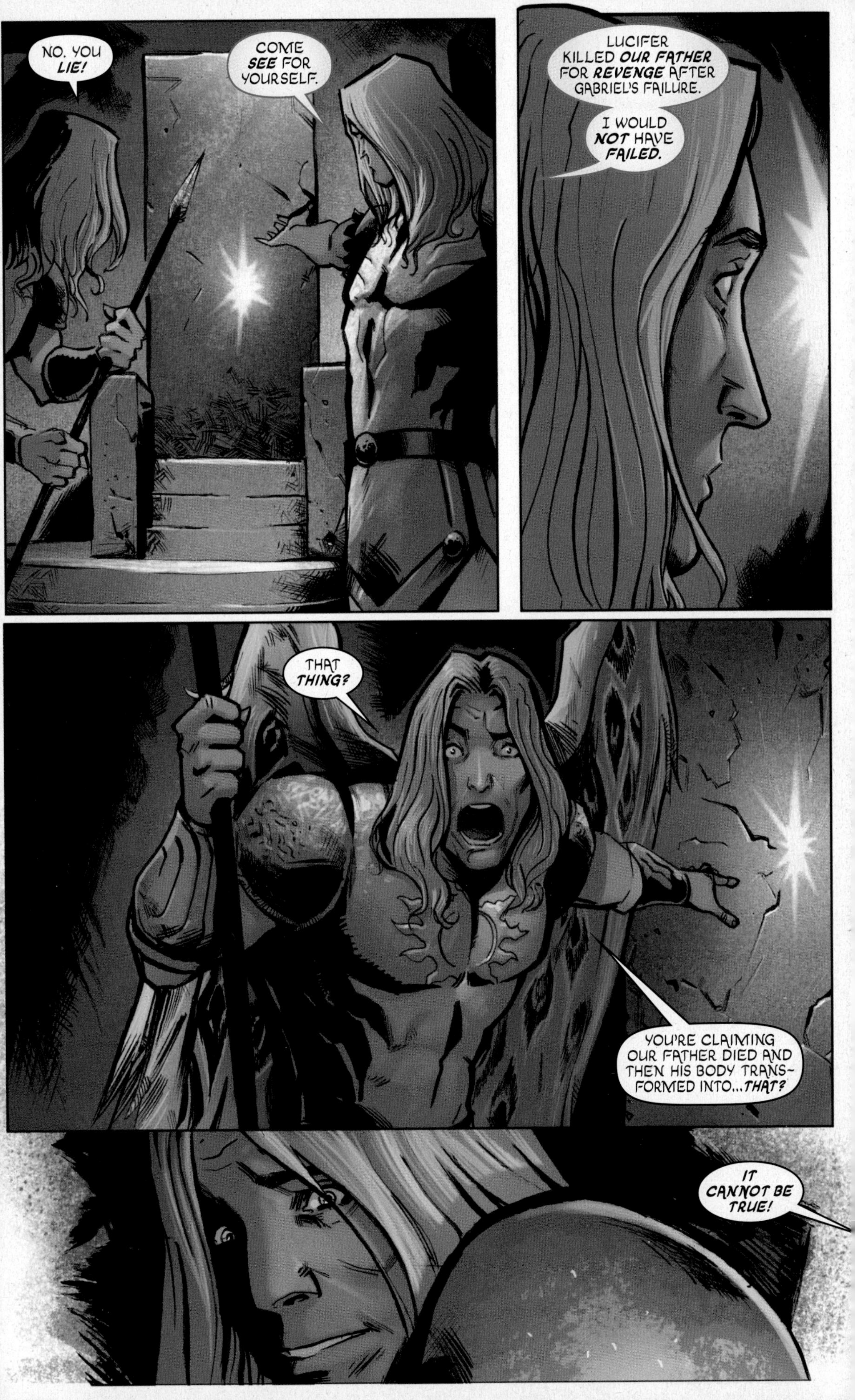

NO. YOU LIE!
COME SEE FOR YOURSELF.
LUCIFER KILLED OUR FATHER FOR REVENGE AFTER GABRIEL'S FAILURE.
I WOULD NOT HAVE FAILED.
THAT THING?
YOU'RE CLAIMING OUR FATHER DIED AND THEN HIS BODY TRANS-FORMED INTO...THAT?
IT CANNOT BE TRUE!

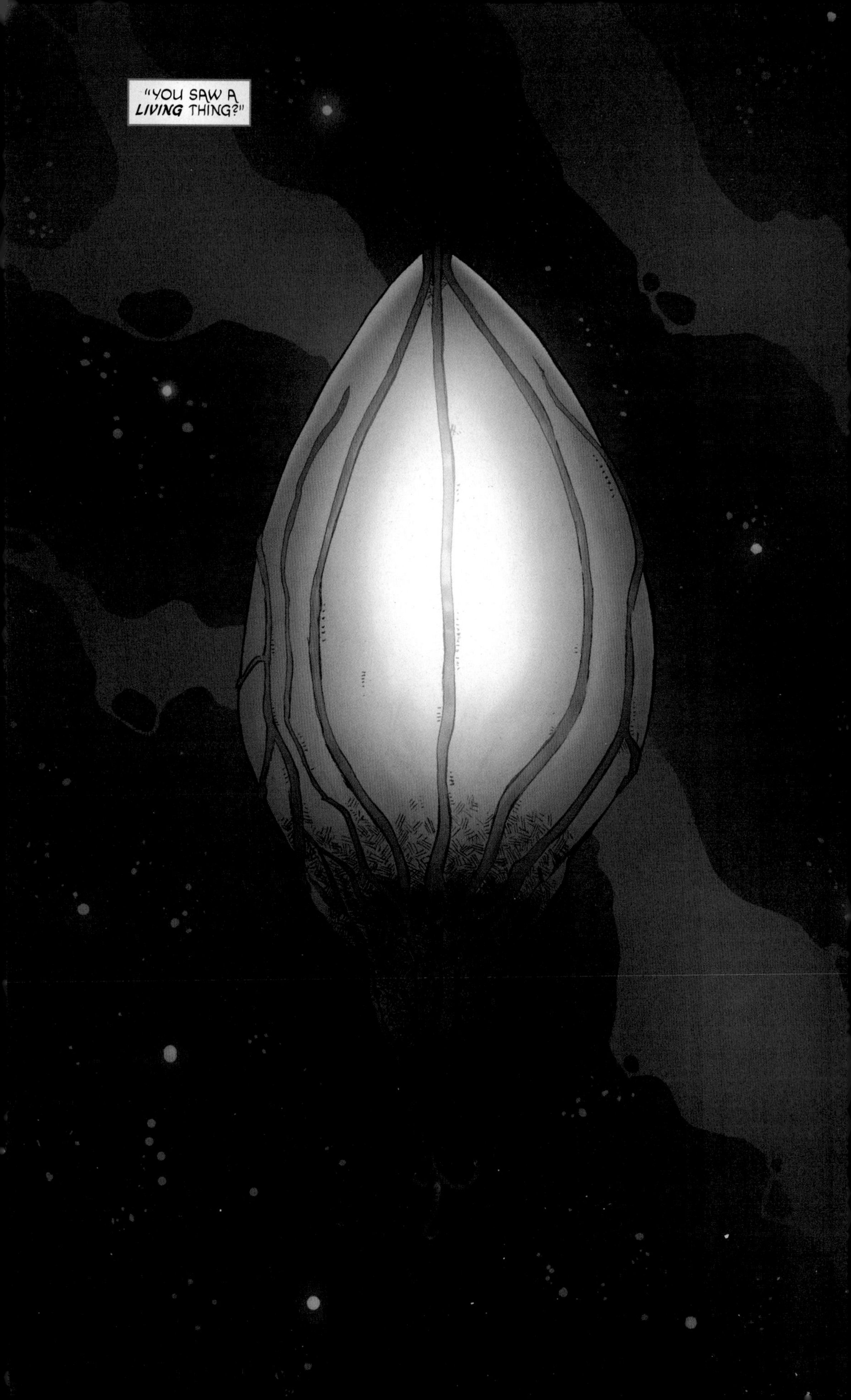
"YOU SAW A LIVING THING?"

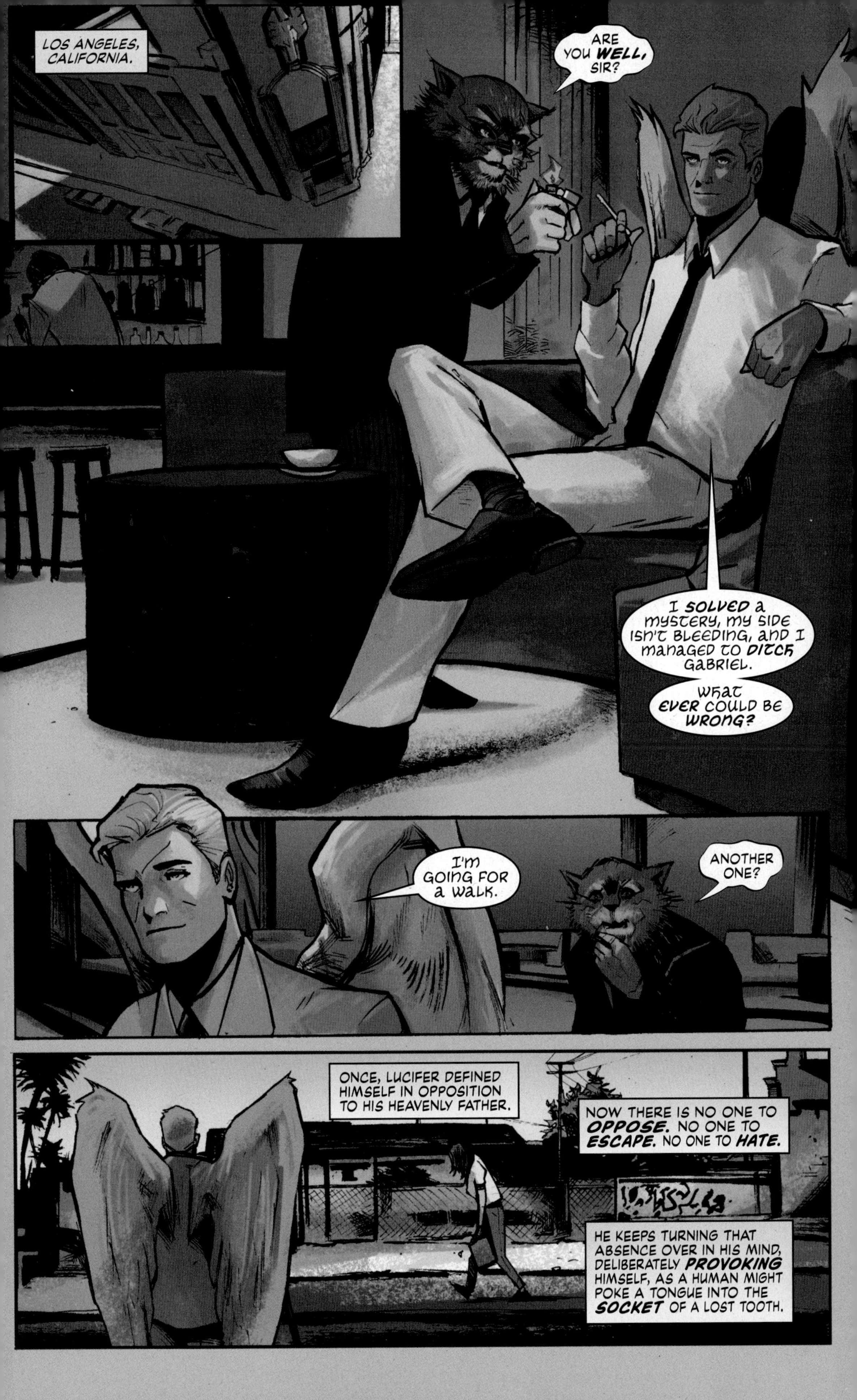
LOS ANGELES, CALIFORNIA.
ARE YOU WELL, SIR?
I SOLVED A MYSTERY, MY SIDE ISN'T BLEEDING, AND I MANAGED TO DITCH GABRIEL.
WHAT EVER COULD BE WRONG?
I'M GOING FOR A WALK.
ANOTHER ONE?
ONCE, LUCIFER DEFINED HIMSELF IN OPPOSITION TO HIS HEAVENLY FATHER.
NOW THERE IS NO ONE TO OPPOSE. NO ONE TO ESCAPE. NO ONE TO HATE.
HE KEEPS TURNING THAT ABSENCE OVER IN HIS MIND, DELIBERATELY PROVOKING HIMSELF, AS A HUMAN MIGHT POKE A TONGUE INTO THE SOCKET OF A LOST TOOTH.

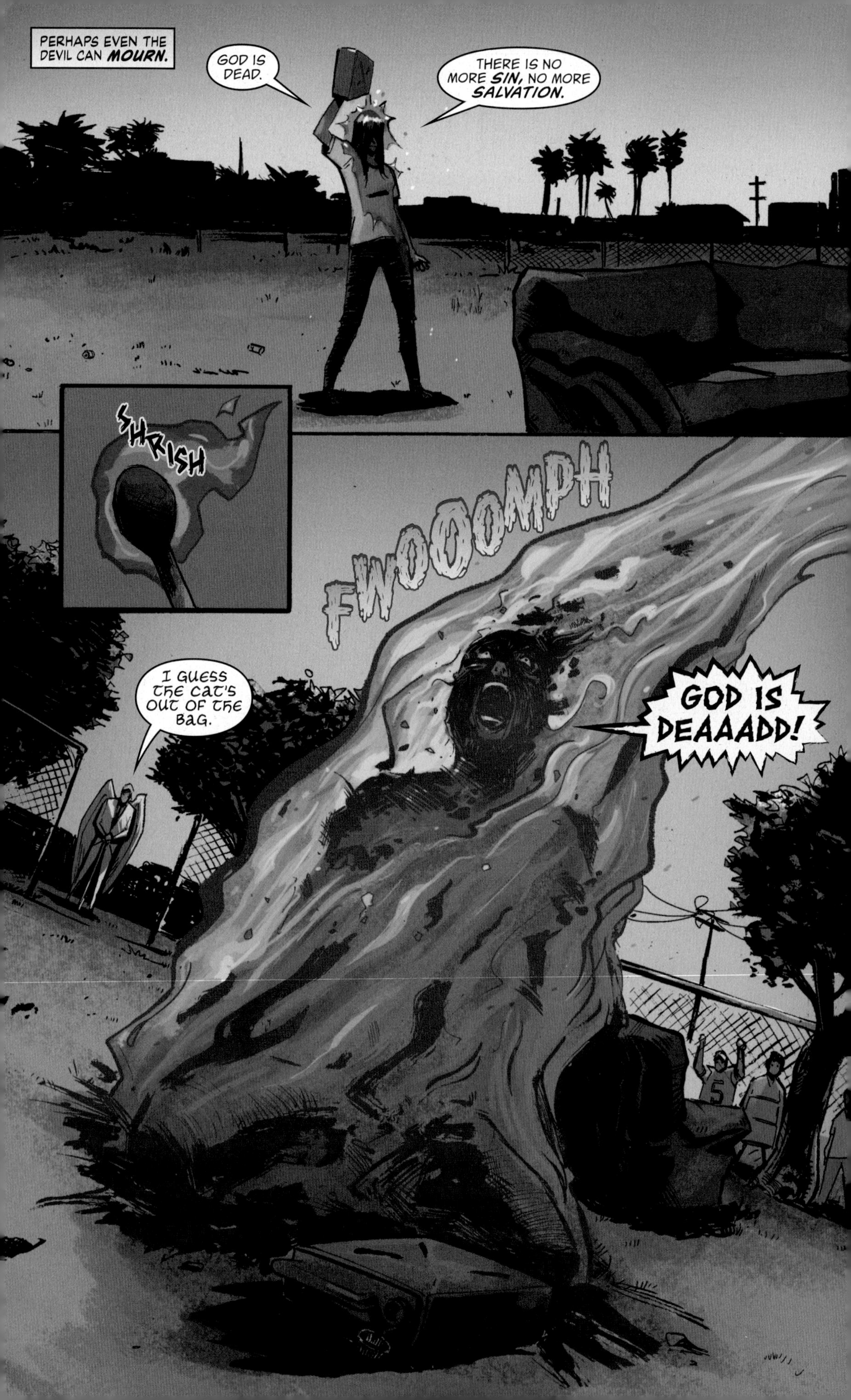
PERHAPS EVEN THE DEVIL CAN MOURN.
GOD IS DEAD.
THERE IS NO MORE SIN, NO MORE SALVATION.
SHRISH
FWOOOOMPH
I GUESS THE CAT'S OUT OF THE BAG.
GOD IS DEAAADD!

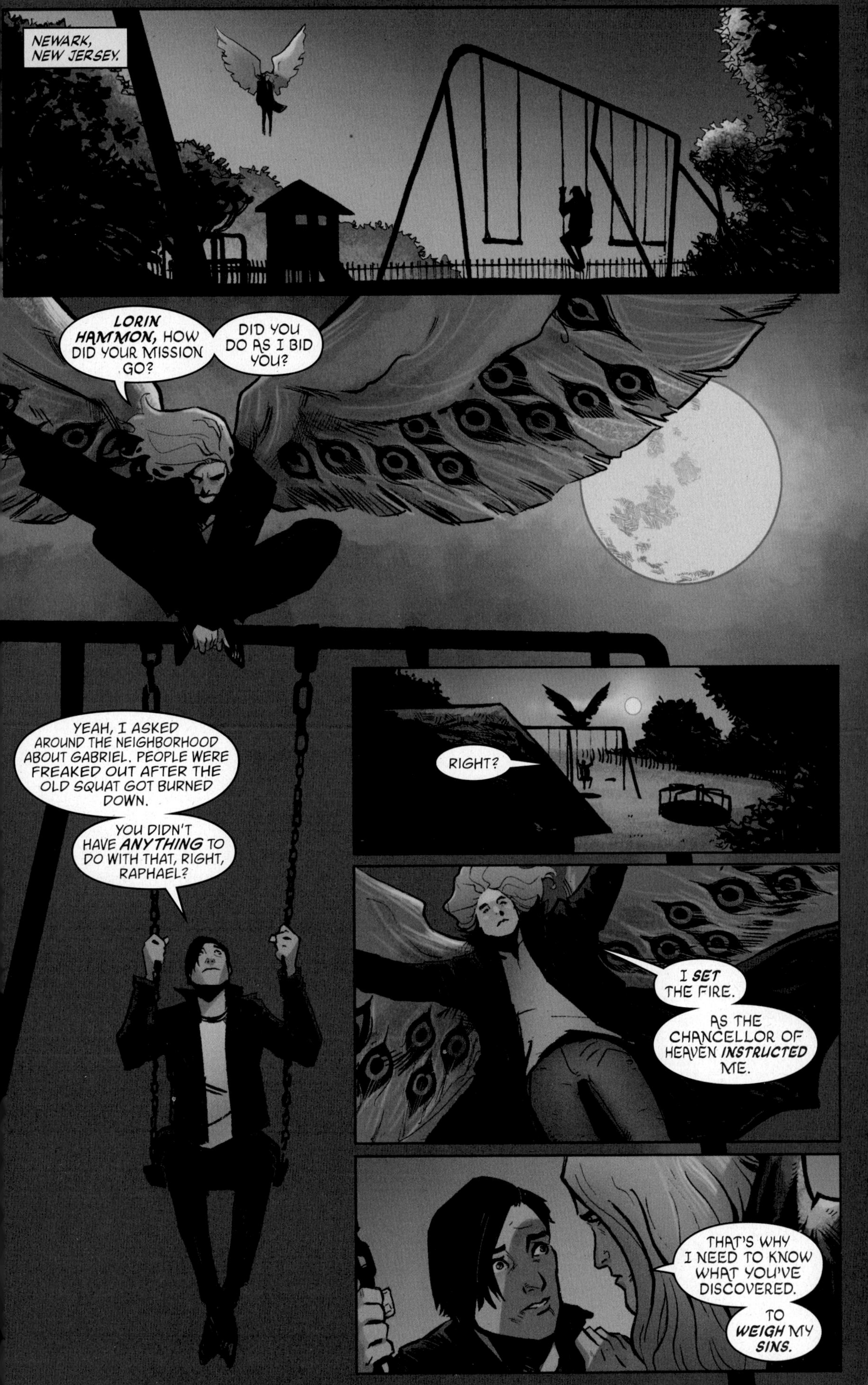
NEWARK, NEW JERSEY.
LORIN HAMMON, HOW DID YOUR MISSION GO?
DID YOU DO AS I BID YOU?
YEAH, I ASKED AROUND THE NEIGHBORHOOD ABOUT GABRIEL. PEOPLE WERE FREAKED OUT AFTER THE OLD SQUAT GOT BURNED DOWN.
YOU DIDN'T HAVE ANYTHING TO DO WITH THAT, RIGHT, RAPHAEL?
RIGHT?
I SET THE FIRE.
AS THE CHANCELLOR OF HEAVEN INSTRUCTED ME.
THAT'S WHY I NEED TO KNOW WHAT YOU'VE DISCOVERED.
TO WEIGH MY SINS.

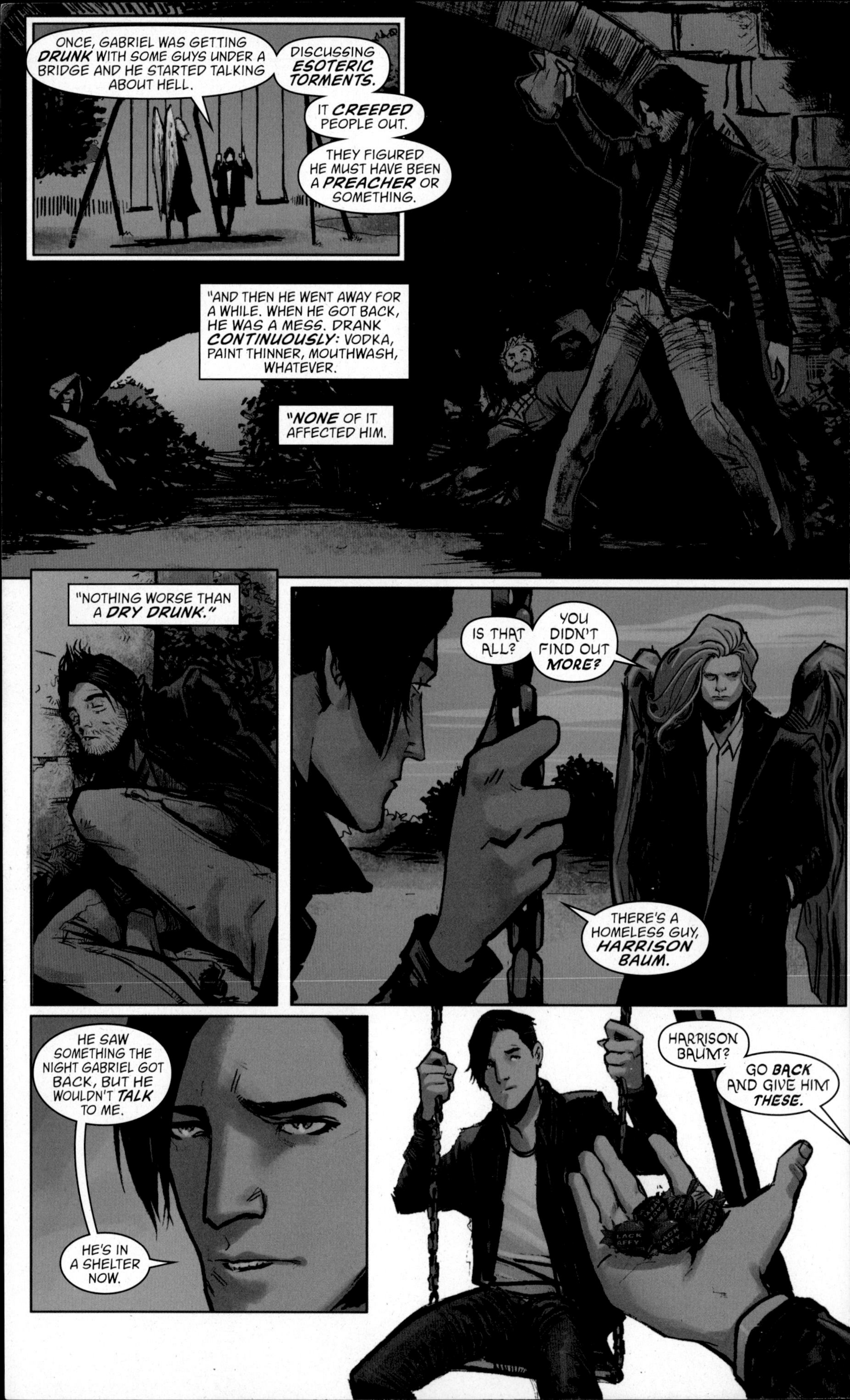

ONCE, GABRIEL WAS GETTING DRUNK WITH SOME GUYS UNDER A BRIDGE AND HE STARTED TALKING ABOUT HELL.
DISCUSSING ESOTERIC TORMENTS.
IT CREEPED PEOPLE OUT.
THEY FIGURED HE MUST HAVE BEEN A PREACHER OR SOMETHING.
"AND THEN HE WENT AWAY FOR A WHILE. WHEN HE GOT BACK, HE WAS A MESS. DRANK CONTINUOUSLY: VODKA, PAINT THINNER, MOUTHWASH, WHATEVER.
"NONE OF IT AFFECTED HIM.
"NOTHING WORSE THAN A DRY DRUNK."
IS THAT ALL?
YOU DIDN'T FIND OUT MORE?
THERE'S A HOMELESS GUY, HARRISON BAUM.
HE SAW SOMETHING THE NIGHT GABRIEL GOT BACK, BUT HE WOULDN'T TALK TO ME.
HE'S IN A SHELTER NOW.
HARRISON BAUM?
GO BACK AND GIVE HIM THESE.

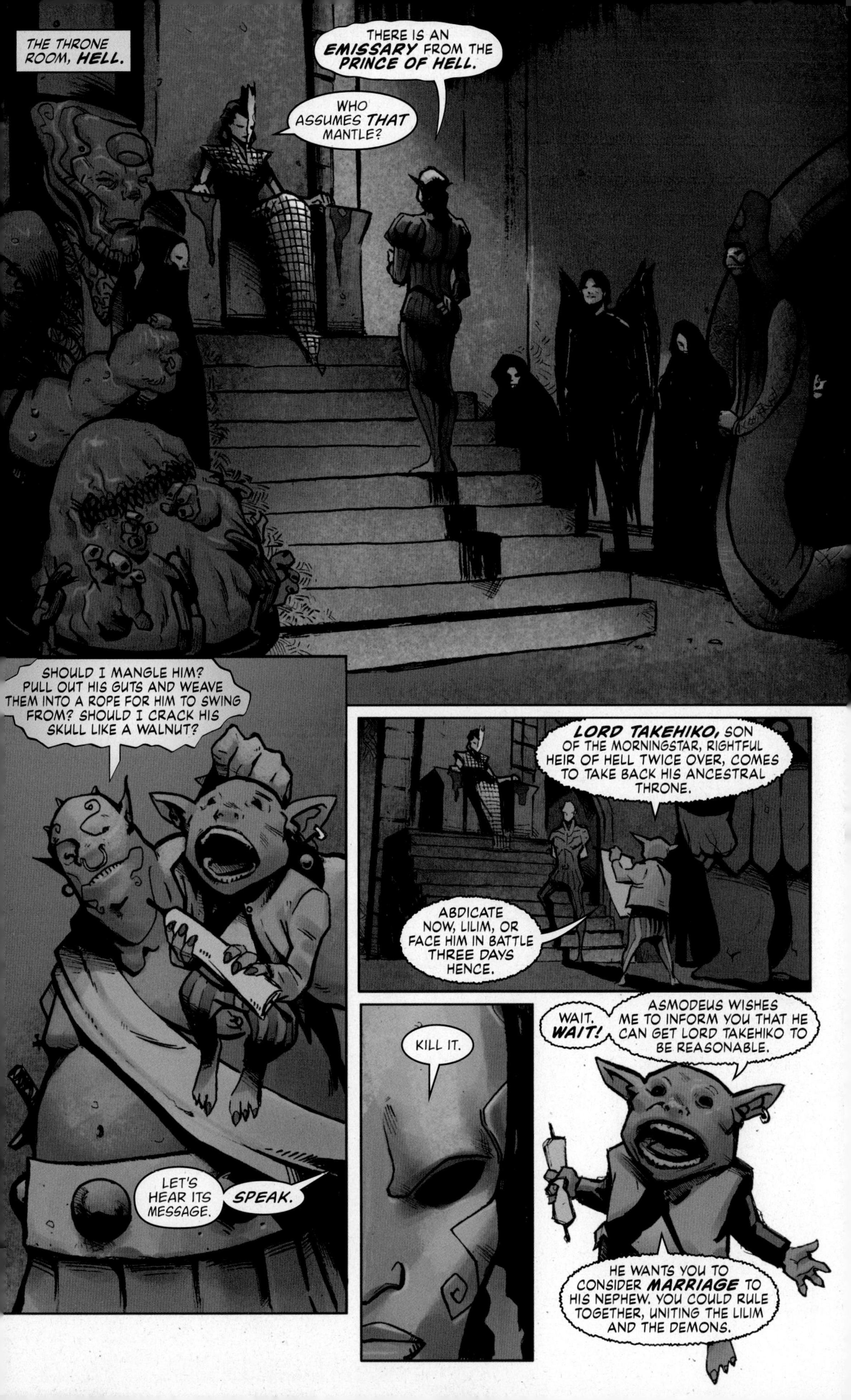
THE THRONE ROOM, HELL.
THERE IS AN EMISSARY FROM THE PRINCE OF HELL.
WHO ASSUMES THAT MANTLE?
SHOULD I MANGLE HIM? PULL OUT HIS GUTS AND WEAVE THEM INTO A ROPE FOR HIM TO SWING FROM? SHOULD I CRACK HIS SKULL LIKE A WALNUT?
LET'S HEAR ITS MESSAGE.
SPEAK.
LORD TAKEHIKO, SON OF THE MORNINGSTAR, RIGHTFUL HEIR OF HELL TWICE OVER, COMES TO TAKE BACK HIS ANCESTRAL THRONE.
ABDICATE NOW, LILIM, OR FACE HIM IN BATTLE THREE DAYS HENCE.
KILL IT.
WAIT. WAIT!
ASMODEUS WISHES ME TO INFORM YOU THAT HE CAN GET LORD TAKEHIKO TO BE REASONABLE.
HE WANTS YOU TO CONSIDER MARRIAGE TO HIS NEPHEW. YOU COULD RULE TOGETHER, UNITING THE LILIM AND THE DEMONS.

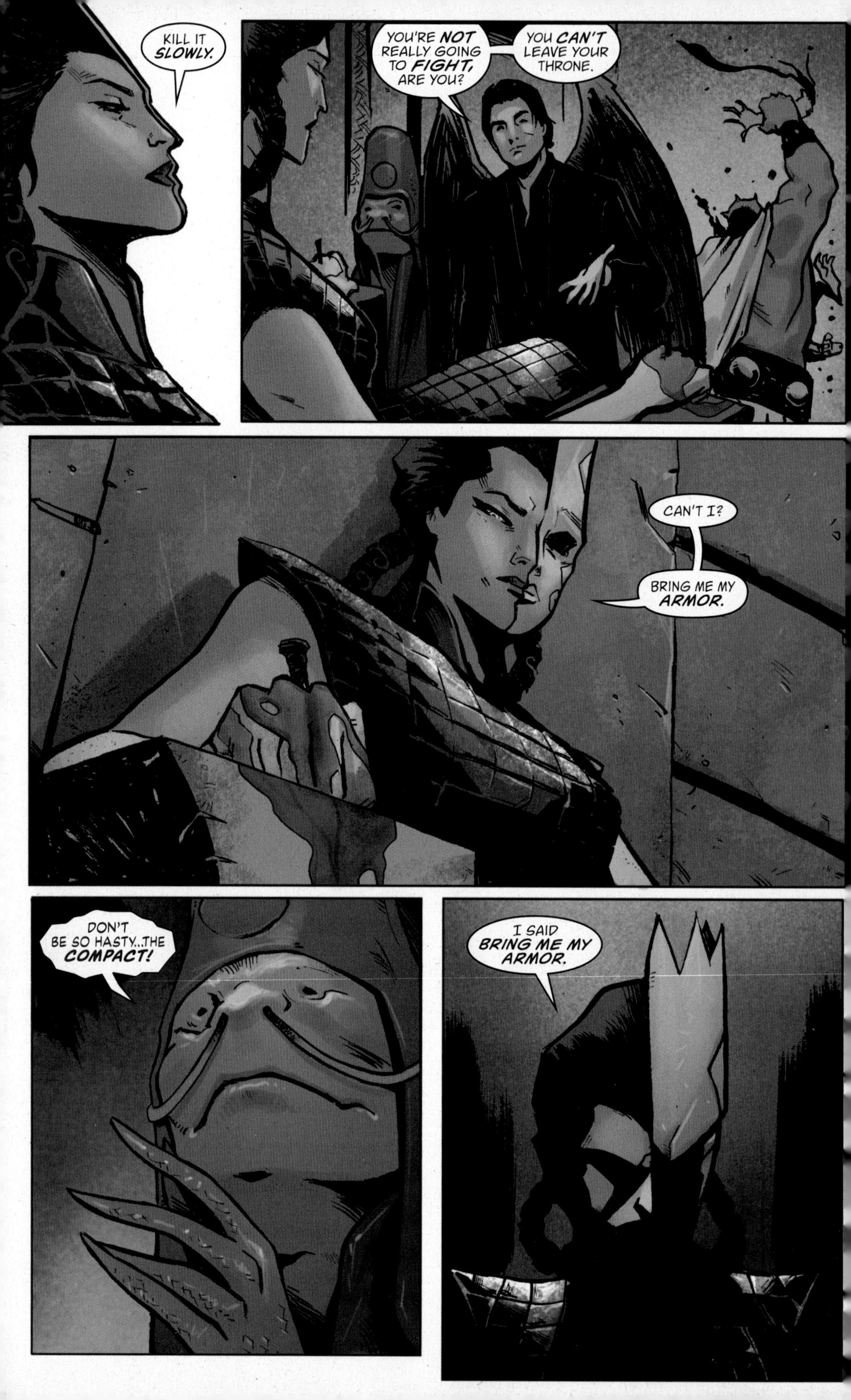
KILL IT SLOWLY.
YOU'RE NOT REALLY GOING TO FIGHT, ARE YOU?
YOU CAN'T LEAVE YOUR THRONE.
CAN'T I?
BRING ME MY ARMOR.
DON'T BE SO HASTY...THE COMPACT!
I SAID BRING ME MY ARMOR.

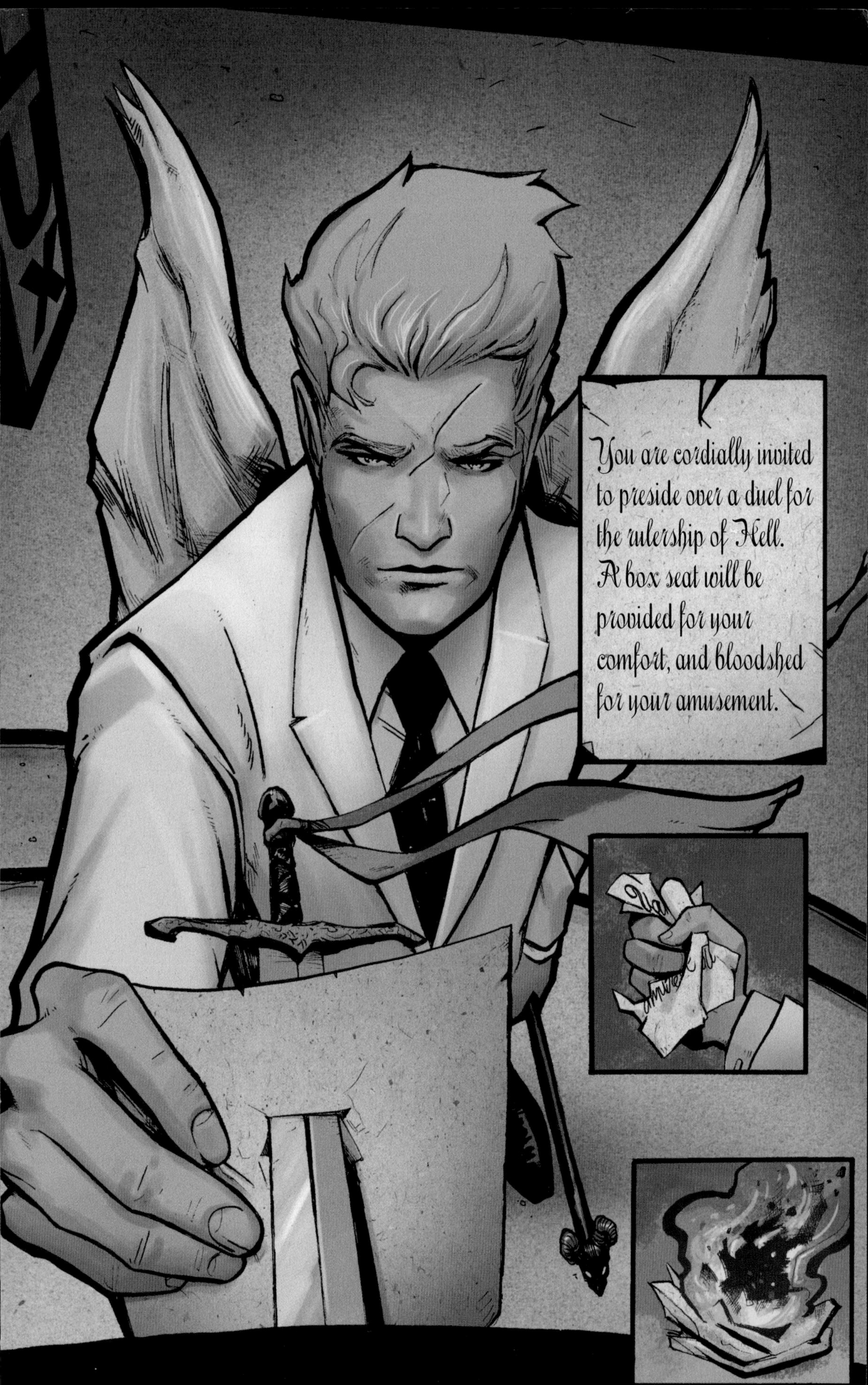

You are cordially invited to preside over a duel for the rulership of Hell. A box seat will be provided for your comfort, and bloodshed for your amusement.

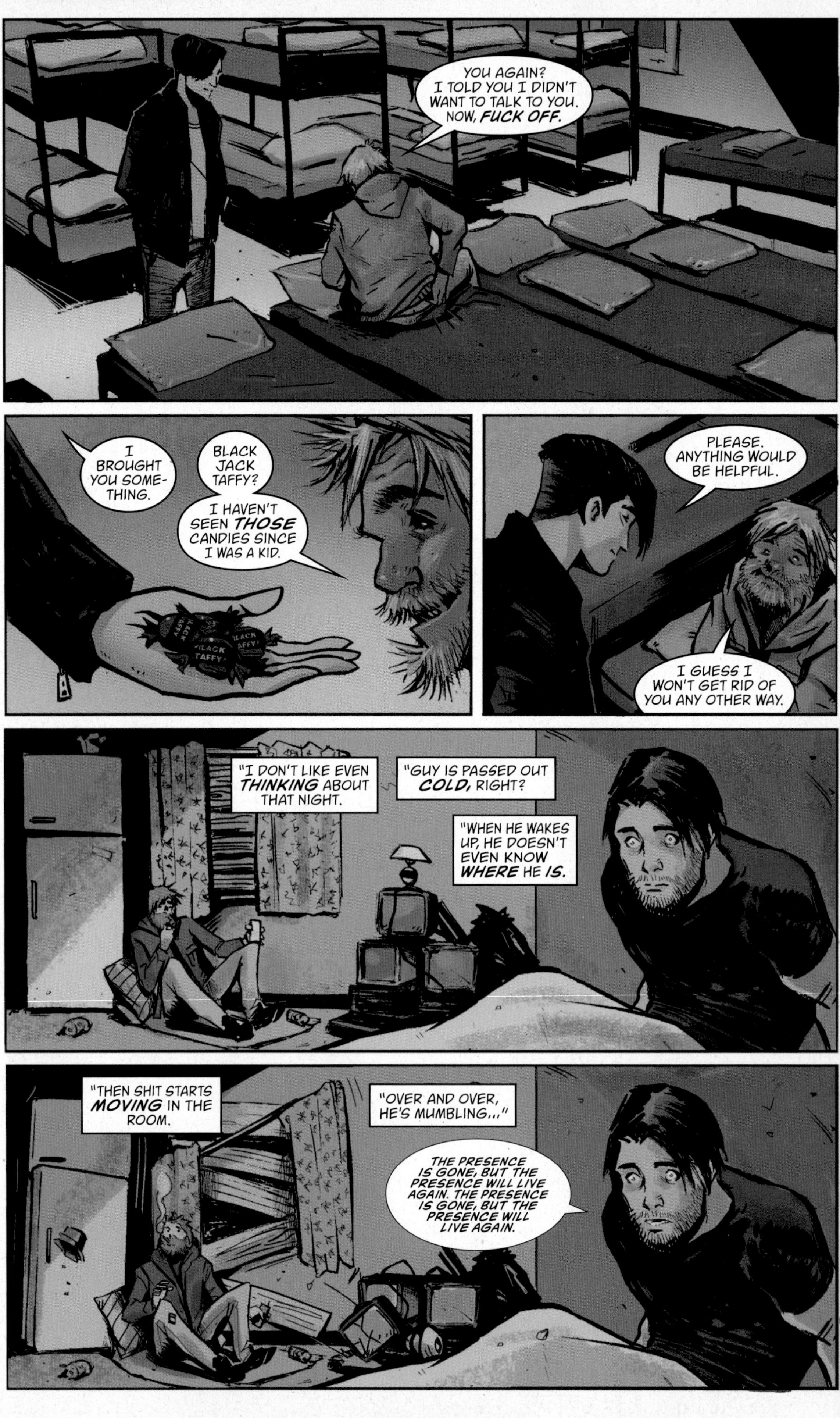
YOU AGAIN? I TOLD YOU I DIDN'T WANT TO TALK TO YOU. NOW, FUCK OFF.
I BROUGHT YOU SOME-THING.
BLACK JACK TAFFY?
I HAVEN'T SEEN THOSE CANDIES SINCE I WAS A KID.
BLACK TAFFY
PLEASE. ANYTHING WOULD BE HELPFUL.
I GUESS I WON'T GET RID OF YOU ANY OTHER WAY.
"I DON'T LIKE EVEN THINKING ABOUT THAT NIGHT.
"GUY IS PASSED OUT COLD, RIGHT?
"WHEN HE WAKES UP, HE DOESN'T EVEN KNOW WHERE HE IS.
"THEN SHIT STARTS MOVING IN THE ROOM.
"OVER AND OVER, HE'S MUMBLING..."
THE PRESENCE IS GONE, BUT THE PRESENCE WILL LIVE AGAIN. THE PRESENCE IS GONE, BUT THE PRESENCE WILL LIVE AGAIN.

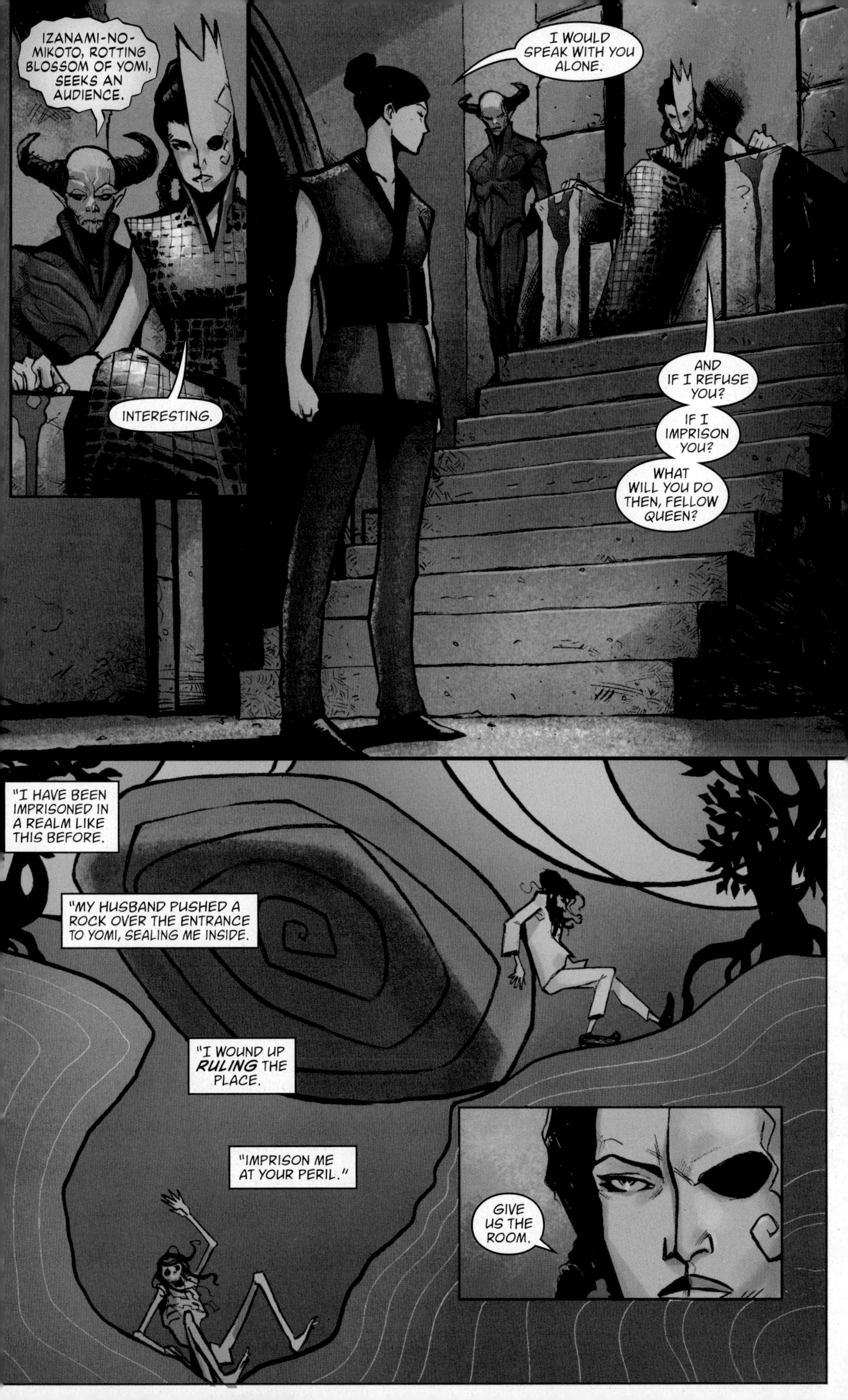
IZANAMI-NO-MIKOTO, ROTTING BLOSSOM OF YOMI, SEEKS AN AUDIENCE.
INTERESTING.
I WOULD SPEAK WITH YOU ALONE.
AND IF I REFUSE YOU?
IF I IMPRISON YOU?
WHAT WILL YOU DO THEN, FELLOW QUEEN?
"I HAVE BEEN IMPRISONED IN A REALM LIKE THIS BEFORE.
"MY HUSBAND PUSHED A ROCK OVER THE ENTRANCE TO YOMI, SEALING ME INSIDE.
"I WOUND UP ***RULING*** THE PLACE.
"IMPRISON ME AT YOUR PERIL."
GIVE US THE ROOM.

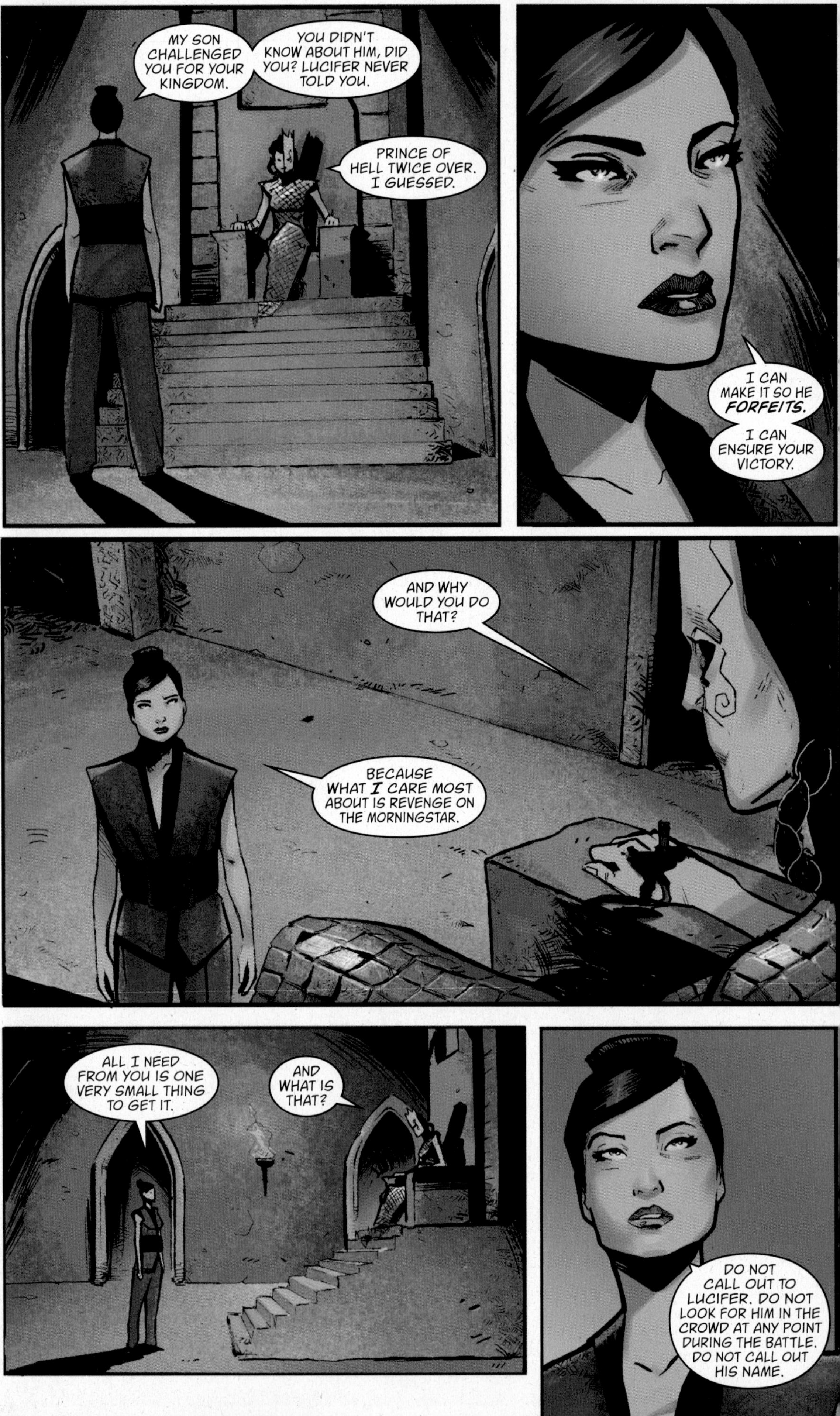
MY SON CHALLENGED YOU FOR YOUR KINGDOM.
YOU DIDN'T KNOW ABOUT HIM, DID YOU? LUCIFER NEVER TOLD YOU.
PRINCE OF HELL TWICE OVER. I GUESSED.
I CAN MAKE IT SO HE FORFEITS.
I CAN ENSURE YOUR VICTORY.
AND WHY WOULD YOU DO THAT?
BECAUSE WHAT I CARE MOST ABOUT IS REVENGE ON THE MORNINGSTAR.
ALL I NEED FROM YOU IS ONE VERY SMALL THING TO GET IT.
AND WHAT IS THAT?
DO NOT CALL OUT TO LUCIFER. DO NOT LOOK FOR HIM IN THE CROWD AT ANY POINT DURING THE BATTLE. DO NOT CALL OUT HIS NAME.

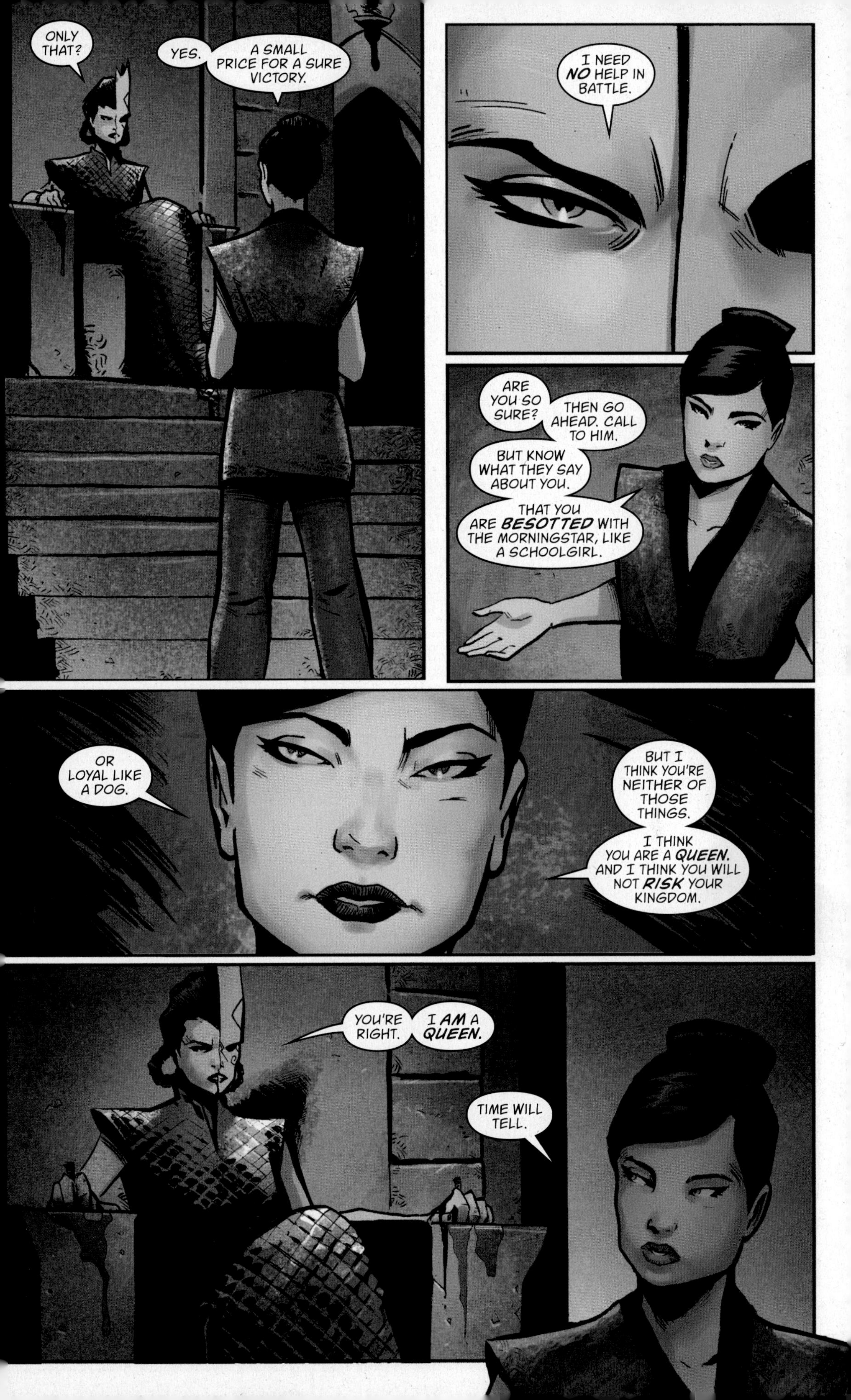
ONLY THAT?
YES.
A SMALL PRICE FOR A SURE VICTORY.
I NEED NO HELP IN BATTLE.
ARE YOU SO SURE?
THEN GO AHEAD. CALL TO HIM.
BUT KNOW WHAT THEY SAY ABOUT YOU.
THAT YOU ARE BESOTTED WITH THE MORNINGSTAR, LIKE A SCHOOLGIRL.
OR LOYAL LIKE A DOG.
BUT I THINK YOU'RE NEITHER OF THOSE THINGS.
I THINK YOU ARE A QUEEN. AND I THINK YOU WILL NOT RISK YOUR KINGDOM.
YOU'RE RIGHT.
I AM A QUEEN.
TIME WILL TELL.

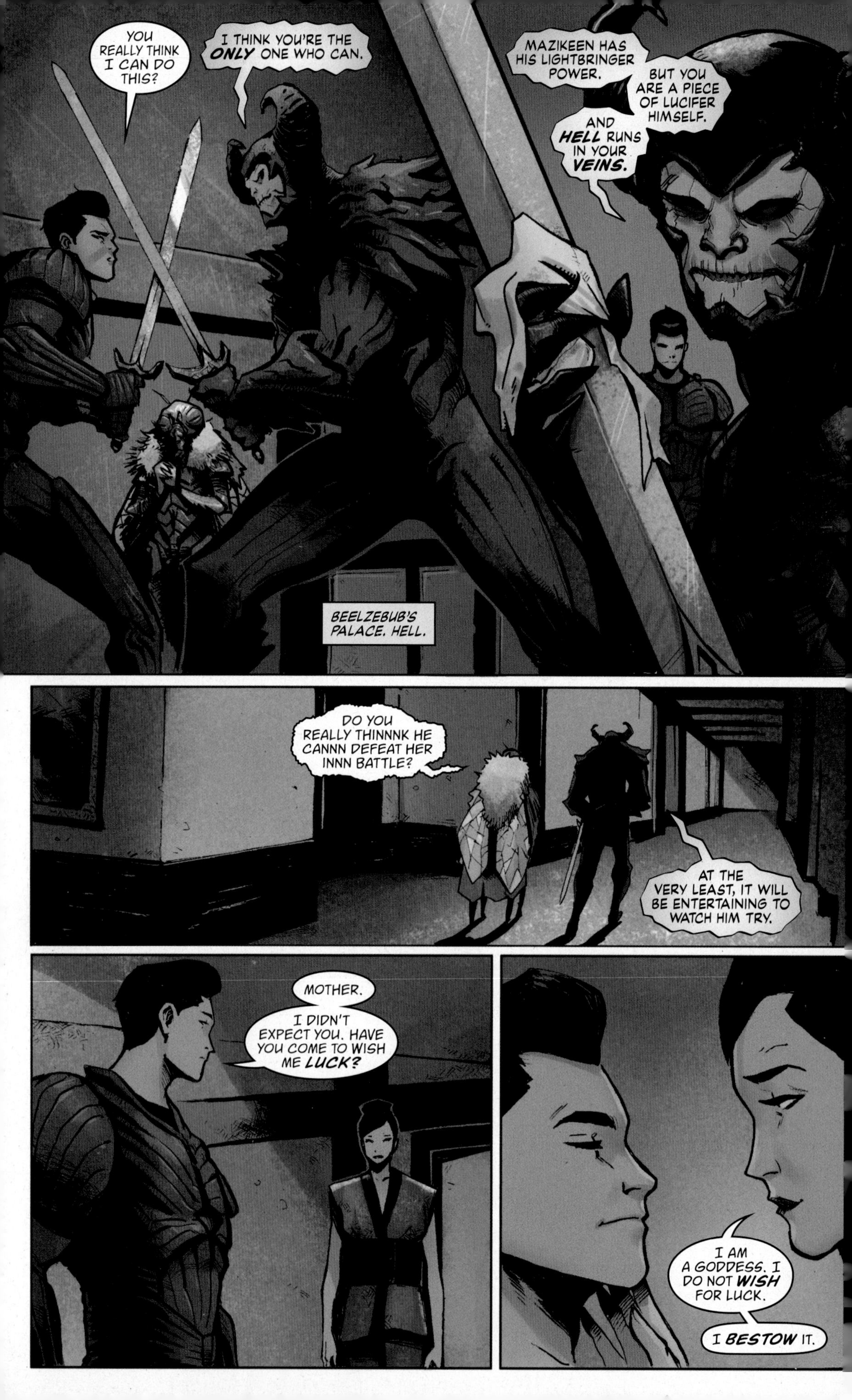
YOU REALLY THINK I CAN DO THIS?
I THINK YOU'RE THE ONLY ONE WHO CAN.
MAZIKEEN HAS HIS LIGHTBRINGER POWER.
BUT YOU ARE A PIECE OF LUCIFER HIMSELF.
AND HELL RUNS IN YOUR VEINS.
BEELZEBUB'S PALACE. HELL.
DO YOU REALLY THINNNK HE CANNN DEFEAT HER INNN BATTLE?
AT THE VERY LEAST, IT WILL BE ENTERTAINING TO WATCH HIM TRY.
MOTHER.
I DIDN'T EXPECT YOU. HAVE YOU COME TO WISH ME LUCK?
I AM A GODDESS. I DO NOT WISH FOR LUCK.
I BESTOW IT.

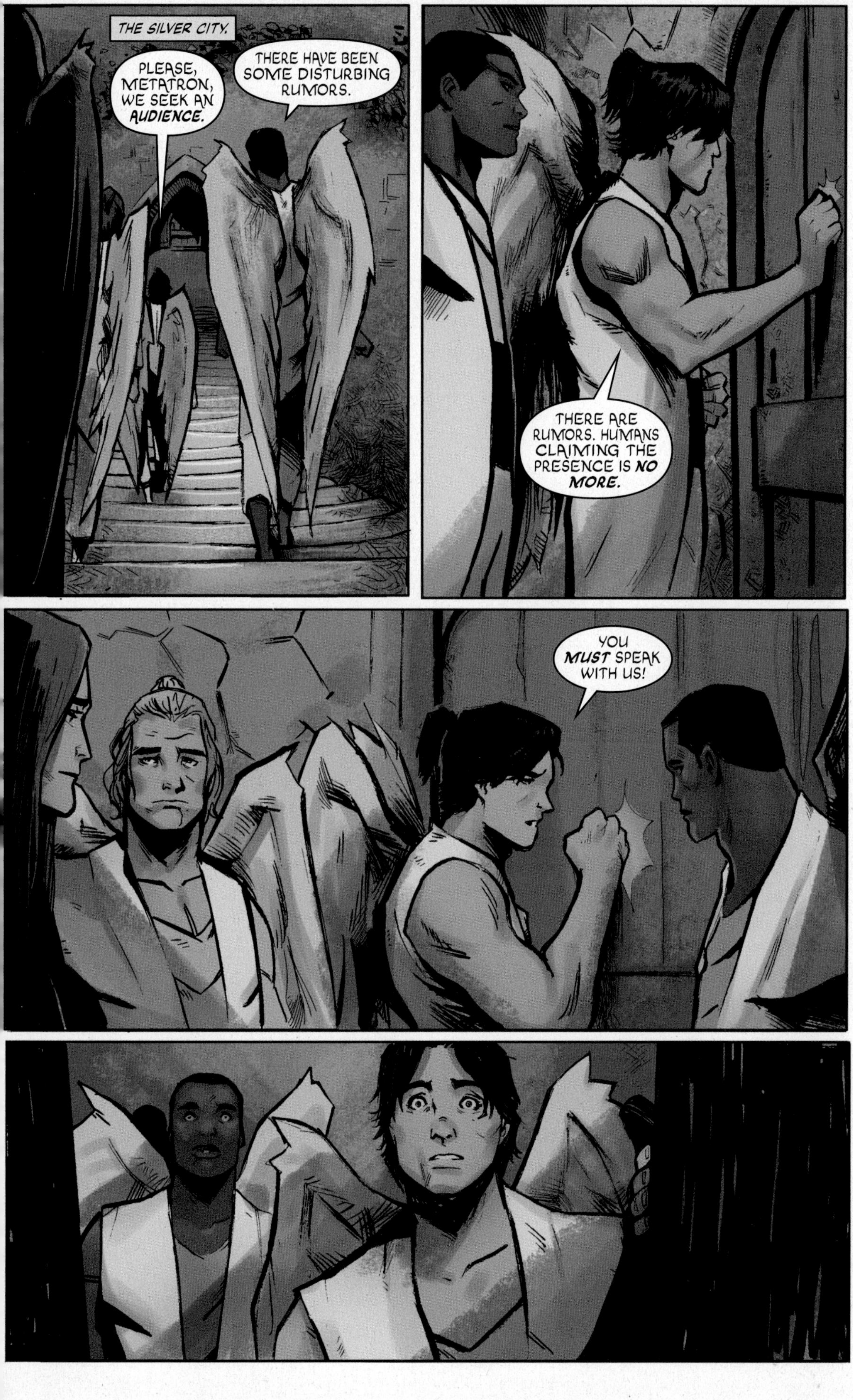
THE SILVER CITY.
PLEASE, METATRON, WE SEEK AN AUDIENCE.
THERE HAVE BEEN SOME DISTURBING RUMORS.
THERE ARE RUMORS. HUMANS CLAIMING THE PRESENCE IS NO MORE.
YOU MUST SPEAK WITH US!

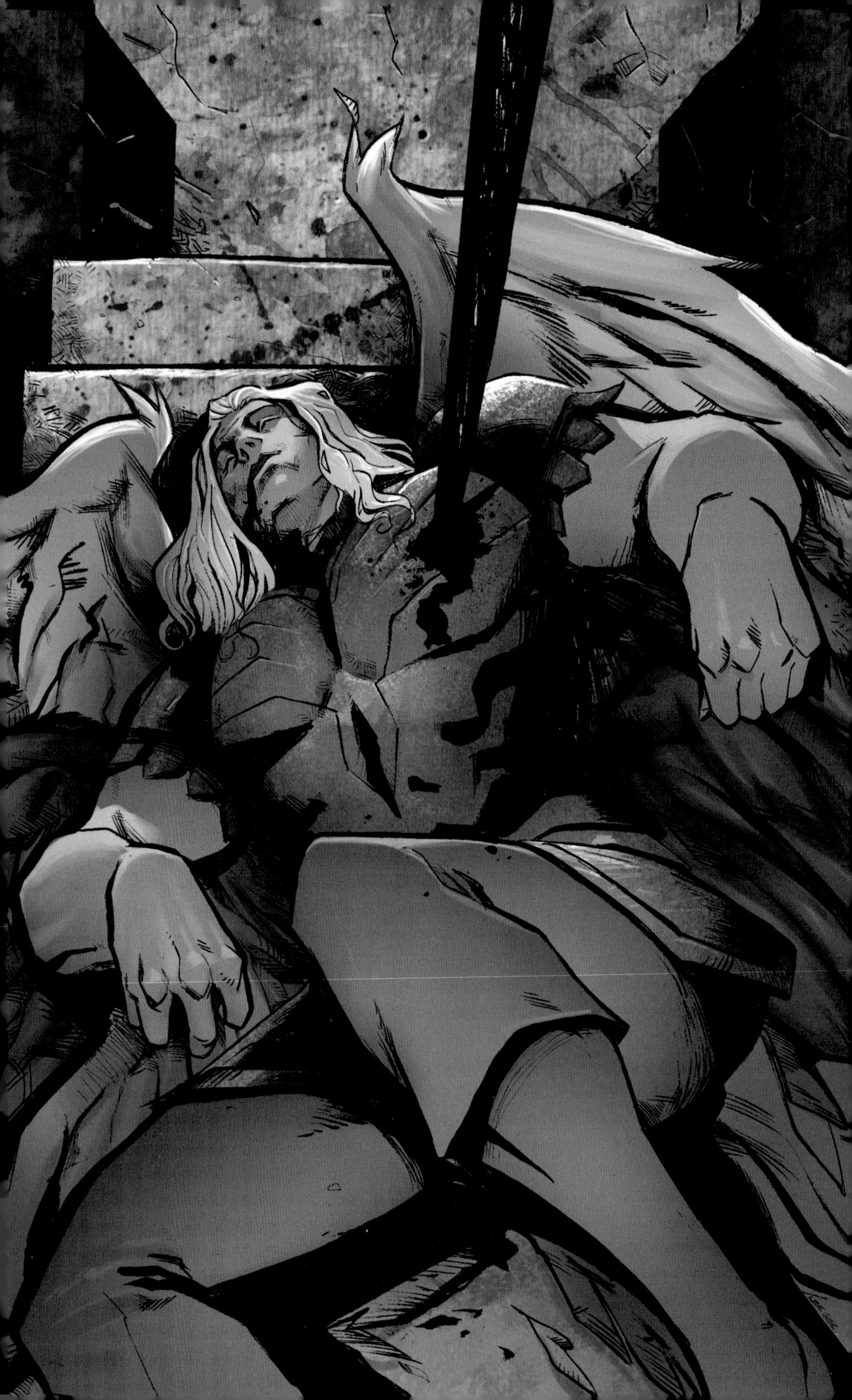

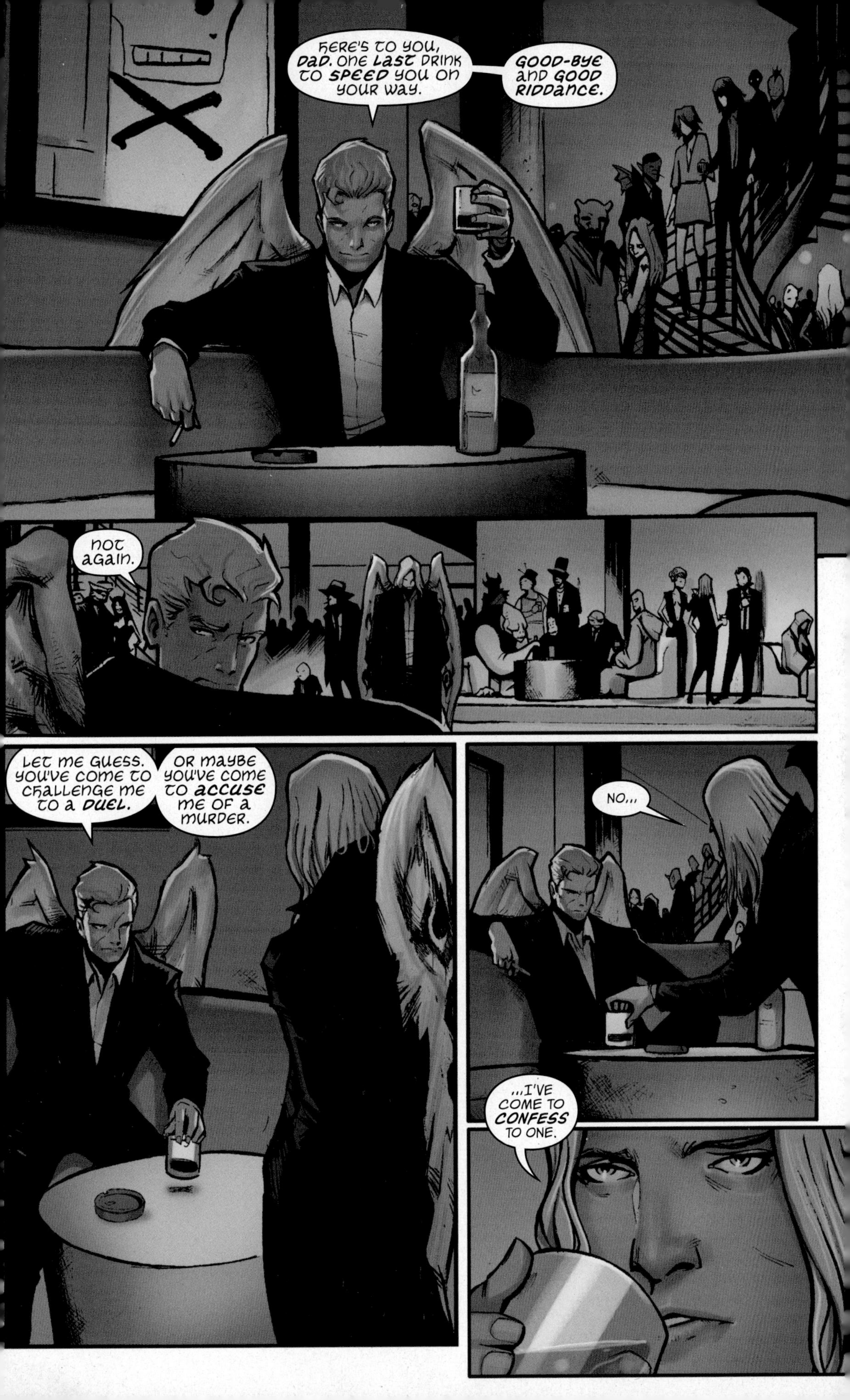
HERE'S TO YOU, DAD. ONE LAST DRINK TO SPEED YOU ON YOUR WAY.
GOOD-BYE AND GOOD RIDDANCE.
NOT AGAIN.
LET ME GUESS. YOU'VE COME TO CHALLENGE ME TO A DUEL.
OR MAYBE YOU'VE COME TO ACCUSE ME OF A MURDER.
NO...
...I'VE COME TO CONFESS TO ONE.

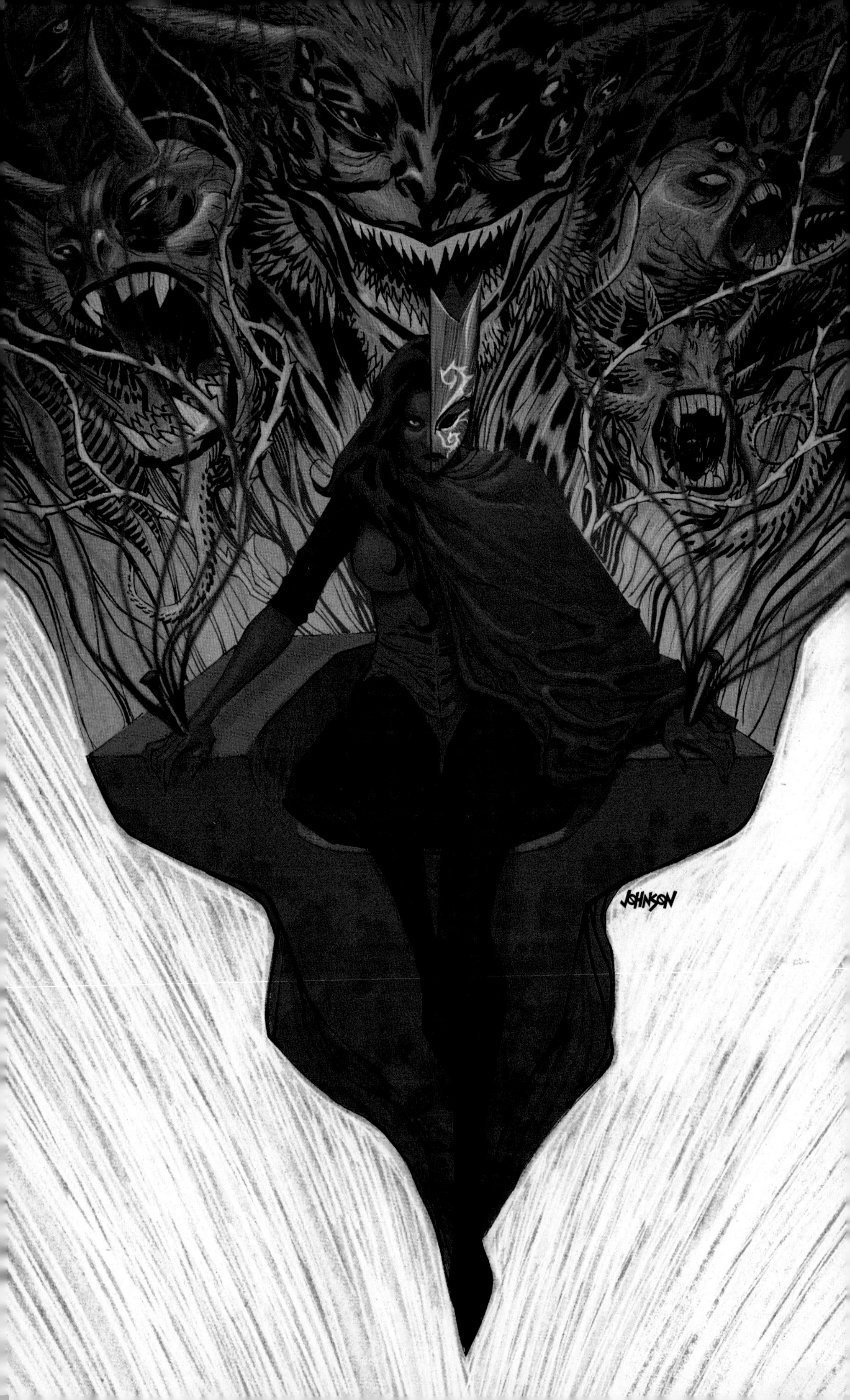
JOHNSON

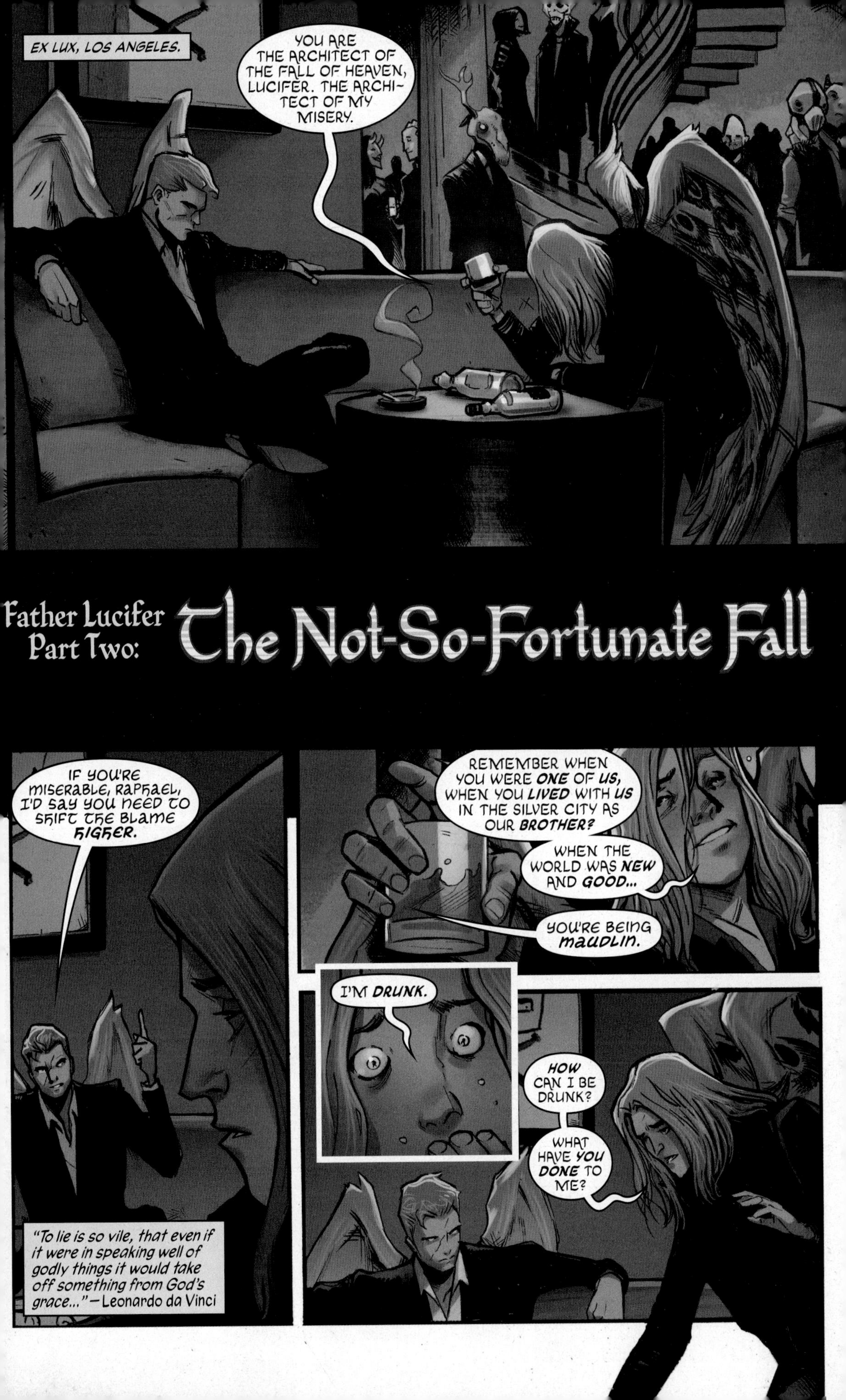
EX LUX, LOS ANGELES.
YOU ARE THE ARCHITECT OF THE FALL OF HEAVEN, LUCIFER. THE ARCHITECT OF MY MISERY.
Father Lucifer Part Two: The Not-So-Fortunate Fall
IF YOU'RE MISERABLE, RAPHAEL, I'D SAY YOU NEED TO SHIFT THE BLAME HIGHER.
REMEMBER WHEN YOU WERE ONE OF US, WHEN YOU LIVED WITH US IN THE SILVER CITY AS OUR BROTHER?
WHEN THE WORLD WAS NEW AND GOOD...
YOU'RE BEING MAUDLIN.
I'M DRUNK.
HOW CAN I BE DRUNK?
WHAT HAVE YOU DONE TO ME?
"To lie is so vile, that even if it were in speaking well of godly things it would take off something from God's grace..."—Leonardo da Vinci

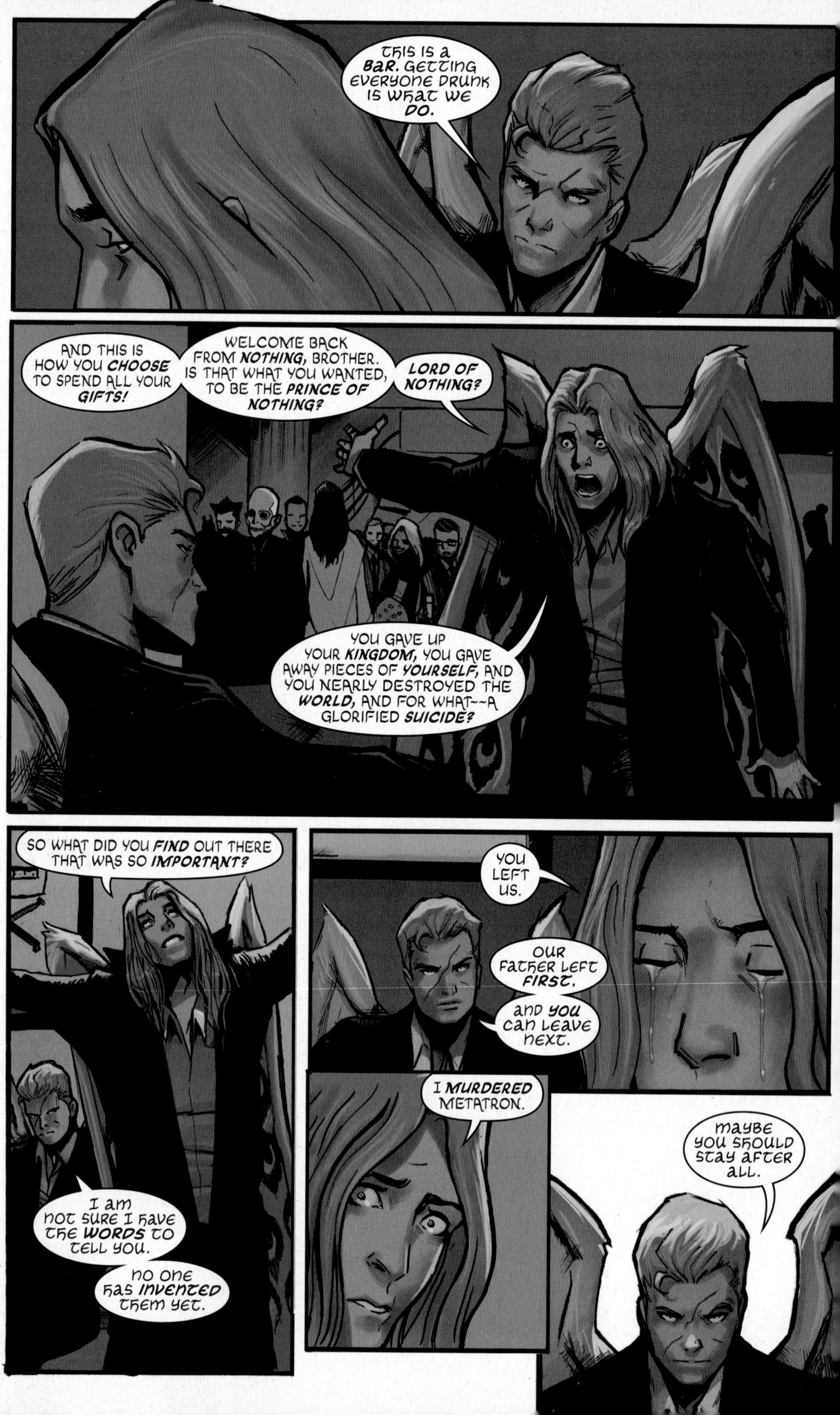
THIS IS A BAR. GETTING EVERYONE DRUNK IS WHAT WE DO.
AND THIS IS HOW YOU CHOOSE TO SPEND ALL YOUR GIFTS!
WELCOME BACK FROM NOTHING, BROTHER. IS THAT WHAT YOU WANTED, TO BE THE PRINCE OF NOTHING?
LORD OF NOTHING?
YOU GAVE UP YOUR KINGDOM, YOU GAVE AWAY PIECES OF YOURSELF, AND YOU NEARLY DESTROYED THE WORLD, AND FOR WHAT--A GLORIFIED SUICIDE?
SO WHAT DID YOU FIND OUT THERE THAT WAS SO IMPORTANT?
I AM NOT SURE I HAVE THE WORDS TO TELL YOU.
NO ONE HAS INVENTED THEM YET.
YOU LEFT US.
OUR FATHER LEFT FIRST.
AND YOU CAN LEAVE NEXT.
I MURDERED METATRON.
MAYBE YOU SHOULD STAY AFTER ALL.

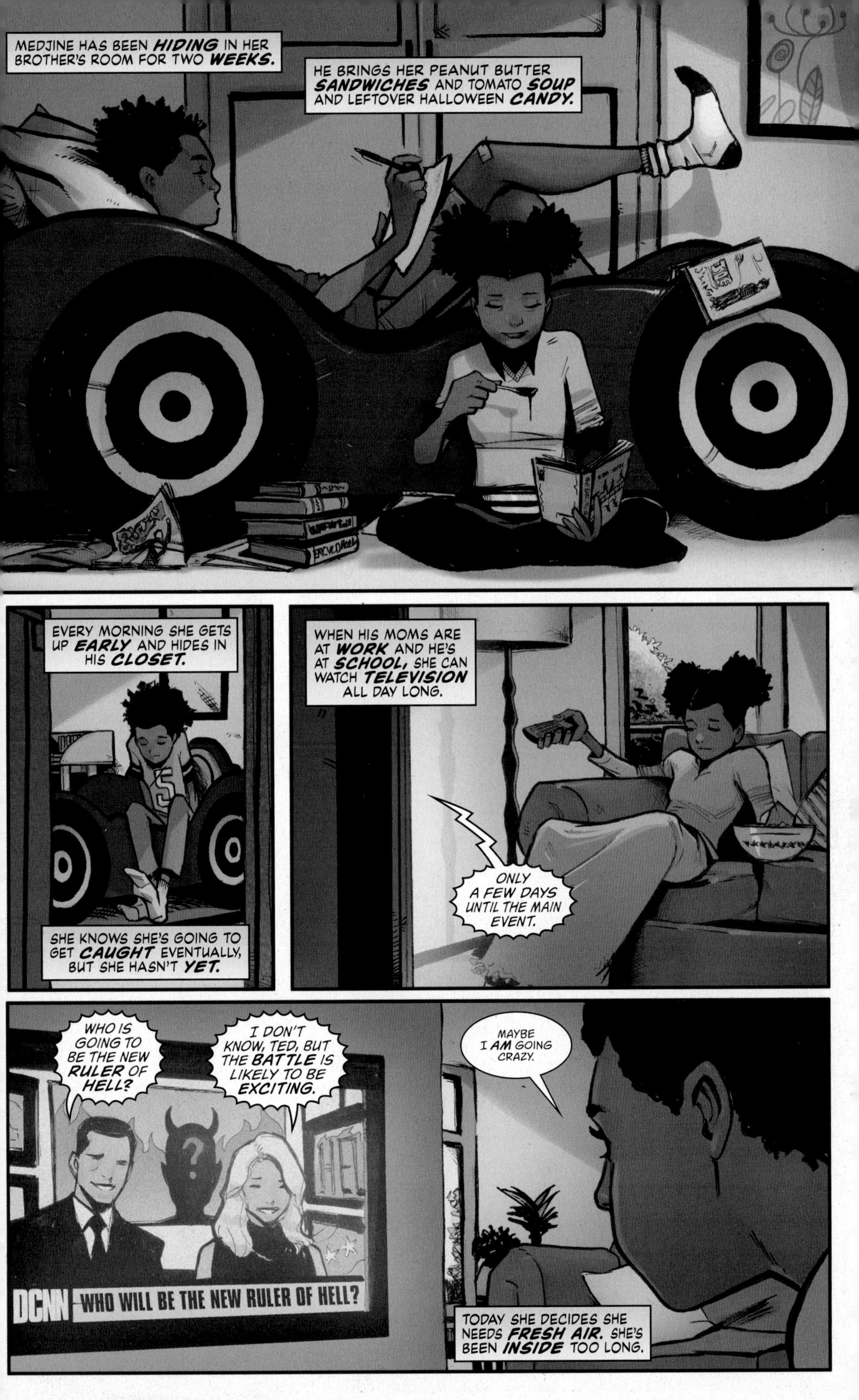
MEDJINE HAS BEEN HIDING IN HER BROTHER'S ROOM FOR TWO WEEKS.
HE BRINGS HER PEANUT BUTTER SANDWICHES AND TOMATO SOUP AND LEFTOVER HALLOWEEN CANDY.
EVERY MORNING SHE GETS UP EARLY AND HIDES IN HIS CLOSET.
SHE KNOWS SHE'S GOING TO GET CAUGHT EVENTUALLY, BUT SHE HASN'T YET.
WHEN HIS MOMS ARE AT WORK AND HE'S AT SCHOOL, SHE CAN WATCH TELEVISION ALL DAY LONG.
ONLY A FEW DAYS UNTIL THE MAIN EVENT.
WHO IS GOING TO BE THE NEW RULER OF HELL?
I DON'T KNOW, TED, BUT THE BATTLE IS LIKELY TO BE EXCITING.
DCNN WHO WILL BE THE NEW RULER OF HELL?
MAYBE I AM GOING CRAZY.
TODAY SHE DECIDES SHE NEEDS FRESH AIR. SHE'S BEEN INSIDE TOO LONG.

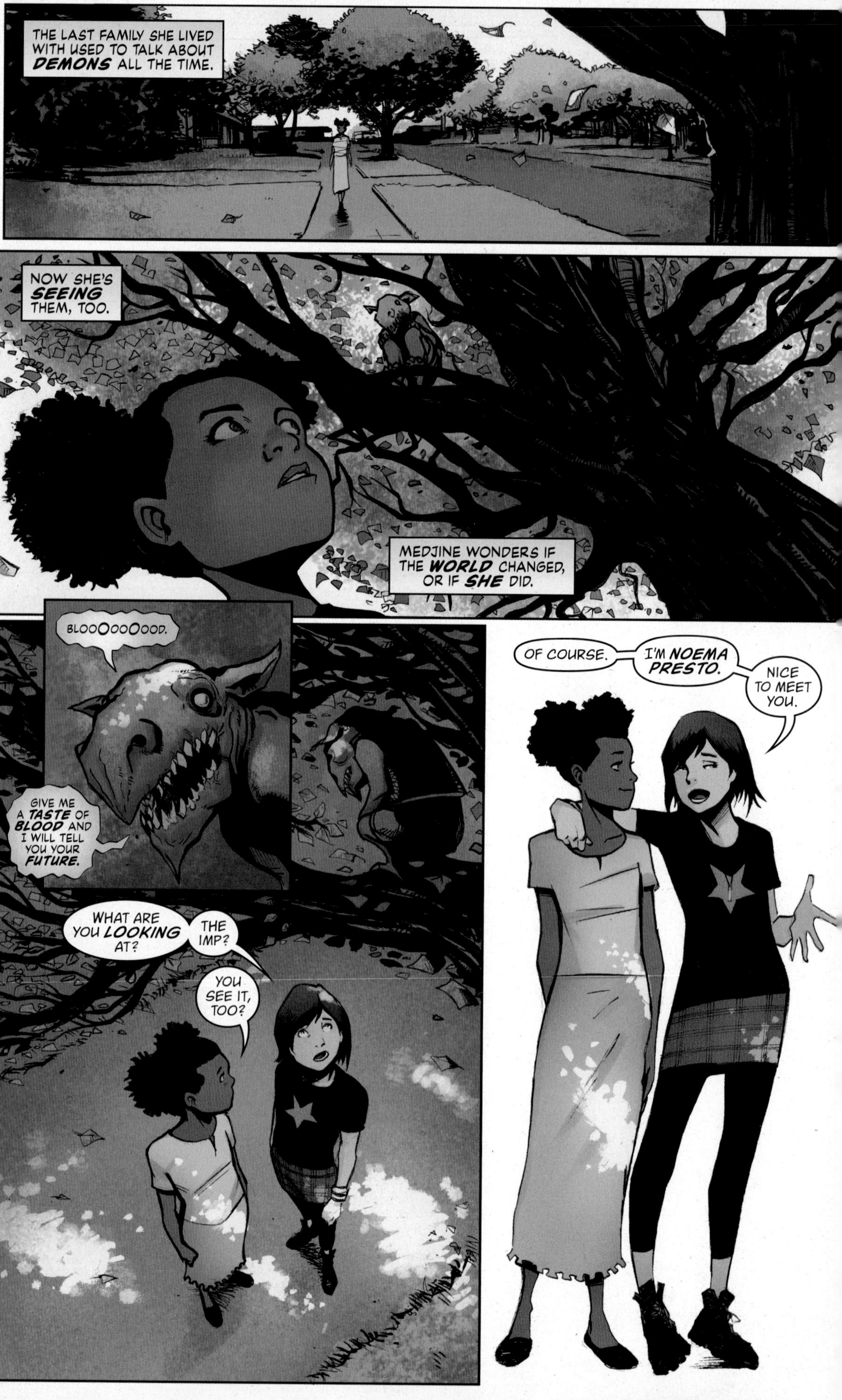
THE LAST FAMILY SHE LIVED WITH USED TO TALK ABOUT DEMONS ALL THE TIME.
NOW SHE'S SEEING THEM, TOO.
MEDJINE WONDERS IF THE WORLD CHANGED, OR IF SHE DID.
BLOOOOOOOOD.
GIVE ME A TASTE OF BLOOD AND I WILL TELL YOU YOUR FUTURE.
WHAT ARE YOU LOOKING AT?
THE IMP?
YOU SEE IT, TOO?
OF COURSE.
I'M NOEMA PRESTO.
NICE TO MEET YOU.

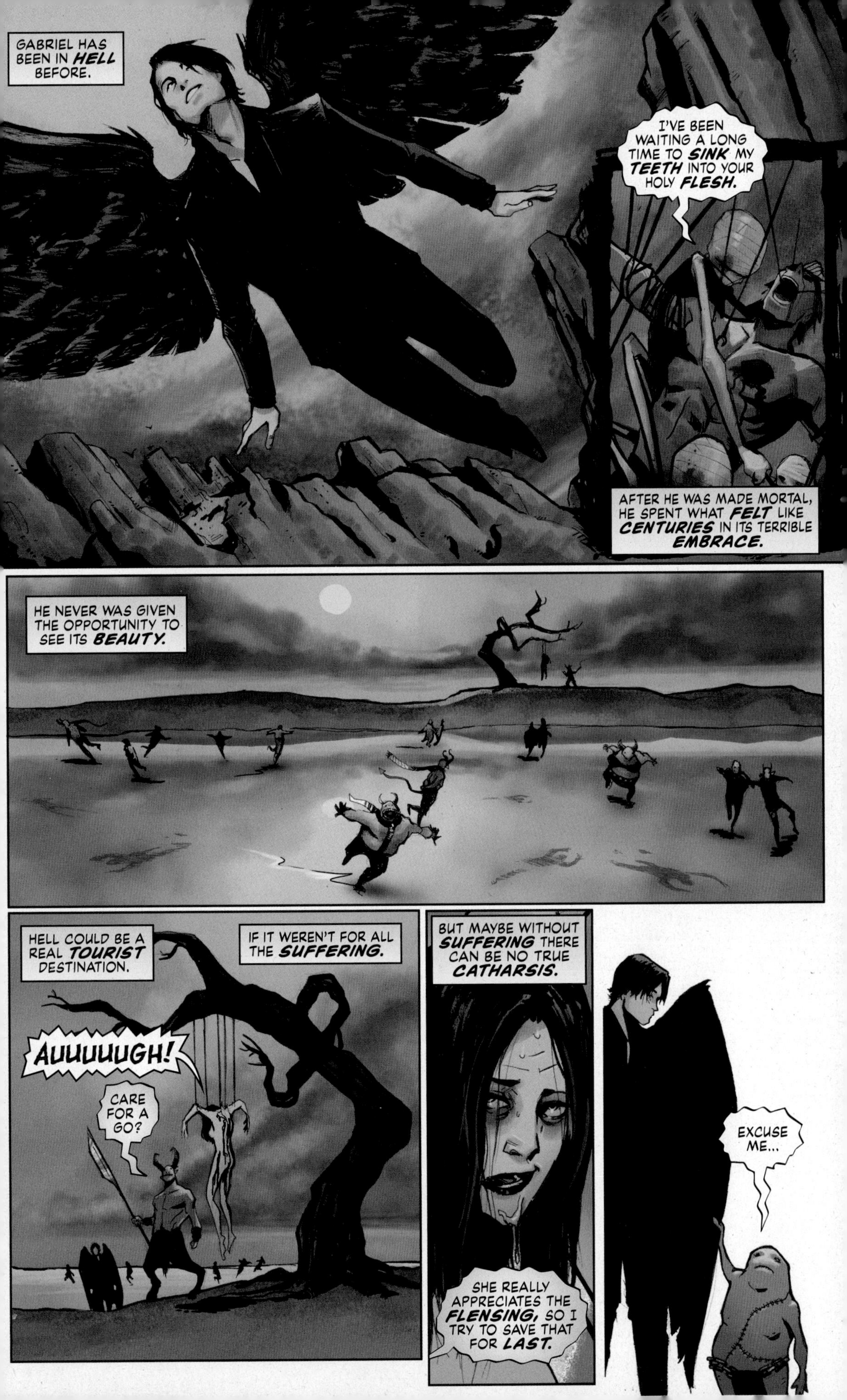
GABRIEL HAS BEEN IN HELL BEFORE.
I'VE BEEN WAITING A LONG TIME TO SINK MY TEETH INTO YOUR HOLY FLESH.
AFTER HE WAS MADE MORTAL, HE SPENT WHAT FELT LIKE CENTURIES IN ITS TERRIBLE EMBRACE.
HE NEVER WAS GIVEN THE OPPORTUNITY TO SEE ITS BEAUTY.
HELL COULD BE A REAL TOURIST DESTINATION.
IF IT WEREN'T FOR ALL THE SUFFERING.
AUUUUUGH!
CARE FOR A GO?
BUT MAYBE WITHOUT SUFFERING THERE CAN BE NO TRUE CATHARSIS.
SHE REALLY APPRECIATES THE FLENSING, SO I TRY TO SAVE THAT FOR LAST.
EXCUSE ME...

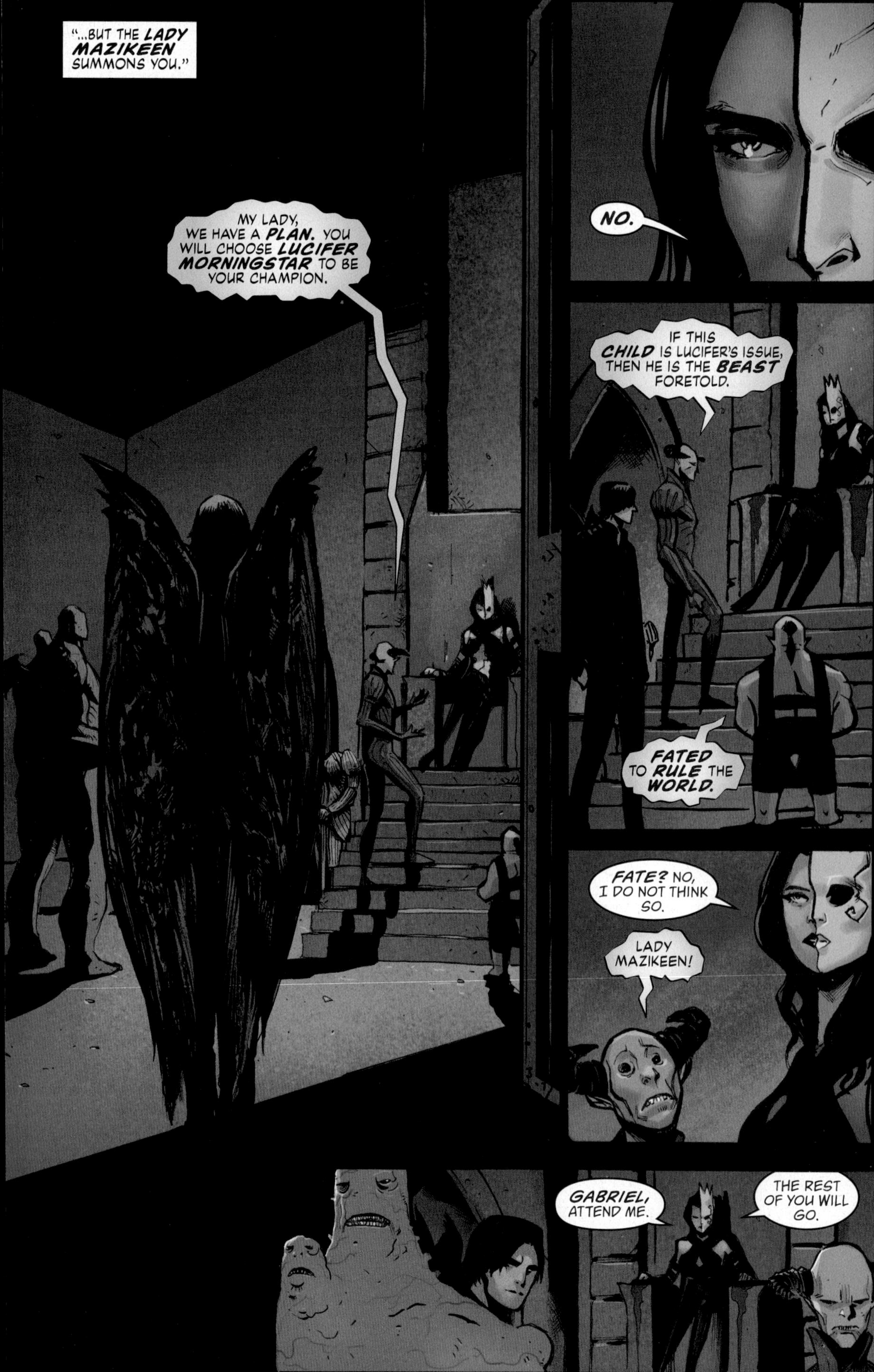
"...BUT THE LADY MAZIKEEN SUMMONS YOU."
MY LADY, WE HAVE A PLAN. YOU WILL CHOOSE LUCIFER MORNINGSTAR TO BE YOUR CHAMPION.
NO.
IF THIS CHILD IS LUCIFER'S ISSUE, THEN HE IS THE BEAST FORETOLD.
FATED TO RULE THE WORLD.
FATE? NO, I DO NOT THINK SO.
LADY MAZIKEEN!
GABRIEL, ATTEND ME.
THE REST OF YOU WILL GO.

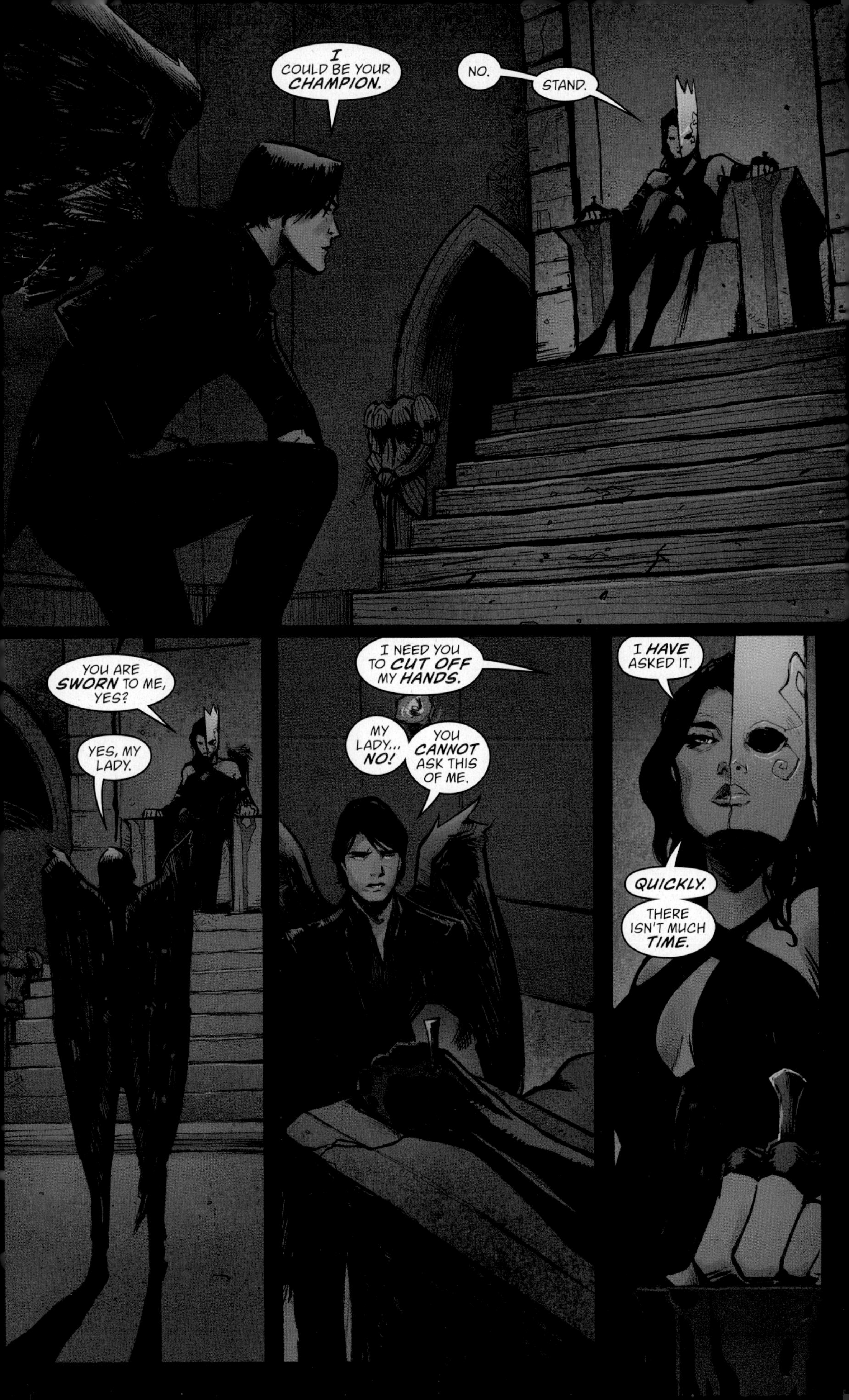
I COULD BE YOUR CHAMPION.
NO.
STAND.
YOU ARE SWORN TO ME, YES?
YES, MY LADY.
I NEED YOU TO CUT OFF MY HANDS.
MY LADY... NO!
YOU CANNOT ASK THIS OF ME.
I HAVE ASKED IT.
QUICKLY.
THERE ISN'T MUCH TIME.

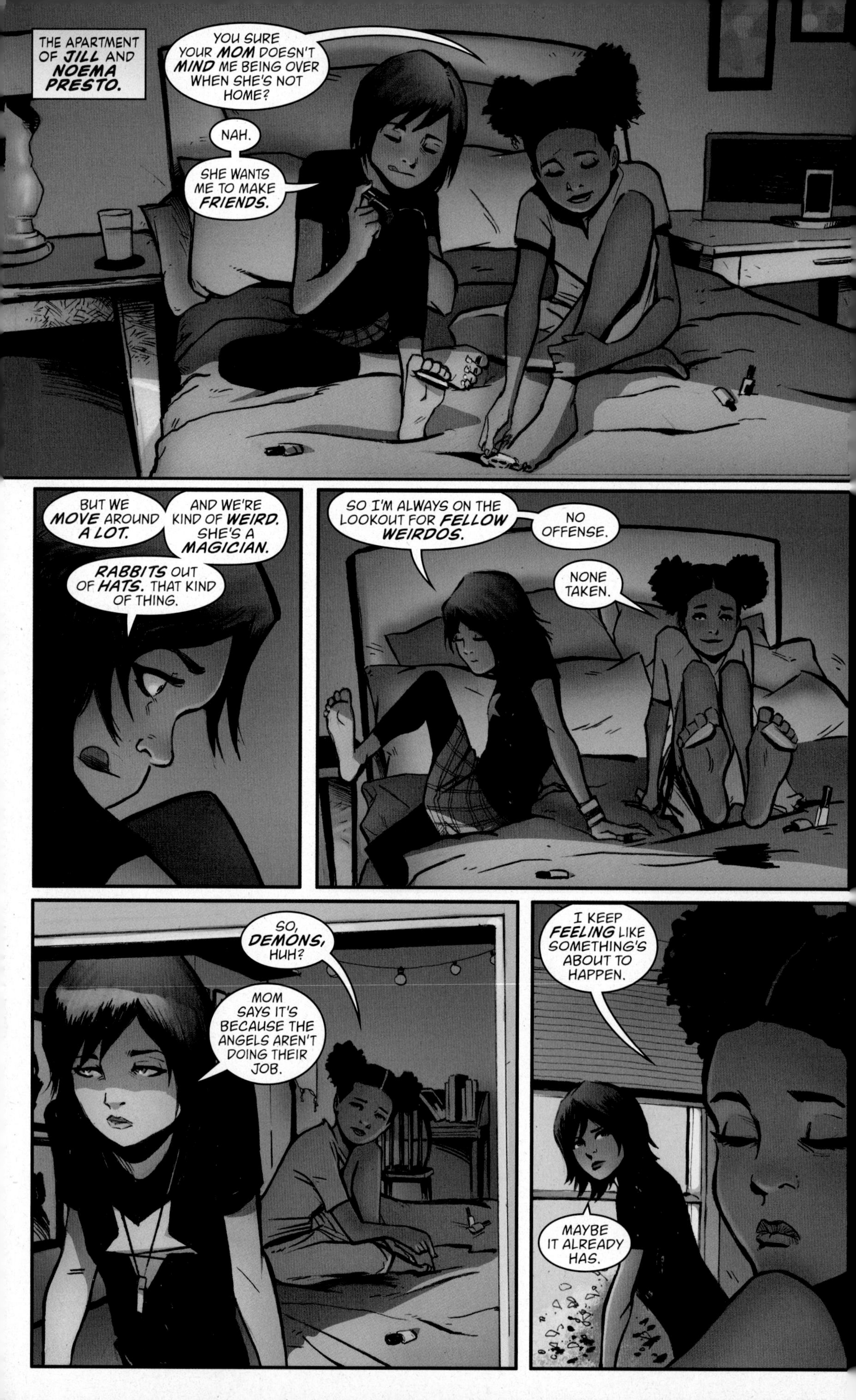

THE APARTMENT OF JILL AND NOEMA PRESTO.
YOU SURE YOUR MOM DOESN'T MIND ME BEING OVER WHEN SHE'S NOT HOME?
NAH.
SHE WANTS ME TO MAKE FRIENDS.
BUT WE MOVE AROUND A LOT.
AND WE'RE KIND OF WEIRD. SHE'S A MAGICIAN.
RABBITS OUT OF HATS. THAT KIND OF THING.
SO I'M ALWAYS ON THE LOOKOUT FOR FELLOW WEIRDOS.
NO OFFENSE.
NONE TAKEN.
SO, DEMONS, HUH?
MOM SAYS IT'S BECAUSE THE ANGELS AREN'T DOING THEIR JOB.
I KEEP FEELING LIKE SOMETHING'S ABOUT TO HAPPEN.
MAYBE IT ALREADY HAS.

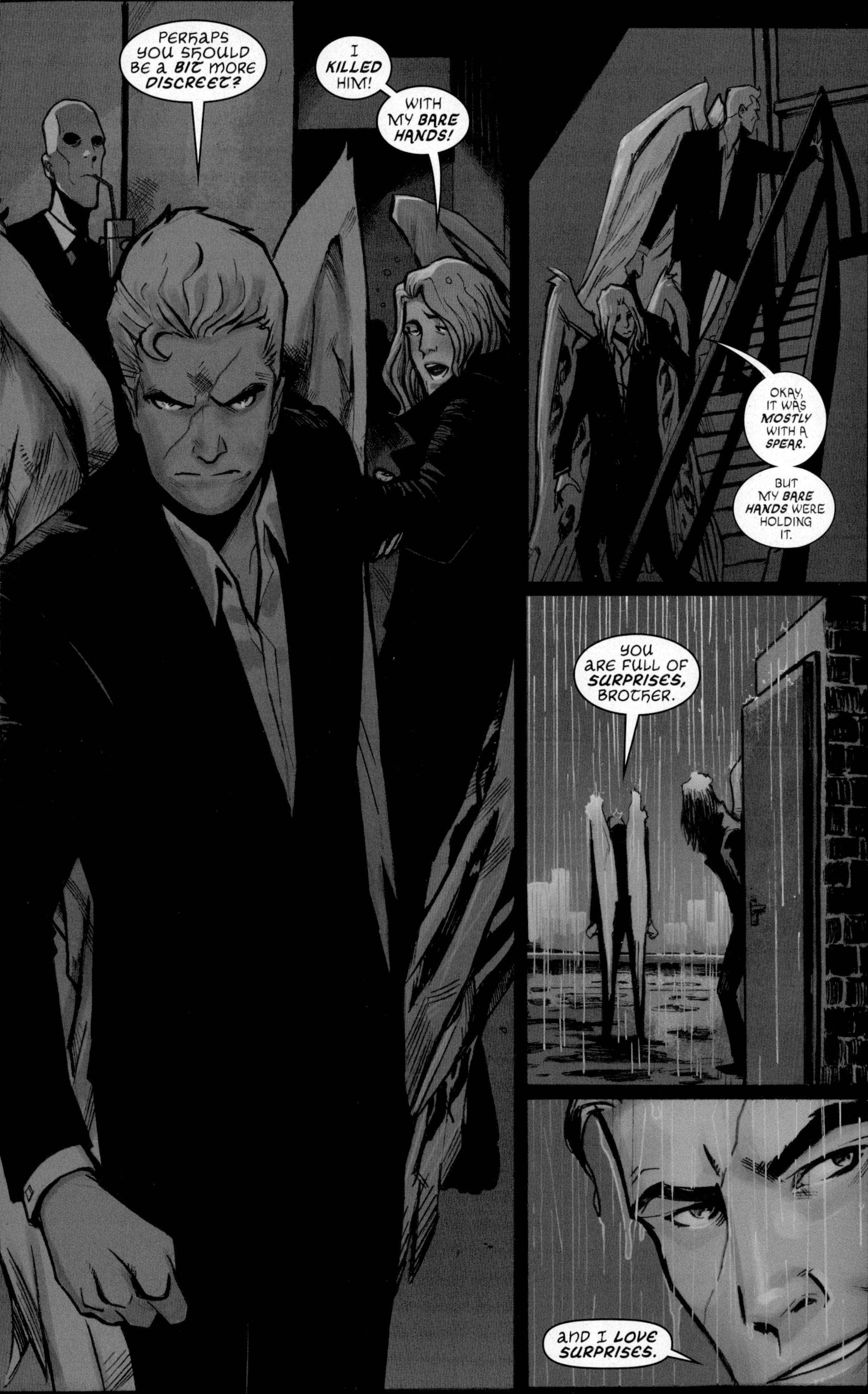
PERHAPS YOU SHOULD BE A BIT MORE DISCREET?
I KILLED HIM!
WITH MY BARE HANDS!
OKAY, IT WAS MOSTLY WITH A SPEAR.
BUT MY BARE HANDS WERE HOLDING IT.
YOU ARE FULL OF SURPRISES, BROTHER.
AND I LOVE SURPRISES.

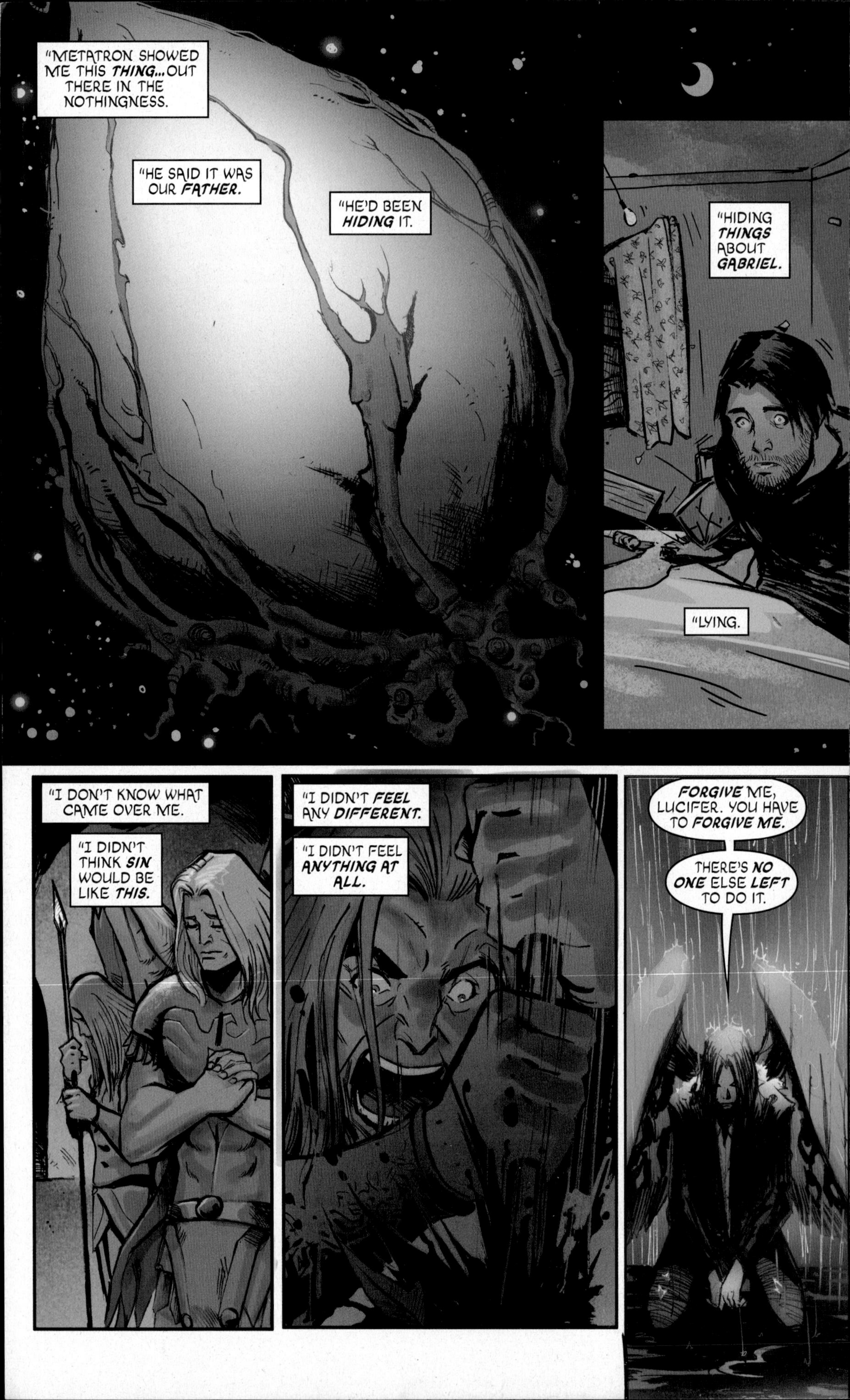
"METATRON SHOWED ME THIS THING...OUT THERE IN THE NOTHINGNESS.
"HE SAID IT WAS OUR FATHER.
"HE'D BEEN HIDING IT.
"HIDING THINGS ABOUT GABRIEL.
"LYING.
"I DON'T KNOW WHAT CAME OVER ME.
"I DIDN'T THINK SIN WOULD BE LIKE THIS.
"I DIDN'T FEEL ANY DIFFERENT.
"I DIDN'T FEEL ANYTHING AT ALL.
FORGIVE ME, LUCIFER. YOU HAVE TO FORGIVE ME.
THERE'S NO ONE ELSE LEFT TO DO IT.

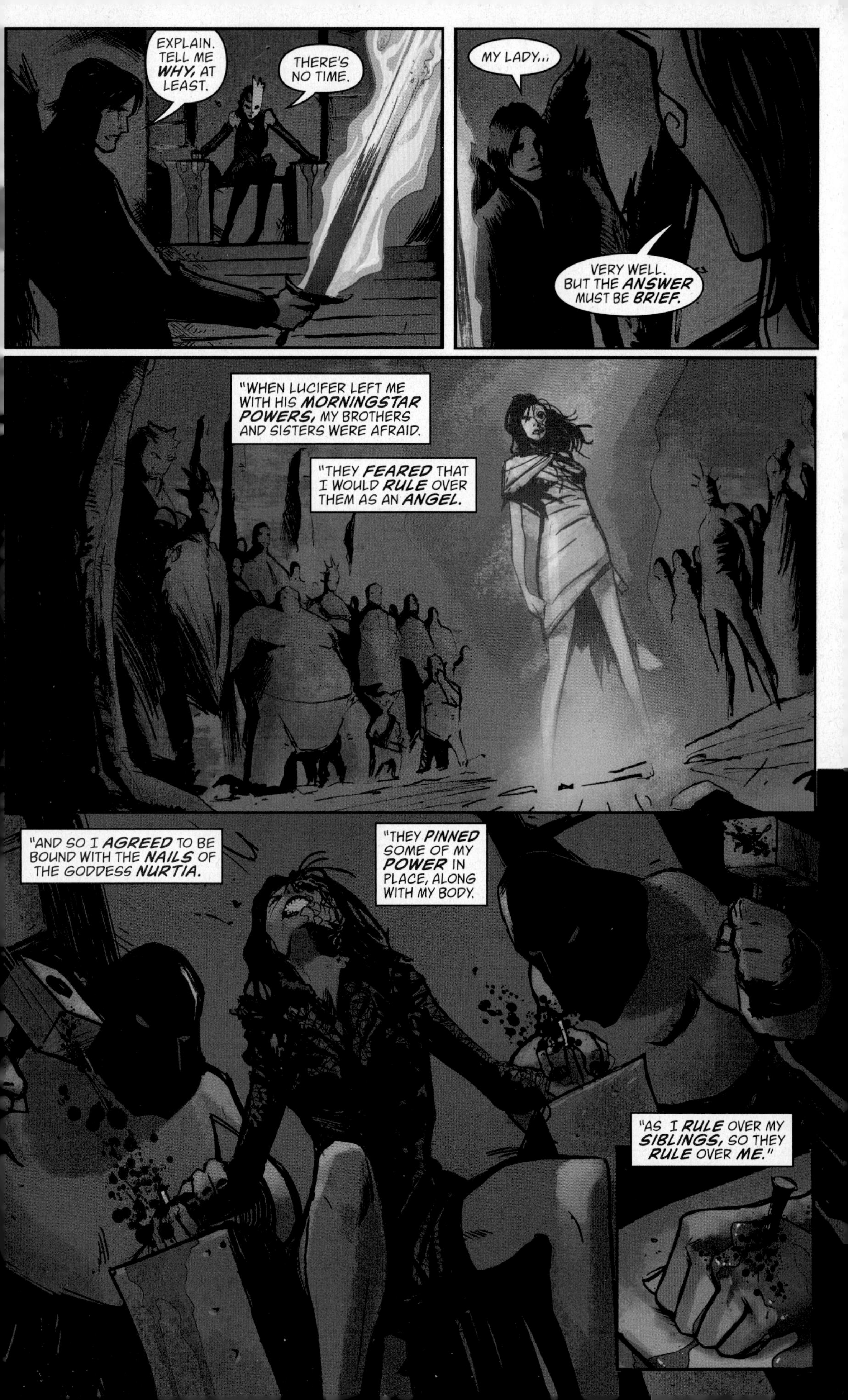
EXPLAIN. TELL ME WHY, AT LEAST.
THERE'S NO TIME.
MY LADY...
VERY WELL. BUT THE ANSWER MUST BE BRIEF.
"WHEN LUCIFER LEFT ME WITH HIS MORNINGSTAR POWERS, MY BROTHERS AND SISTERS WERE AFRAID.
"THEY FEARED THAT I WOULD RULE OVER THEM AS AN ANGEL.
"AND SO I AGREED TO BE BOUND WITH THE NAILS OF THE GODDESS NURTIA.
"THEY PINNED SOME OF MY POWER IN PLACE, ALONG WITH MY BODY.
"AS I RULE OVER MY SIBLINGS, SO THEY RULE OVER ME."

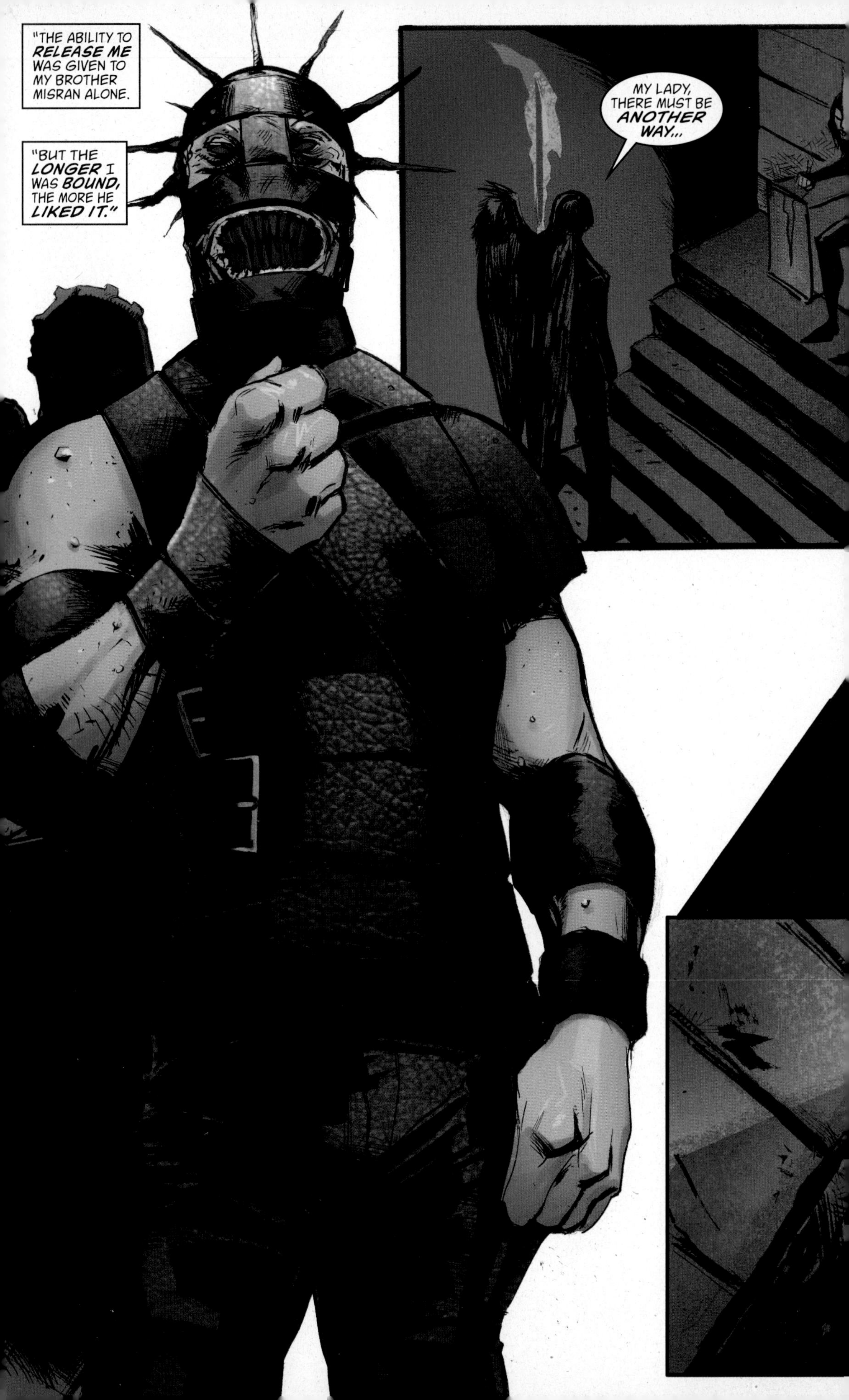
"THE ABILITY TO RELEASE ME WAS GIVEN TO MY BROTHER MISRAN ALONE.
"BUT THE LONGER I WAS BOUND, THE MORE HE LIKED IT."
MY LADY, THERE MUST BE ANOTHER WAY...

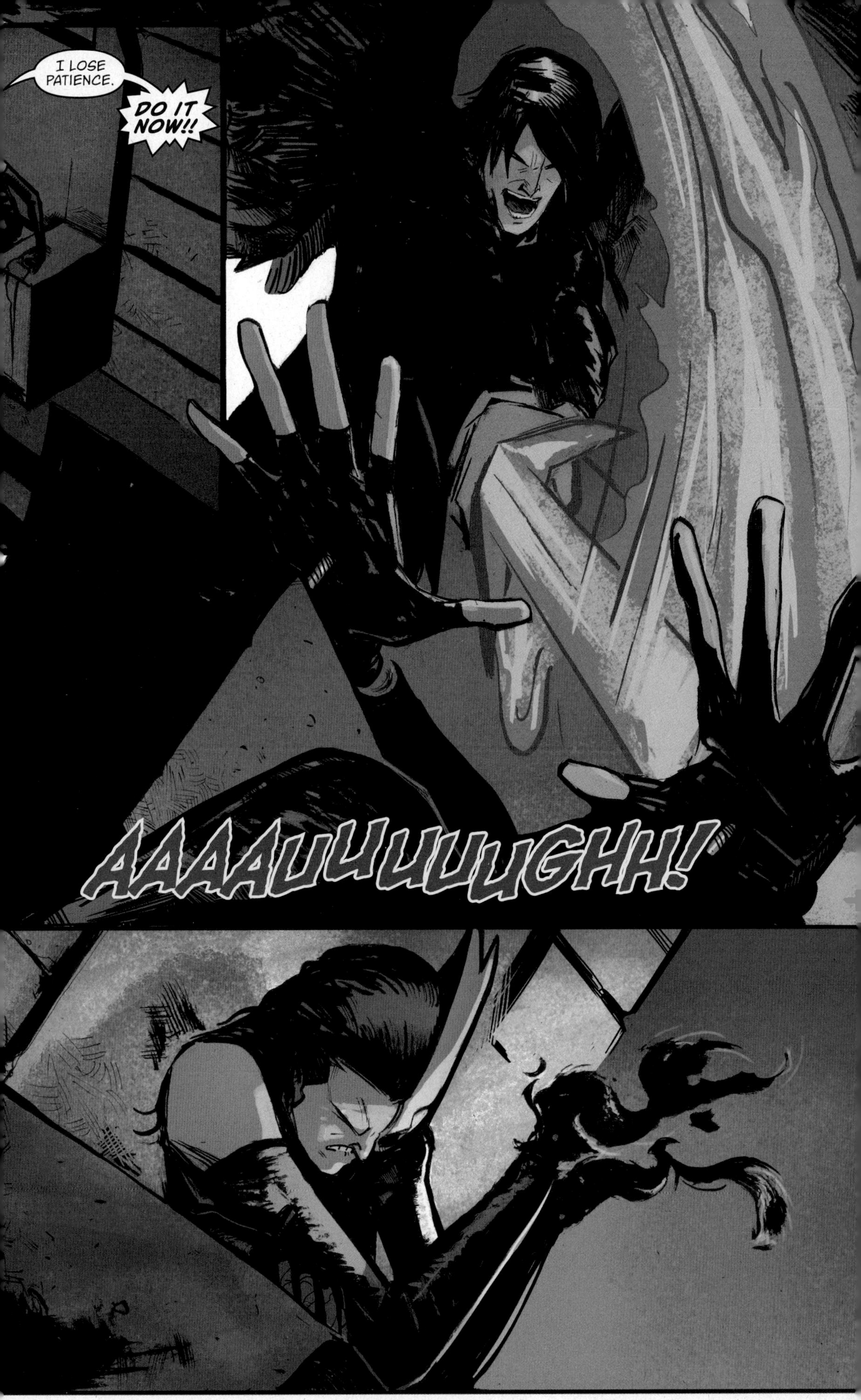
I LOSE PATIENCE.
DO IT NOW!!
AAAAUUUUUGHH!

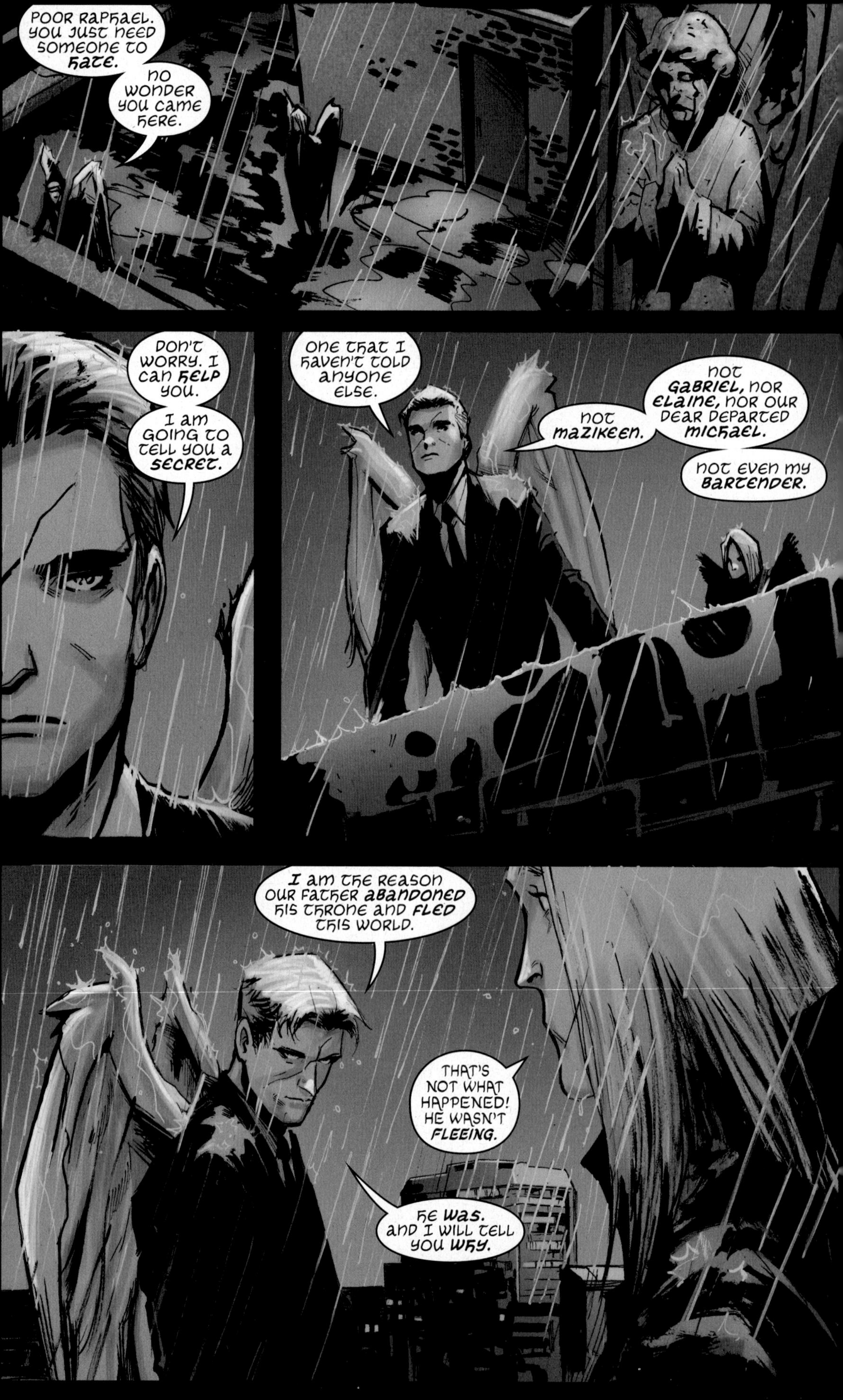

POOR RAPHAEL. YOU JUST NEED SOMEONE TO HATE.
NO WONDER YOU CAME HERE.
DON'T WORRY. I CAN HELP YOU.
I AM GOING TO TELL YOU A SECRET.
ONE THAT I HAVEN'T TOLD ANYONE ELSE.
NOT MAZIKEEN.
NOT GABRIEL, NOR ELAINE, NOR OUR DEAR DEPARTED MICHAEL.
NOT EVEN MY BARTENDER.
I AM THE REASON OUR FATHER ABANDONED HIS THRONE AND FLED THIS WORLD.
THAT'S NOT WHAT HAPPENED! HE WASN'T FLEEING.
HE WAS. AND I WILL TELL YOU WHY.

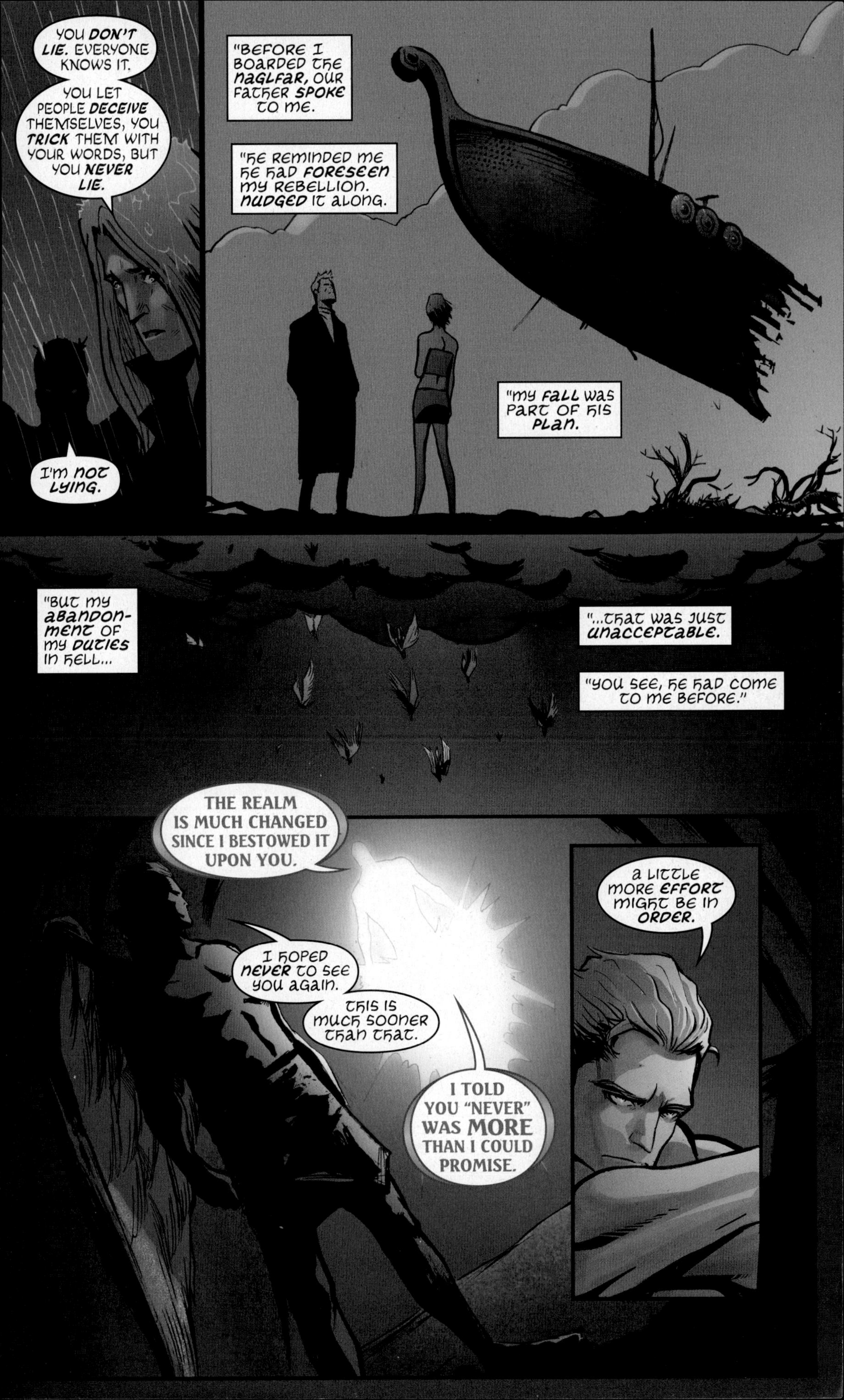
YOU DON'T LIE. EVERYONE KNOWS IT.
YOU LET PEOPLE DECEIVE THEMSELVES, YOU TRICK THEM WITH YOUR WORDS, BUT YOU NEVER LIE.
I'M NOT LYING.
"BEFORE I BOARDED THE NAGLFAR, OUR FATHER SPOKE TO ME.
"HE REMINDED ME HE HAD FORESEEN MY REBELLION. NUDGED IT ALONG.
"MY FALL WAS PART OF HIS PLAN.
"BUT MY ABANDONMENT OF MY DUTIES IN HELL...
"...THAT WAS JUST UNACCEPTABLE.
"YOU SEE, HE HAD COME TO ME BEFORE."
THE REALM IS MUCH CHANGED SINCE I BESTOWED IT UPON YOU.
I HOPED NEVER TO SEE YOU AGAIN.
THIS IS MUCH SOONER THAN THAT.
I TOLD YOU "NEVER" WAS MORE THAN I COULD PROMISE.
A LITTLE MORE EFFORT MIGHT BE IN ORDER.

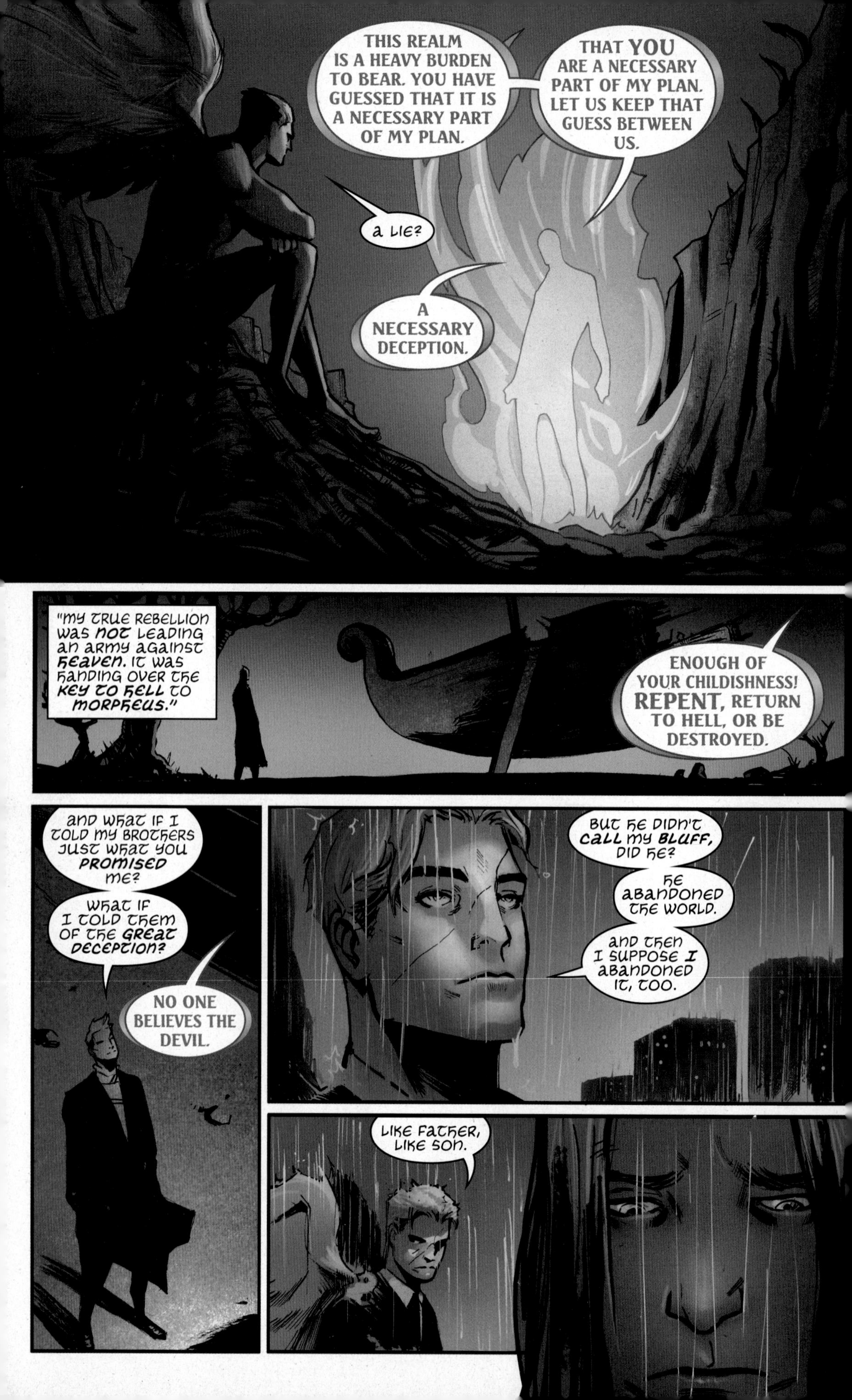
THIS REALM IS A HEAVY BURDEN TO BEAR. YOU HAVE GUESSED THAT IT IS A NECESSARY PART OF MY PLAN.
THAT YOU ARE A NECESSARY PART OF MY PLAN. LET US KEEP THAT GUESS BETWEEN US.
A LIE?
A NECESSARY DECEPTION.
"MY TRUE REBELLION WAS NOT LEADING AN ARMY AGAINST HEAVEN. IT WAS HANDING OVER THE KEY TO HELL TO MORPHEUS."
ENOUGH OF YOUR CHILDISHNESS! REPENT, RETURN TO HELL, OR BE DESTROYED.
AND WHAT IF I TOLD MY BROTHERS JUST WHAT YOU PROMISED ME?
WHAT IF I TOLD THEM OF THE GREAT DECEPTION?
NO ONE BELIEVES THE DEVIL.
BUT HE DIDN'T CALL MY BLUFF, DID HE?
HE ABANDONED THE WORLD.
AND THEN I SUPPOSE I ABANDONED IT, TOO.
LIKE FATHER, LIKE SON.

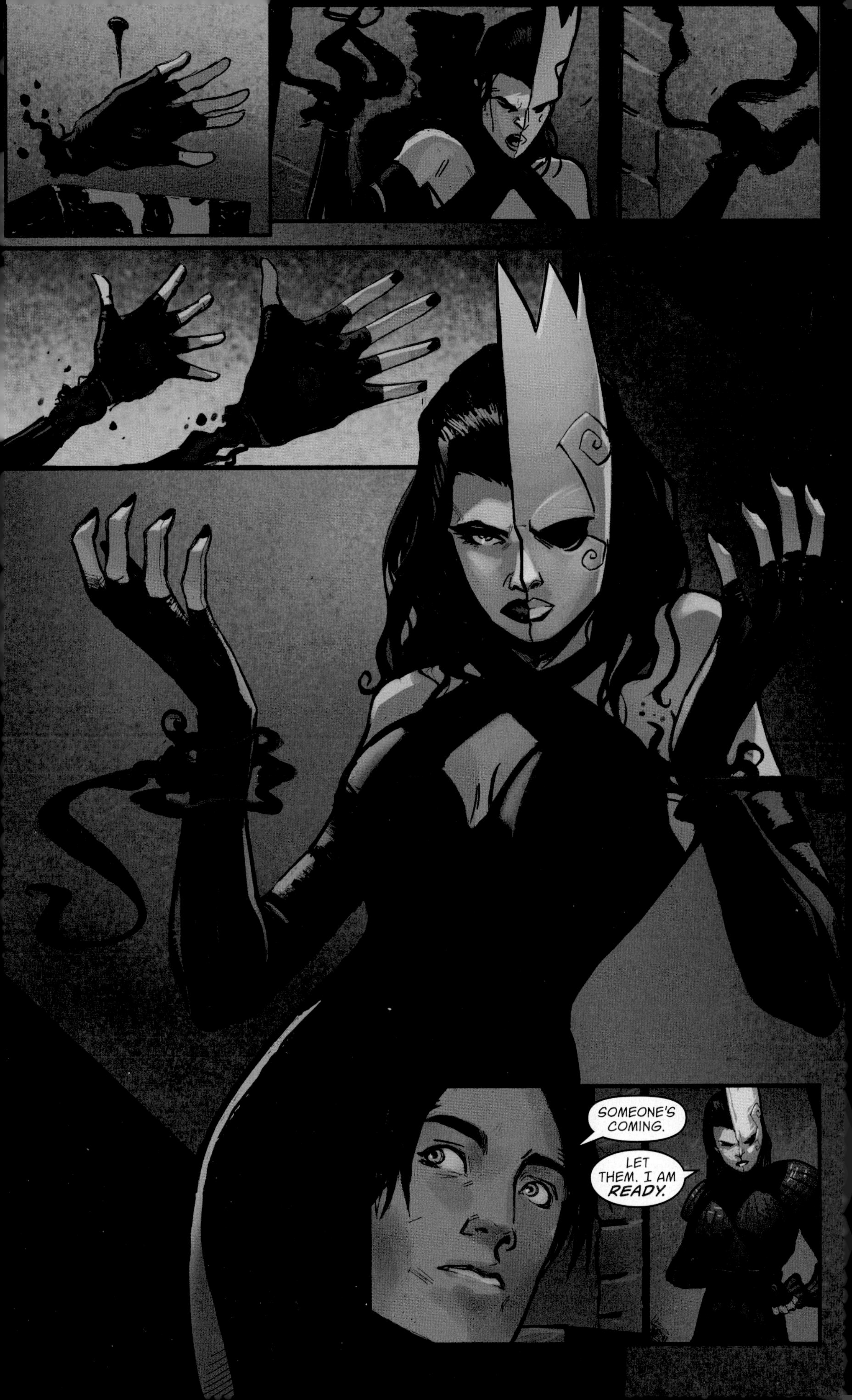
SOMEONE'S COMING.
LET THEM. I AM *READY.*

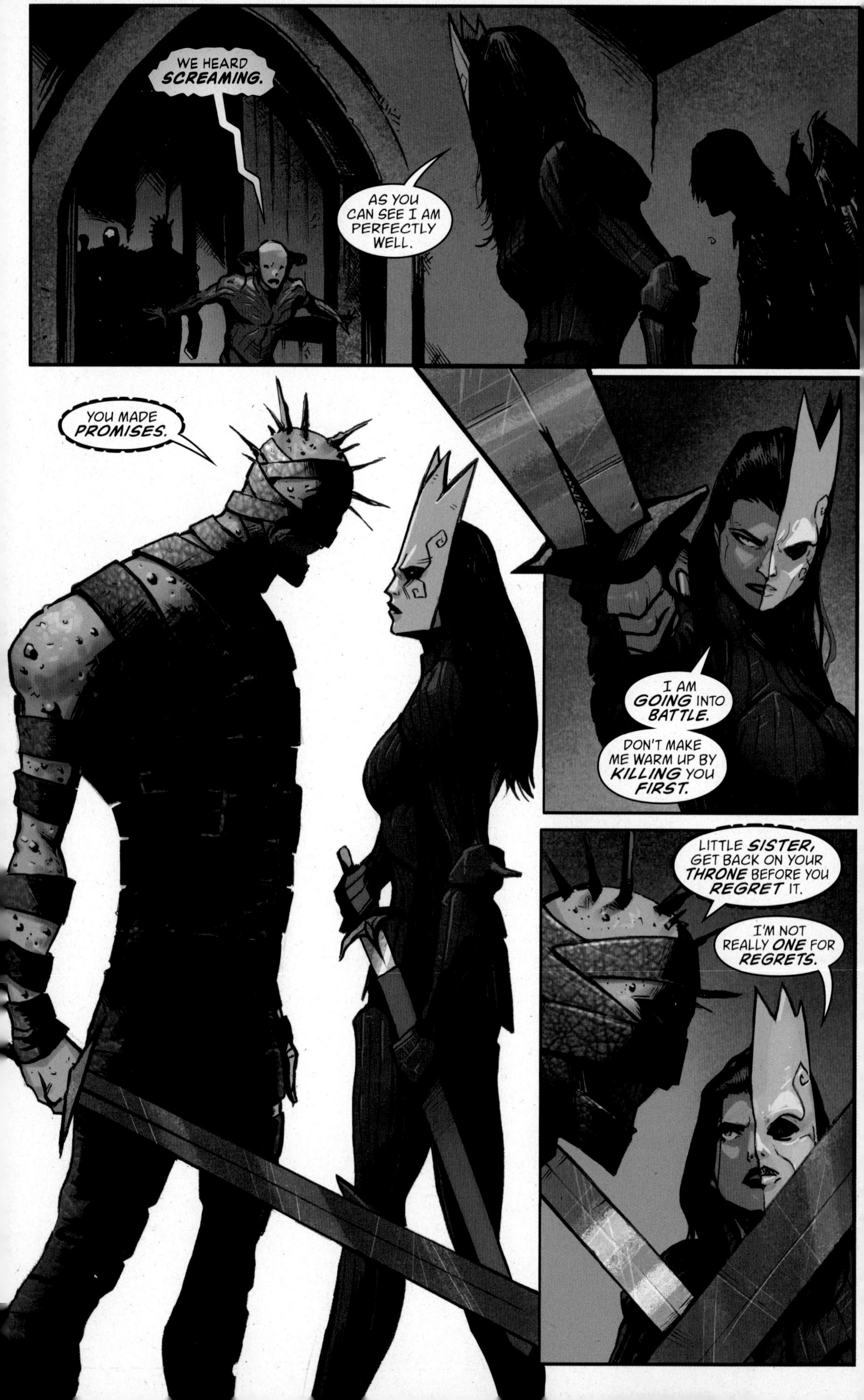
WE HEARD SCREAMING.
AS YOU CAN SEE I AM PERFECTLY WELL.
YOU MADE PROMISES.
I AM GOING INTO BATTLE.
DON'T MAKE ME WARM UP BY KILLING YOU FIRST.
LITTLE SISTER, GET BACK ON YOUR THRONE BEFORE YOU REGRET IT.
I'M NOT REALLY ONE FOR REGRETS.

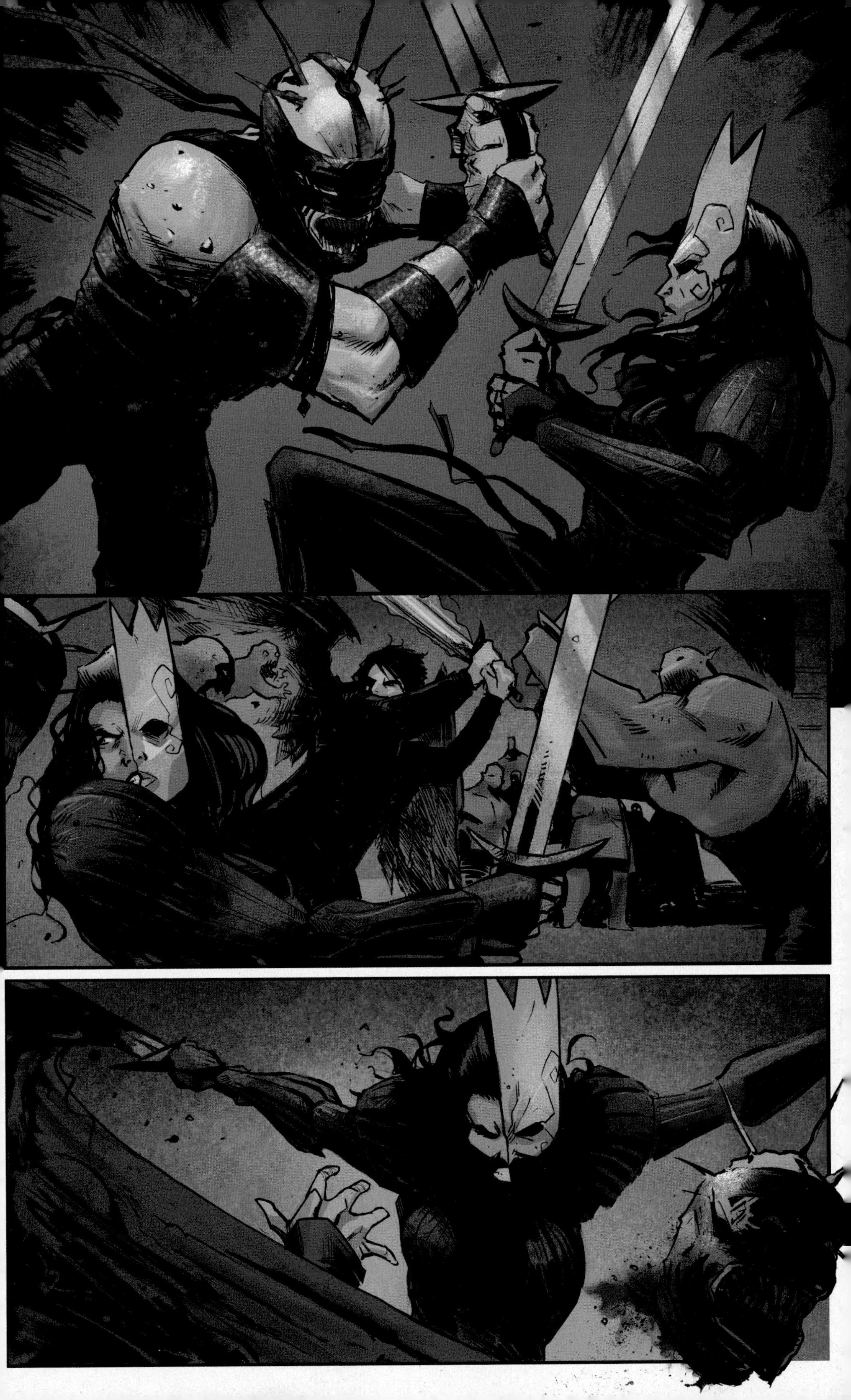

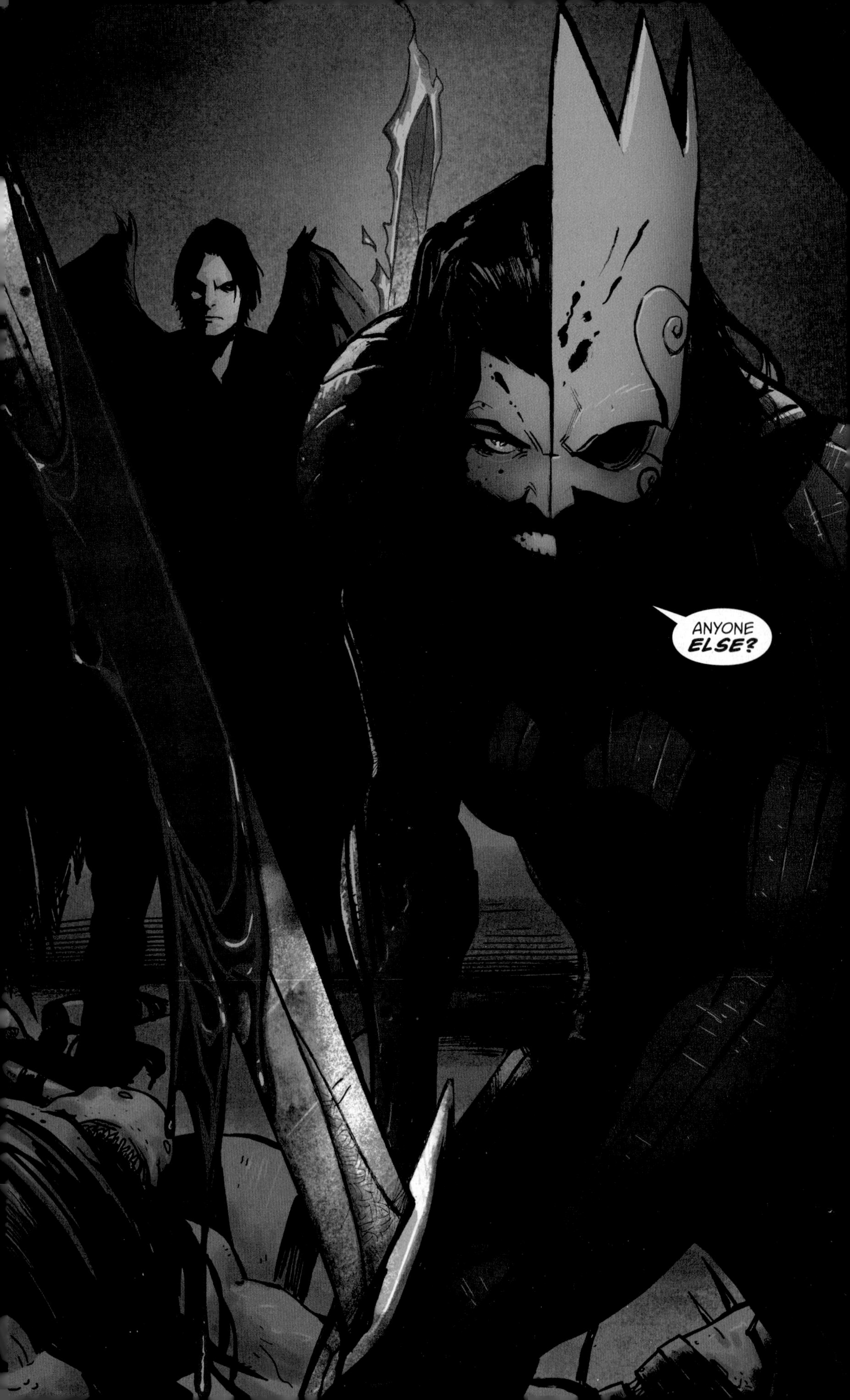
ANYONE ELSE?

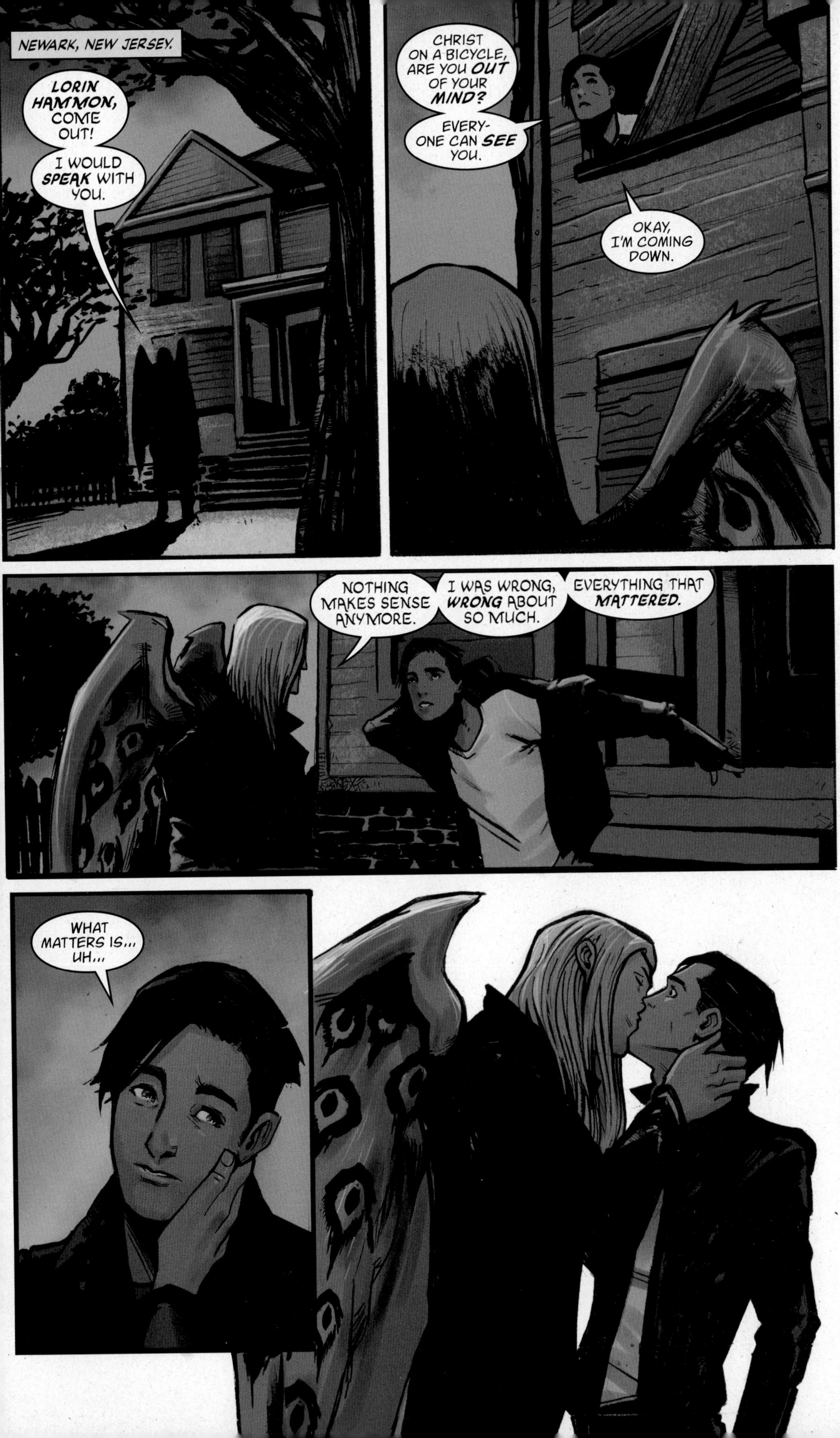
NEWARK, NEW JERSEY.
LORIN HAMMON, COME OUT!
I WOULD SPEAK WITH YOU.
CHRIST ON A BICYCLE, ARE YOU OUT OF YOUR MIND?
EVERY-ONE CAN SEE YOU.
OKAY, I'M COMING DOWN.
NOTHING MAKES SENSE ANYMORE.
I WAS WRONG, WRONG ABOUT SO MUCH.
EVERYTHING THAT MATTERED.
WHAT MATTERS IS... UH...

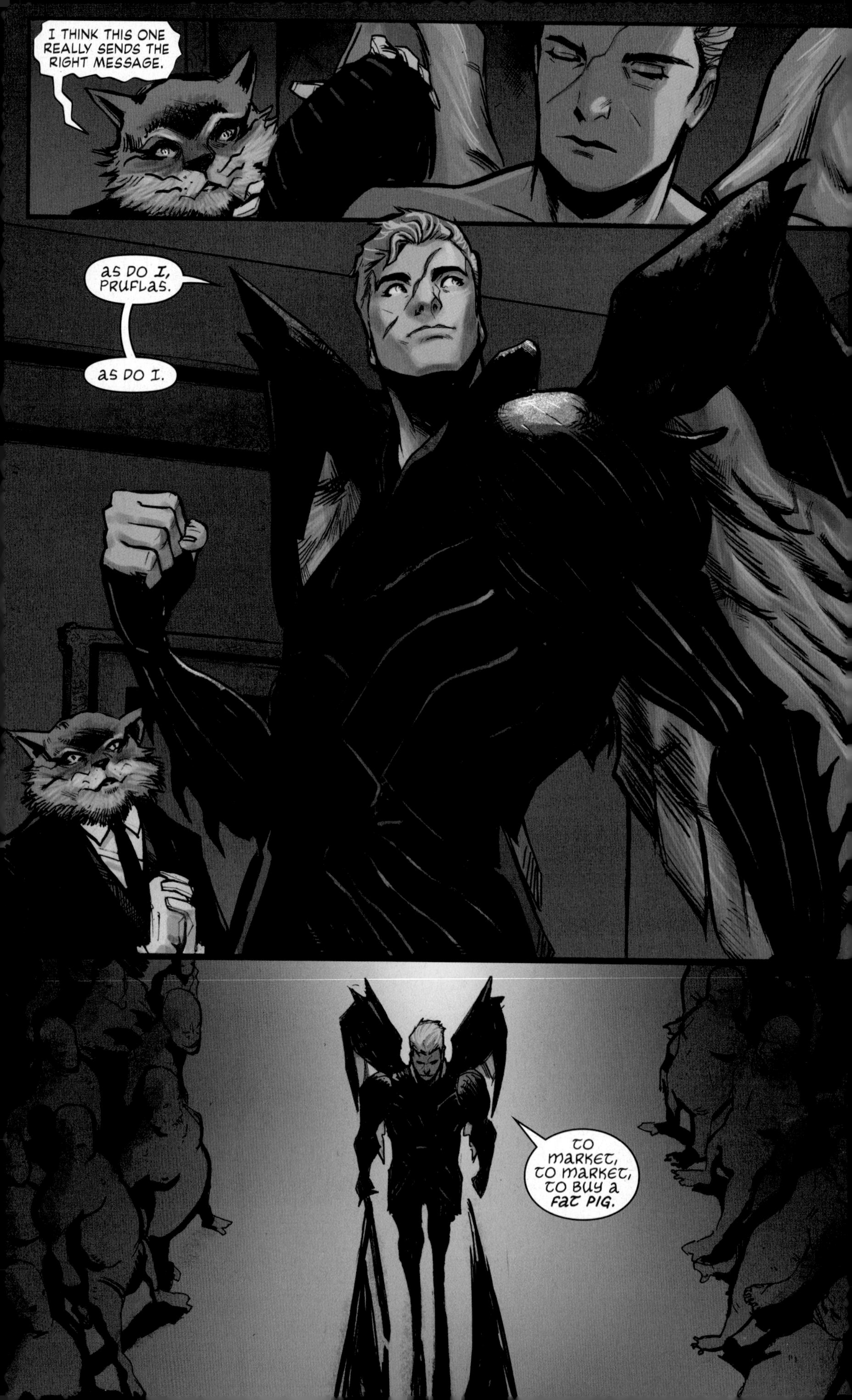
I THINK THIS ONE REALLY SENDS THE RIGHT MESSAGE.
AS DO *I*, PRUFLAS.
AS DO I.
TO MARKET, TO MARKET, TO BUY A *FAT PIG*.

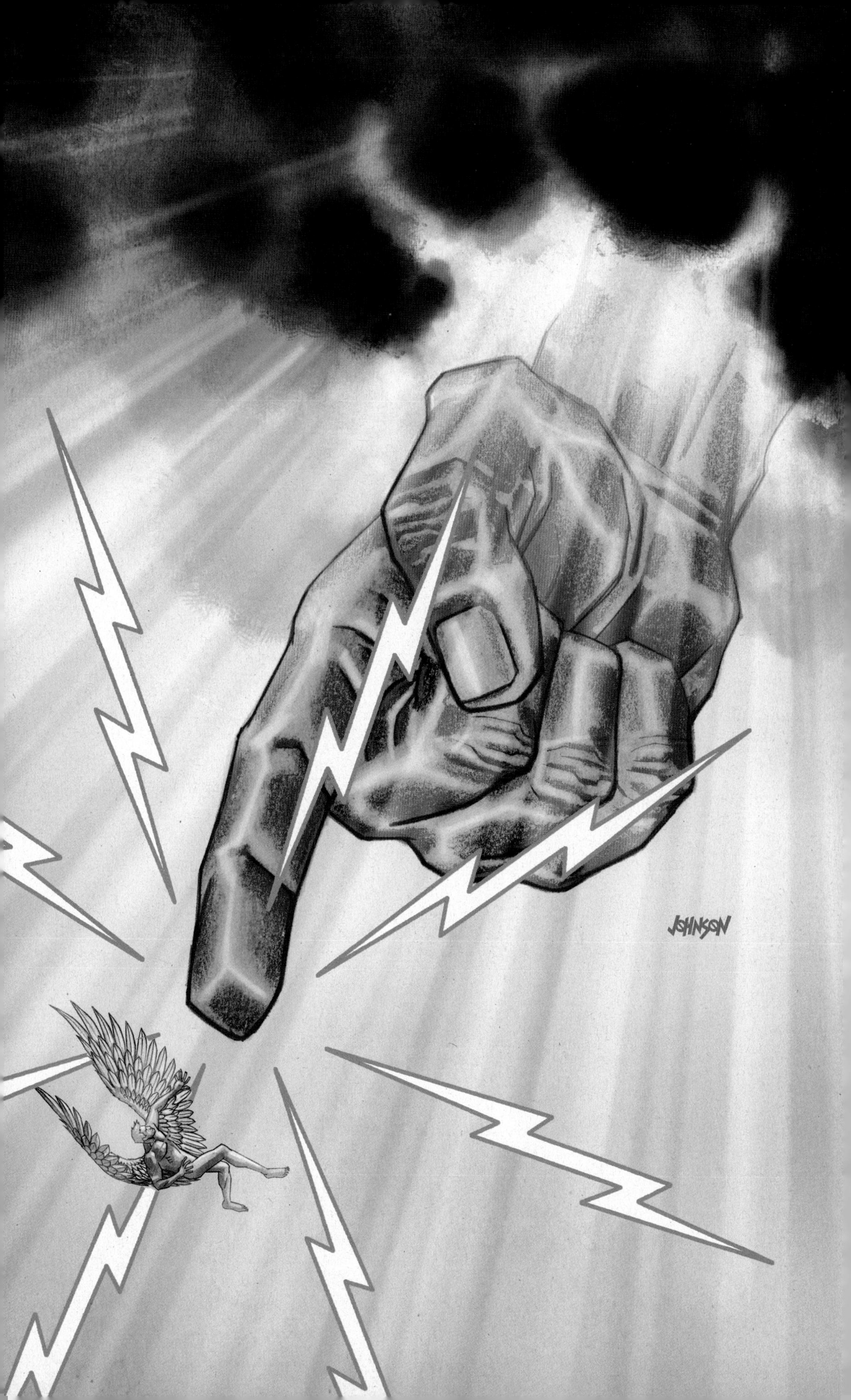
JOHNSON

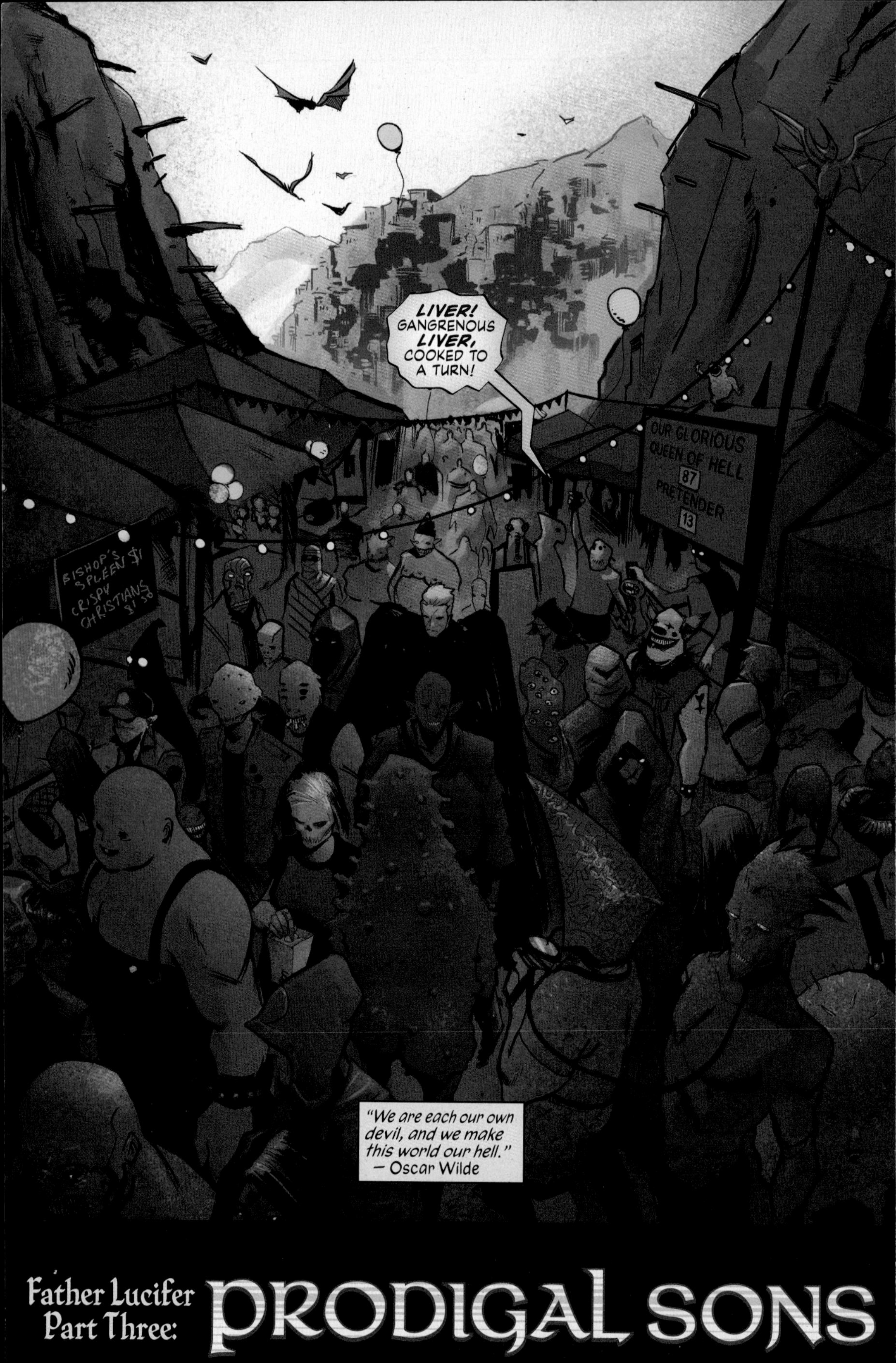
LIVER! GANGRENOUS LIVER, COOKED TO A TURN!
OUR GLORIOUS QUEEN OF HELL 87 PRETENDER 13
BISHOP'S SPLEEN $1 CRISPY CHRISTIANS $1.50
"We are each our own devil, and we make this world our hell."
— Oscar Wilde

Father Lucifer Part Three: PRODIGAL SONS

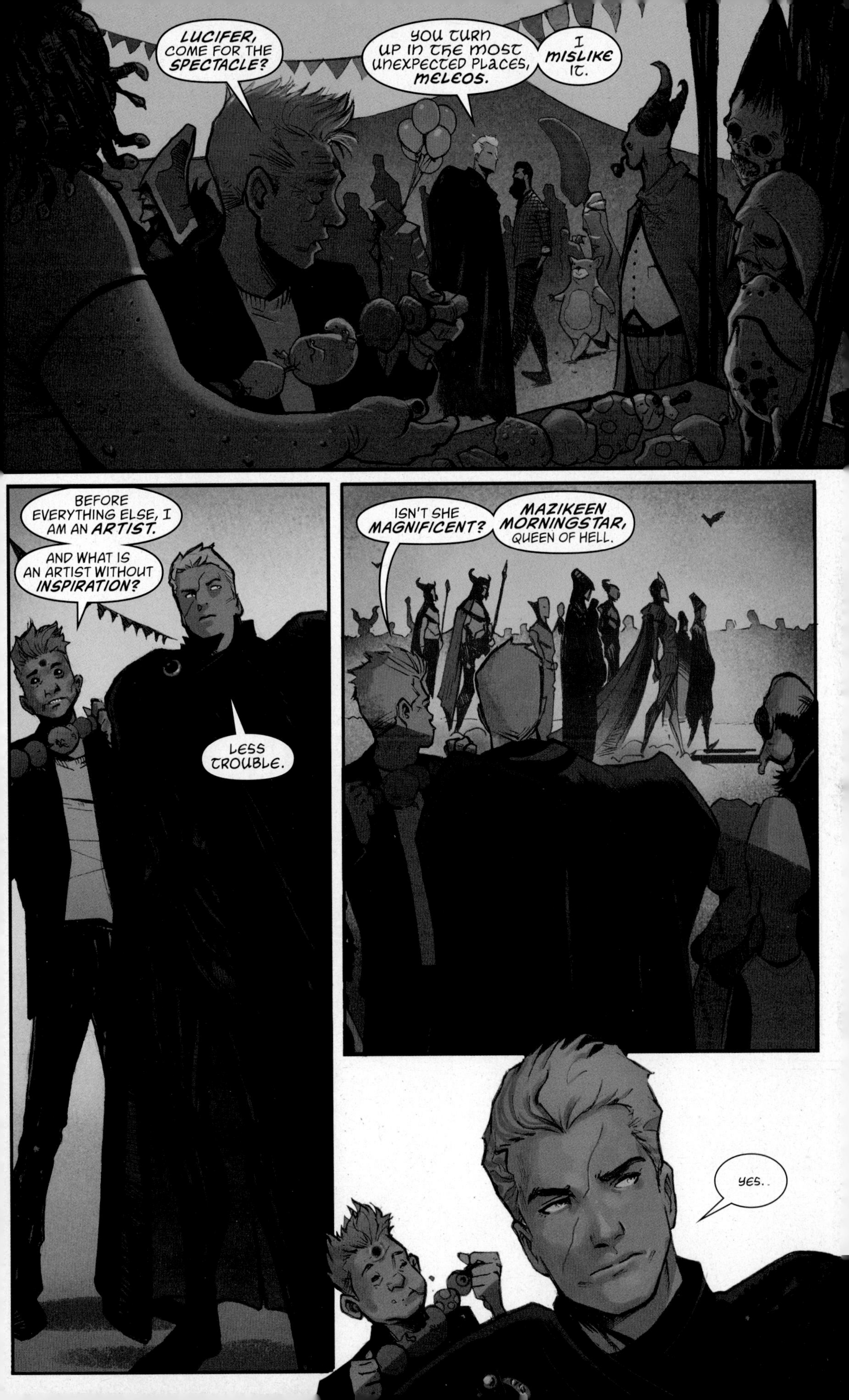
LUCIFER, COME FOR THE SPECTACLE?
YOU TURN UP IN THE MOST UNEXPECTED PLACES, MELEOS.
I MISLIKE IT.
BEFORE EVERYTHING ELSE, I AM AN ARTIST.
AND WHAT IS AN ARTIST WITHOUT INSPIRATION?
LESS TROUBLE.
ISN'T SHE MAGNIFICENT?
MAZIKEEN MORNINGSTAR, QUEEN OF HELL.
YES..

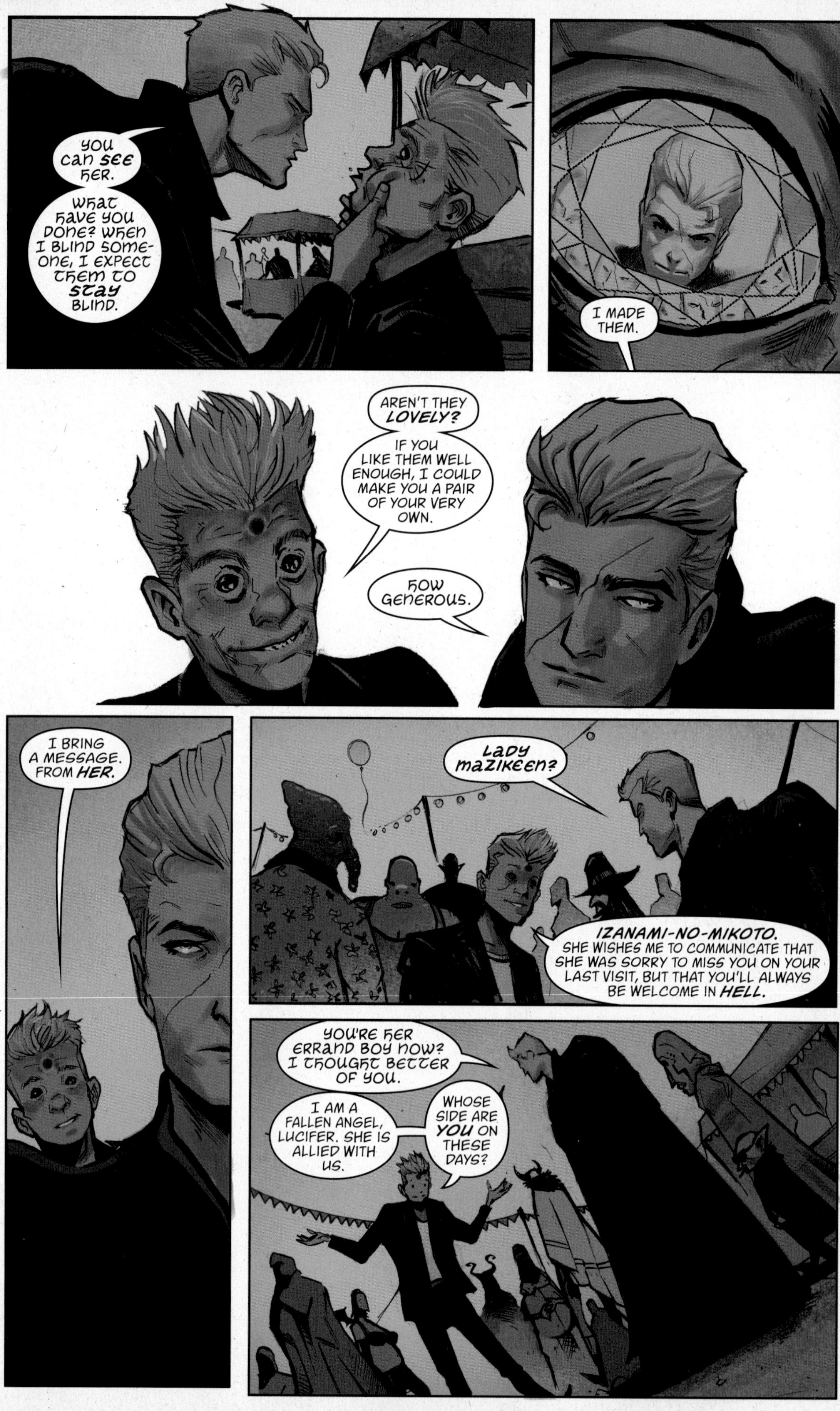

YOU CAN SEE HER.
WHAT HAVE YOU DONE? WHEN I BLIND SOMEONE, I EXPECT THEM TO STAY BLIND.
I MADE THEM.
AREN'T THEY LOVELY?
IF YOU LIKE THEM WELL ENOUGH, I COULD MAKE YOU A PAIR OF YOUR VERY OWN.
HOW GENEROUS.
I BRING A MESSAGE. FROM HER.
LADY MAZIKEEN?
IZANAMI-NO-MIKOTO. SHE WISHES ME TO COMMUNICATE THAT SHE WAS SORRY TO MISS YOU ON YOUR LAST VISIT, BUT THAT YOU'LL ALWAYS BE WELCOME IN HELL.
YOU'RE HER ERRAND BOY NOW? I THOUGHT BETTER OF YOU.
I AM A FALLEN ANGEL, LUCIFER. SHE IS ALLIED WITH US.
WHOSE SIDE ARE YOU ON THESE DAYS?

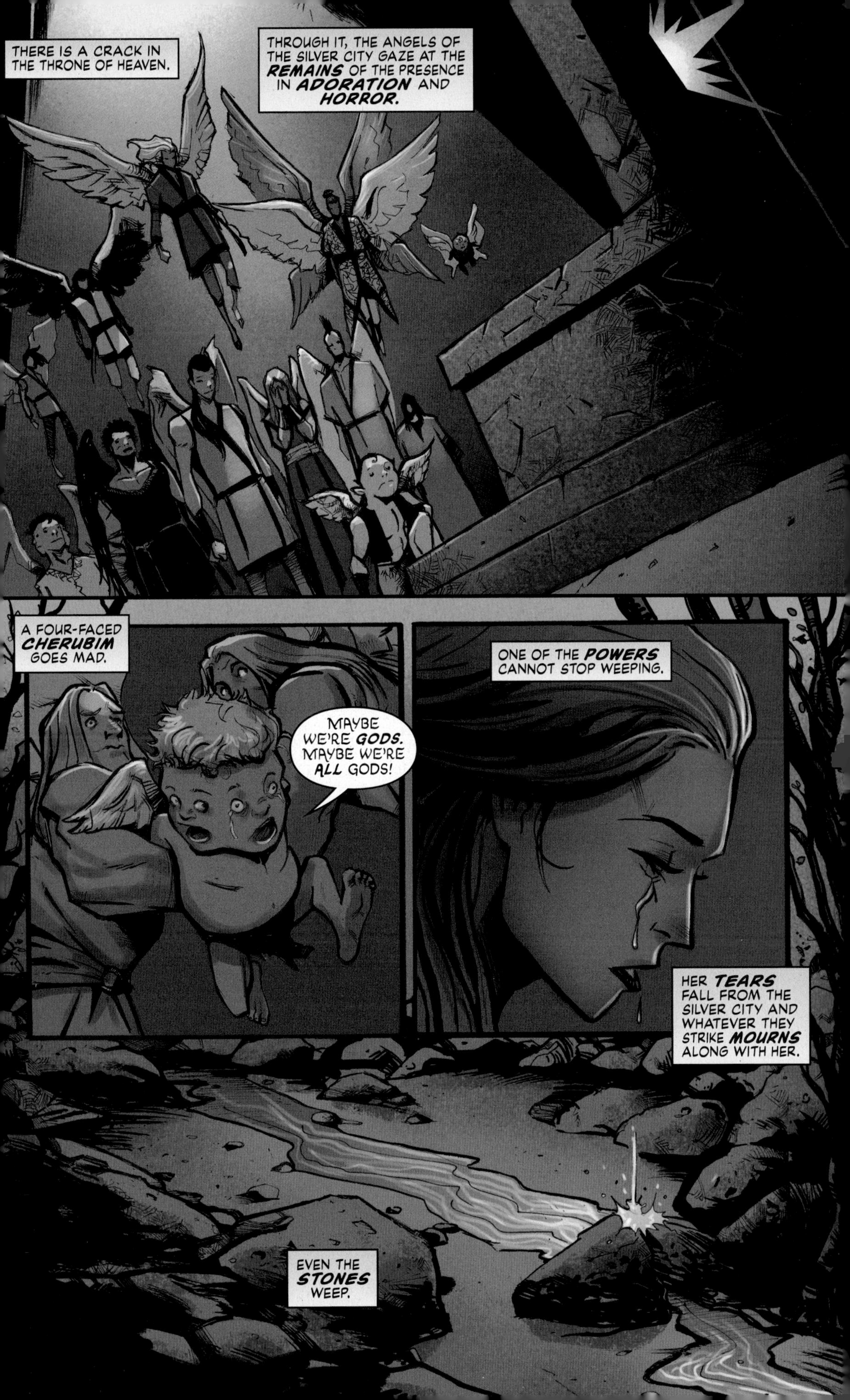
THERE IS A CRACK IN THE THRONE OF HEAVEN.
THROUGH IT, THE ANGELS OF THE SILVER CITY GAZE AT THE REMAINS OF THE PRESENCE IN ADORATION AND HORROR.
A FOUR-FACED CHERUBIM GOES MAD.
MAYBE WE'RE GODS. MAYBE WE'RE ALL GODS!
ONE OF THE POWERS CANNOT STOP WEEPING.
HER TEARS FALL FROM THE SILVER CITY AND WHATEVER THEY STRIKE MOURNS ALONG WITH HER.
EVEN THE STONES WEEP.

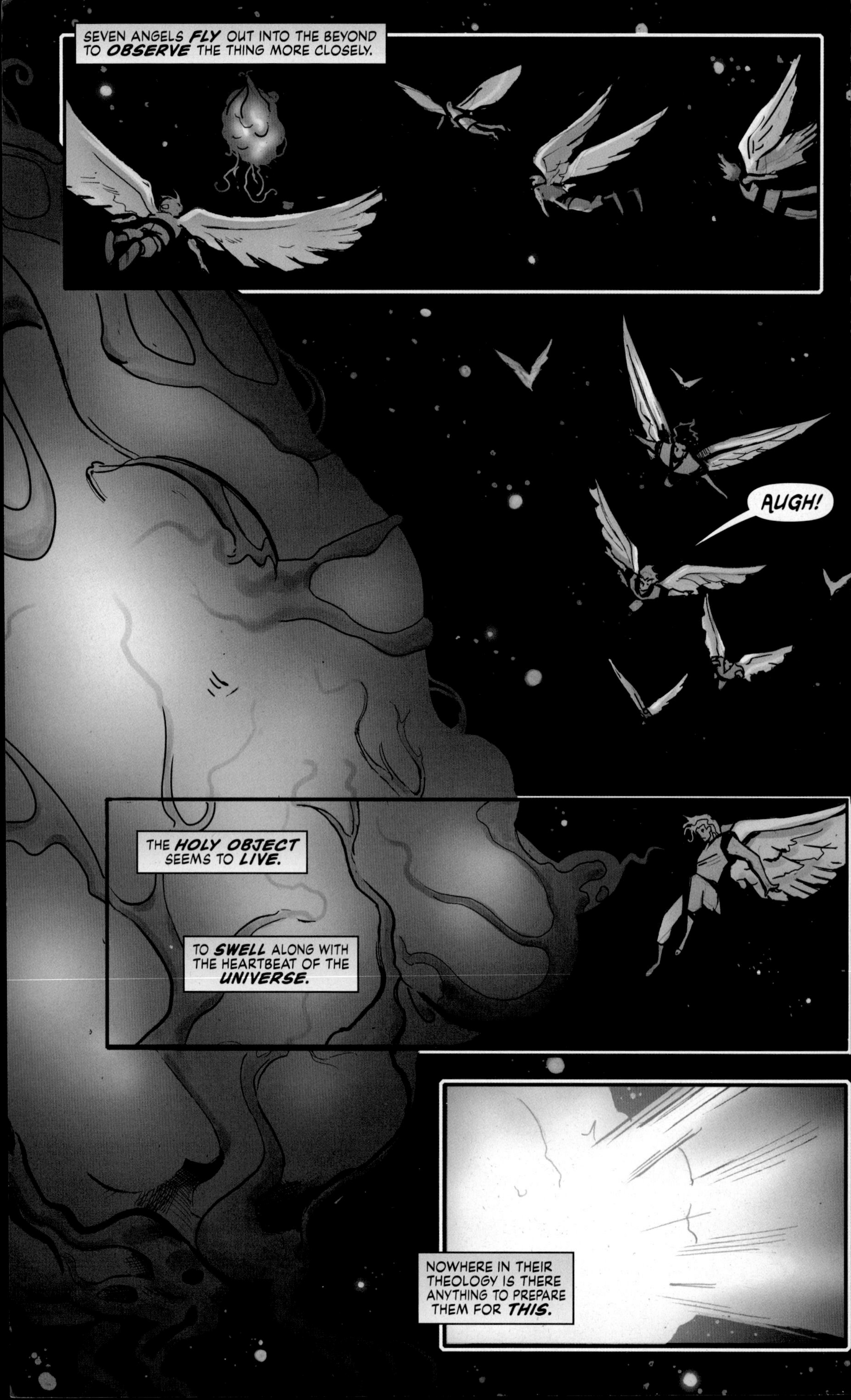
SEVEN ANGELS FLY OUT INTO THE BEYOND TO OBSERVE THE THING MORE CLOSELY.
AUGH!
THE HOLY OBJECT SEEMS TO LIVE.
TO SWELL ALONG WITH THE HEARTBEAT OF THE UNIVERSE.
NOWHERE IN THEIR THEOLOGY IS THERE ANYTHING TO PREPARE THEM FOR THIS.

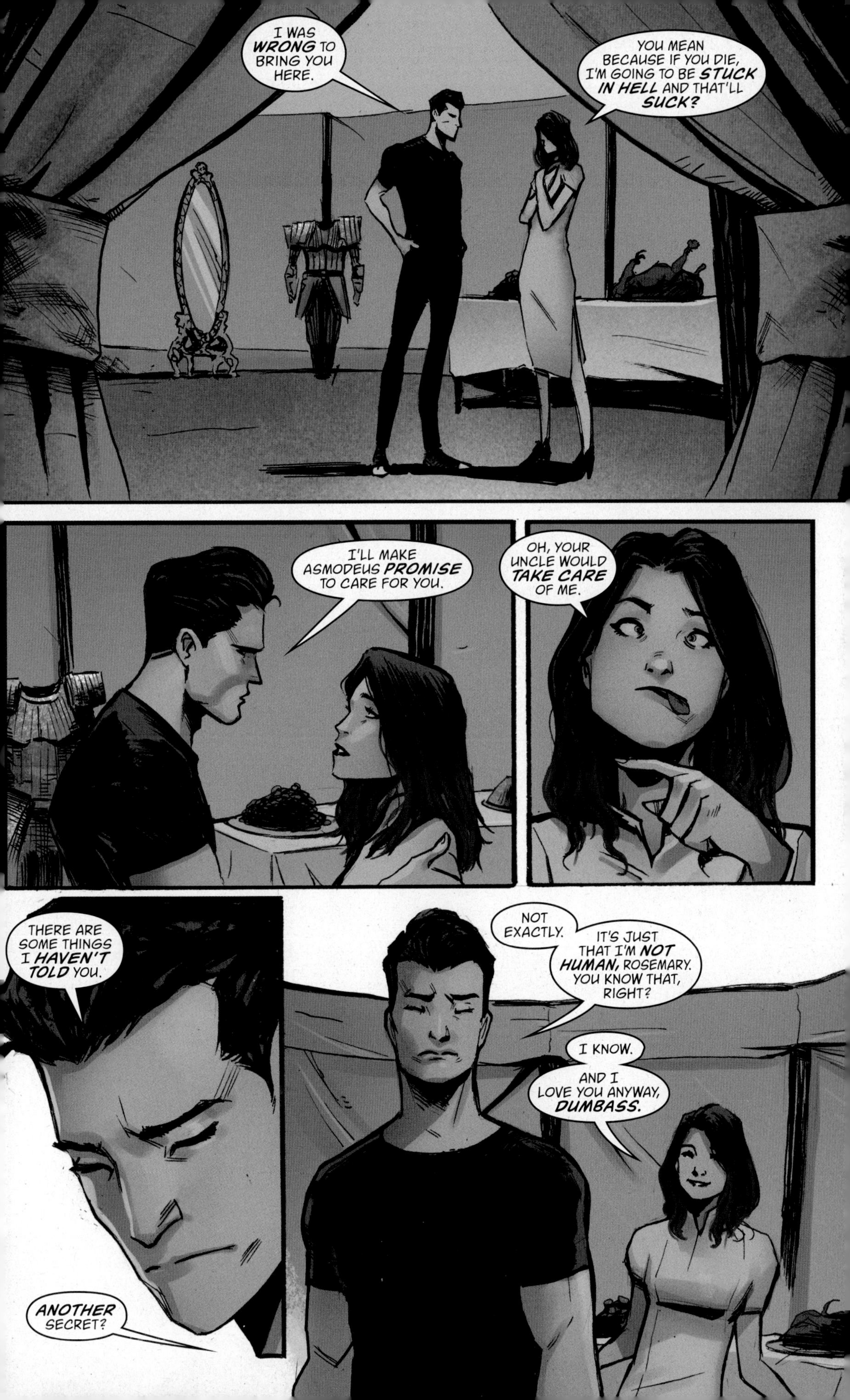
I WAS WRONG TO BRING YOU HERE.
YOU MEAN BECAUSE IF YOU DIE, I'M GOING TO BE STUCK IN HELL AND THAT'LL SUCK?
I'LL MAKE ASMODEUS PROMISE TO CARE FOR YOU.
OH, YOUR UNCLE WOULD TAKE CARE OF ME.
THERE ARE SOME THINGS I HAVEN'T TOLD YOU.
ANOTHER SECRET?
NOT EXACTLY.
IT'S JUST THAT I'M NOT HUMAN, ROSEMARY. YOU KNOW THAT, RIGHT?
I KNOW.
AND I LOVE YOU ANYWAY, DUMBASS.

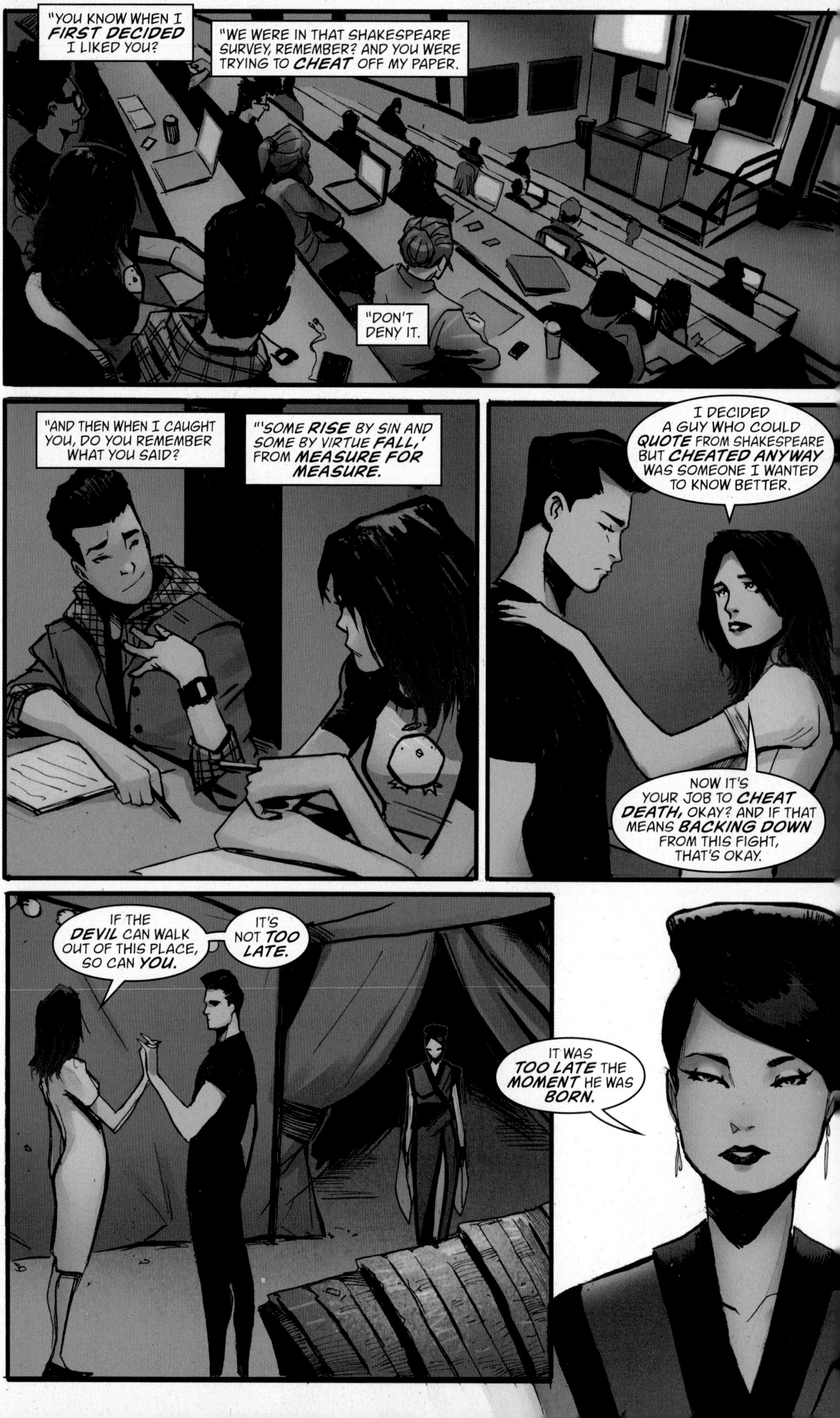
"YOU KNOW WHEN I FIRST DECIDED I LIKED YOU?
"WE WERE IN THAT SHAKESPEARE SURVEY, REMEMBER? AND YOU WERE TRYING TO CHEAT OFF MY PAPER.
"DON'T DENY IT.
"AND THEN WHEN I CAUGHT YOU, DO YOU REMEMBER WHAT YOU SAID?
"'SOME RISE BY SIN AND SOME BY VIRTUE FALL,' FROM MEASURE FOR MEASURE.
I DECIDED A GUY WHO COULD QUOTE FROM SHAKESPEARE BUT CHEATED ANYWAY WAS SOMEONE I WANTED TO KNOW BETTER.
NOW IT'S YOUR JOB TO CHEAT DEATH, OKAY? AND IF THAT MEANS BACKING DOWN FROM THIS FIGHT, THAT'S OKAY.
IF THE DEVIL CAN WALK OUT OF THIS PLACE, SO CAN YOU.
IT'S NOT TOO LATE.
IT WAS TOO LATE THE MOMENT HE WAS BORN.

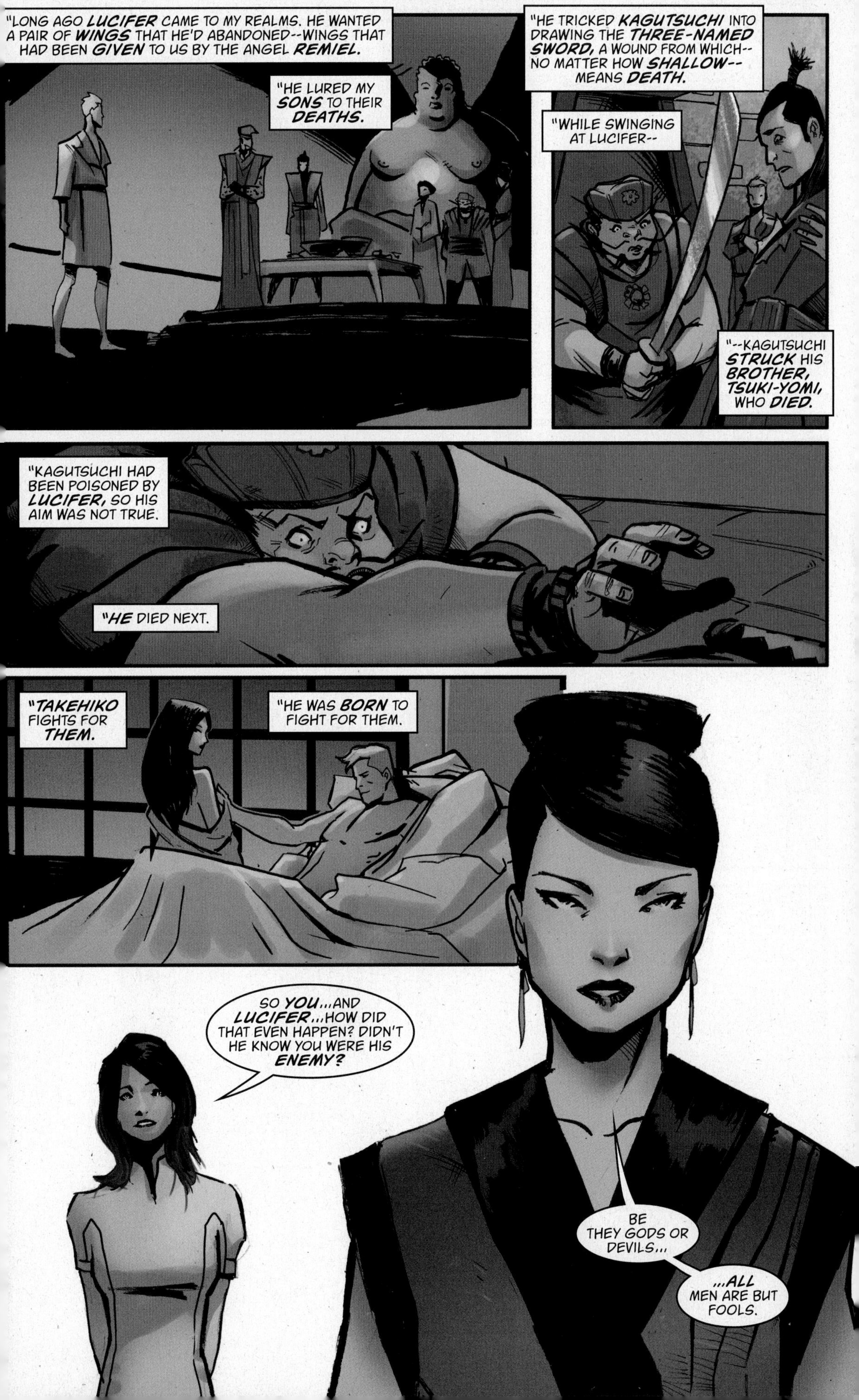
"LONG AGO LUCIFER CAME TO MY REALMS. HE WANTED A PAIR OF WINGS THAT HE'D ABANDONED--WINGS THAT HAD BEEN GIVEN TO US BY THE ANGEL REMIEL.
"HE LURED MY SONS TO THEIR DEATHS.
"HE TRICKED KAGUTSUCHI INTO DRAWING THE THREE-NAMED SWORD, A WOUND FROM WHICH--NO MATTER HOW SHALLOW--MEANS DEATH.
"WHILE SWINGING AT LUCIFER--
"--KAGUTSUCHI STRUCK HIS BROTHER, TSUKI-YOMI, WHO DIED.
"KAGUTSUCHI HAD BEEN POISONED BY LUCIFER, SO HIS AIM WAS NOT TRUE.
"HE DIED NEXT.
"TAKEHIKO FIGHTS FOR THEM.
"HE WAS BORN TO FIGHT FOR THEM.
SO YOU...AND LUCIFER...HOW DID THAT EVEN HAPPEN? DIDN'T HE KNOW YOU WERE HIS ENEMY?
BE THEY GODS OR DEVILS...
...ALL MEN ARE BUT FOOLS.

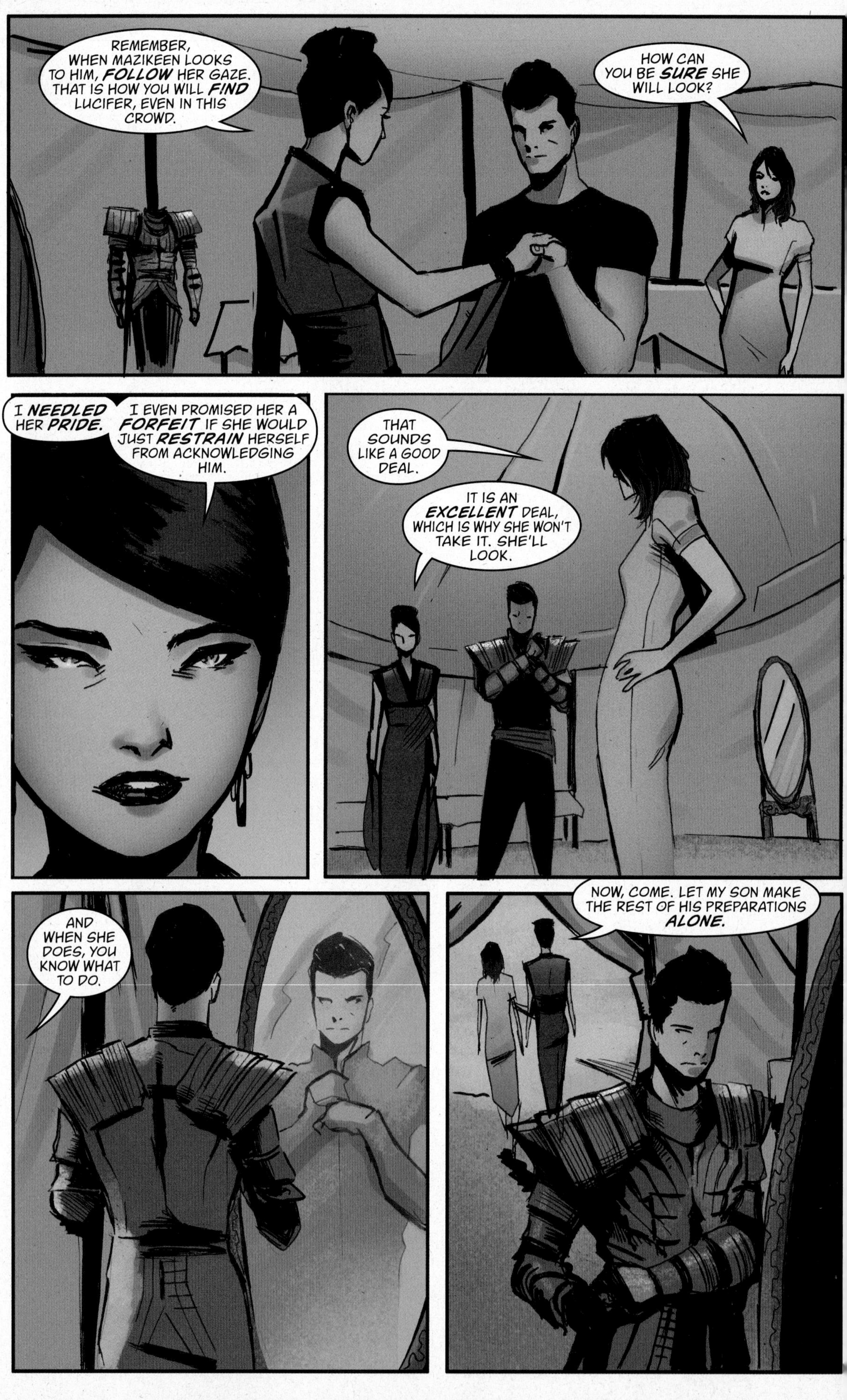
REMEMBER, WHEN MAZIKEEN LOOKS TO HIM, FOLLOW HER GAZE. THAT IS HOW YOU WILL FIND LUCIFER, EVEN IN THIS CROWD.
HOW CAN YOU BE SURE SHE WILL LOOK?
I NEEDLED HER PRIDE.
I EVEN PROMISED HER A FORFEIT IF SHE WOULD JUST RESTRAIN HERSELF FROM ACKNOWLEDGING HIM.
THAT SOUNDS LIKE A GOOD DEAL.
IT IS AN EXCELLENT DEAL, WHICH IS WHY SHE WON'T TAKE IT. SHE'LL LOOK.
AND WHEN SHE DOES, YOU KNOW WHAT TO DO.
NOW, COME. LET MY SON MAKE THE REST OF HIS PREPARATIONS ALONE.

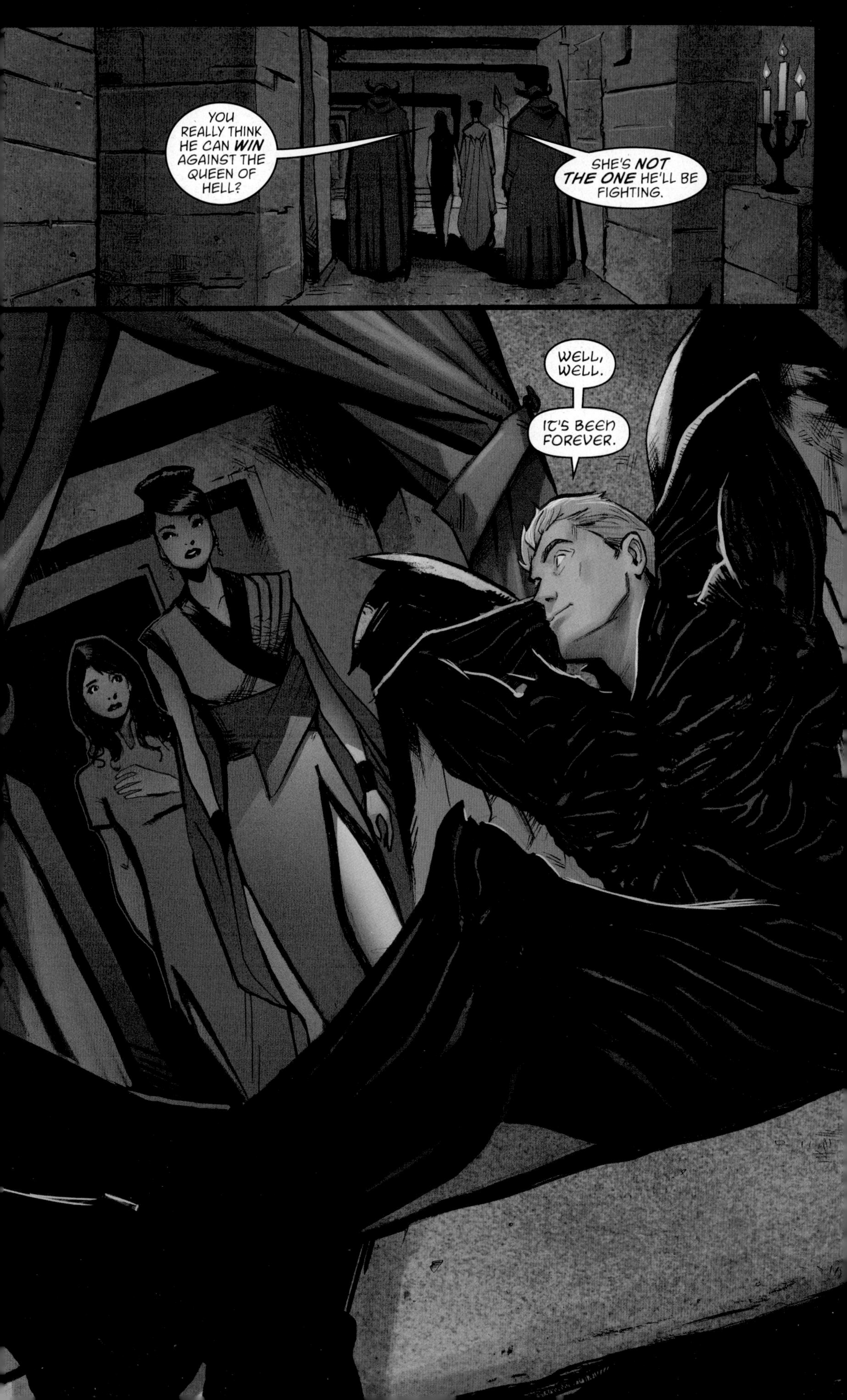
YOU REALLY THINK HE CAN **WIN** AGAINST THE QUEEN OF HELL?
SHE'S **NOT THE ONE** HE'LL BE FIGHTING.
WELL, WELL.
IT'S BEEN FOREVER.

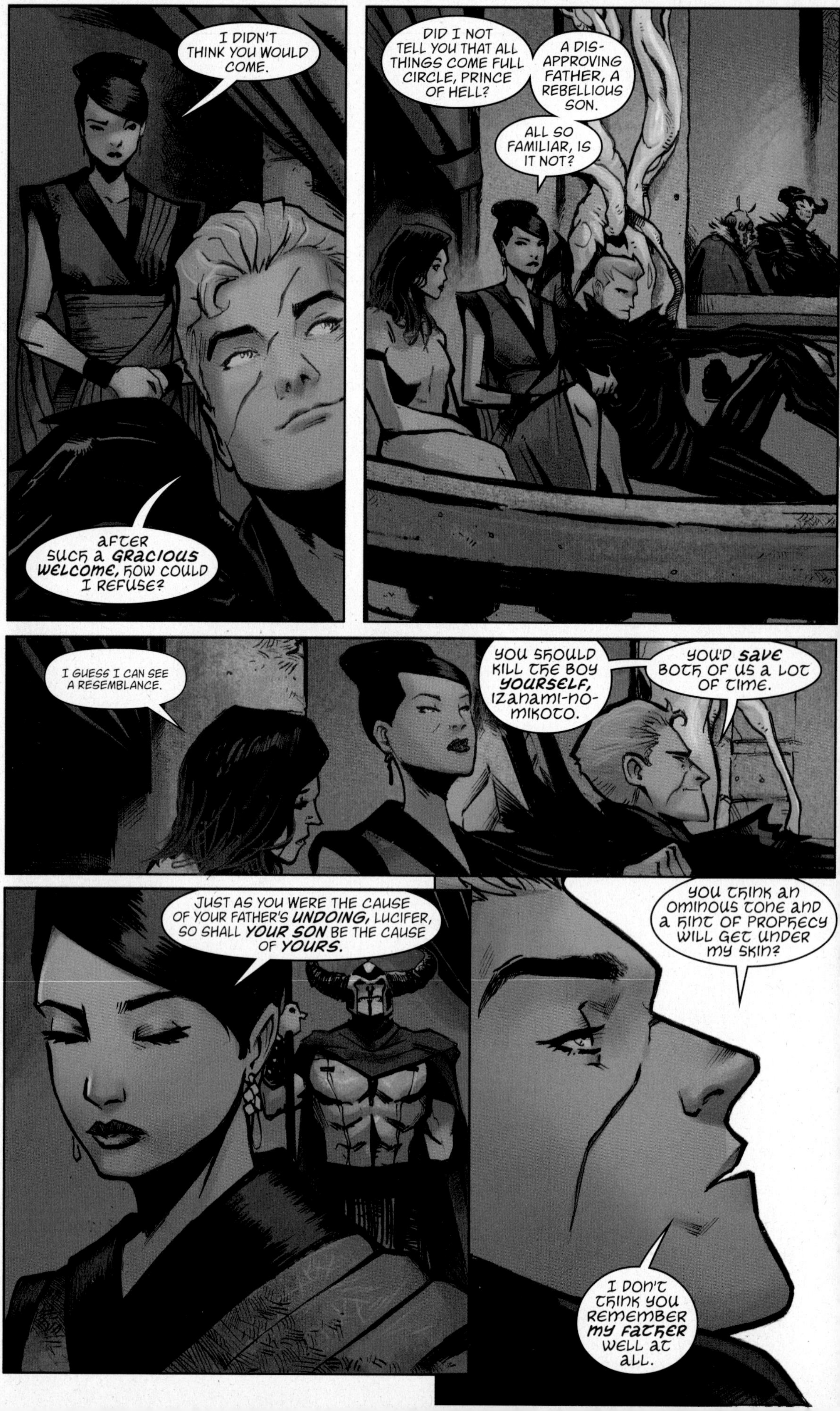
I DIDN'T THINK YOU WOULD COME.
AFTER SUCH A GRACIOUS WELCOME, HOW COULD I REFUSE?
DID I NOT TELL YOU THAT ALL THINGS COME FULL CIRCLE, PRINCE OF HELL?
A DIS-APPROVING FATHER, A REBELLIOUS SON.
ALL SO FAMILIAR, IS IT NOT?
I GUESS I CAN SEE A RESEMBLANCE.
YOU SHOULD KILL THE BOY YOURSELF, IZANAMI-NO-MIKOTO.
YOU'D SAVE BOTH OF US A LOT OF TIME.
JUST AS YOU WERE THE CAUSE OF YOUR FATHER'S UNDOING, LUCIFER, SO SHALL YOUR SON BE THE CAUSE OF YOURS.
YOU THINK AN OMINOUS TONE AND A HINT OF PROPHECY WILL GET UNDER MY SKIN?
I DON'T THINK YOU REMEMBER MY FATHER WELL AT ALL.

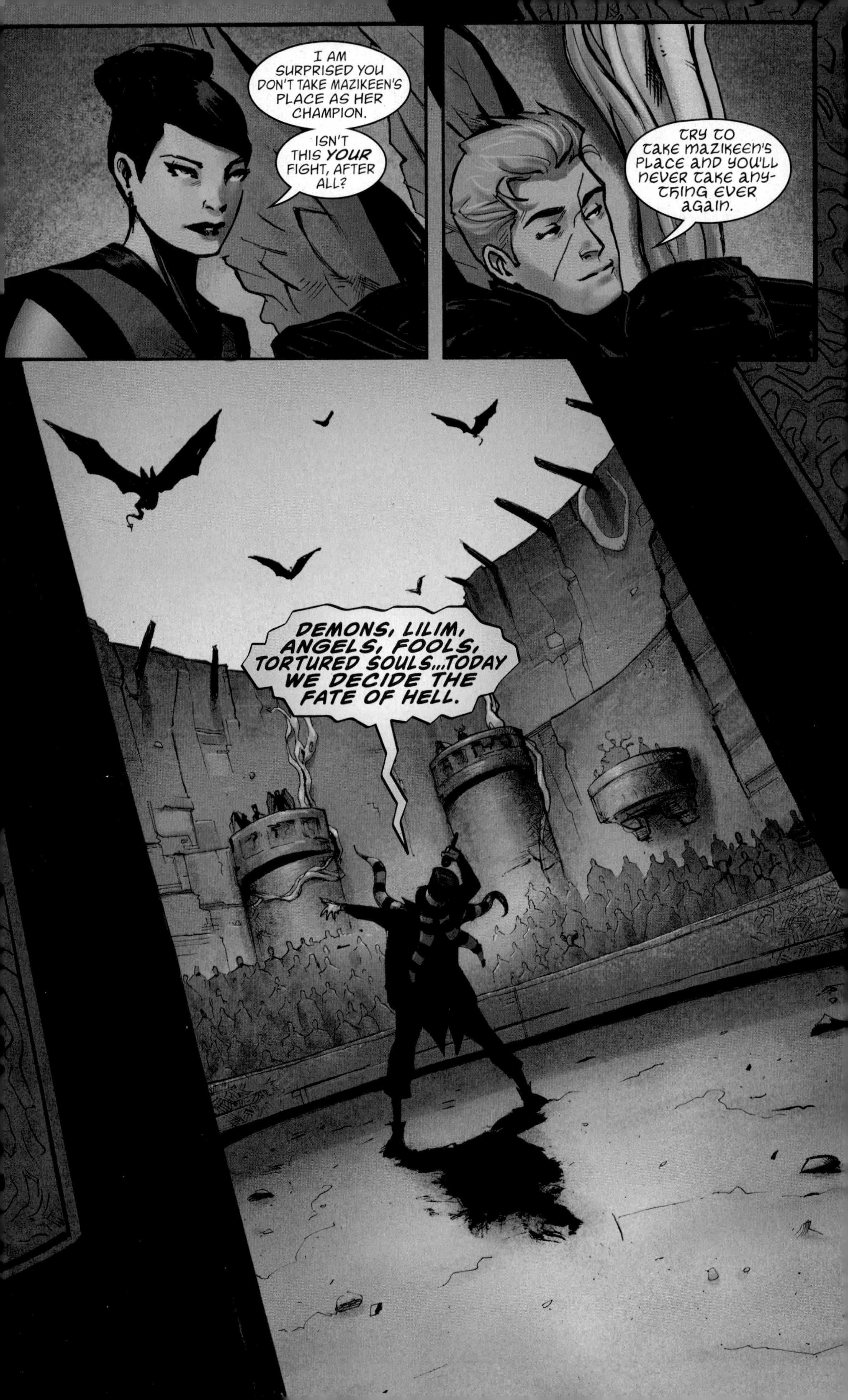
I AM SURPRISED YOU DON'T TAKE MAZIKEEN'S PLACE AS HER CHAMPION.
ISN'T THIS *YOUR* FIGHT, AFTER ALL?
TRY TO TAKE MAZIKEEN'S PLACE AND YOU'LL NEVER TAKE ANY-THING EVER AGAIN.
DEMONS, LILIM, ANGELS, FOOLS, TORTURED SOULS...TODAY WE DECIDE THE FATE OF HELL.

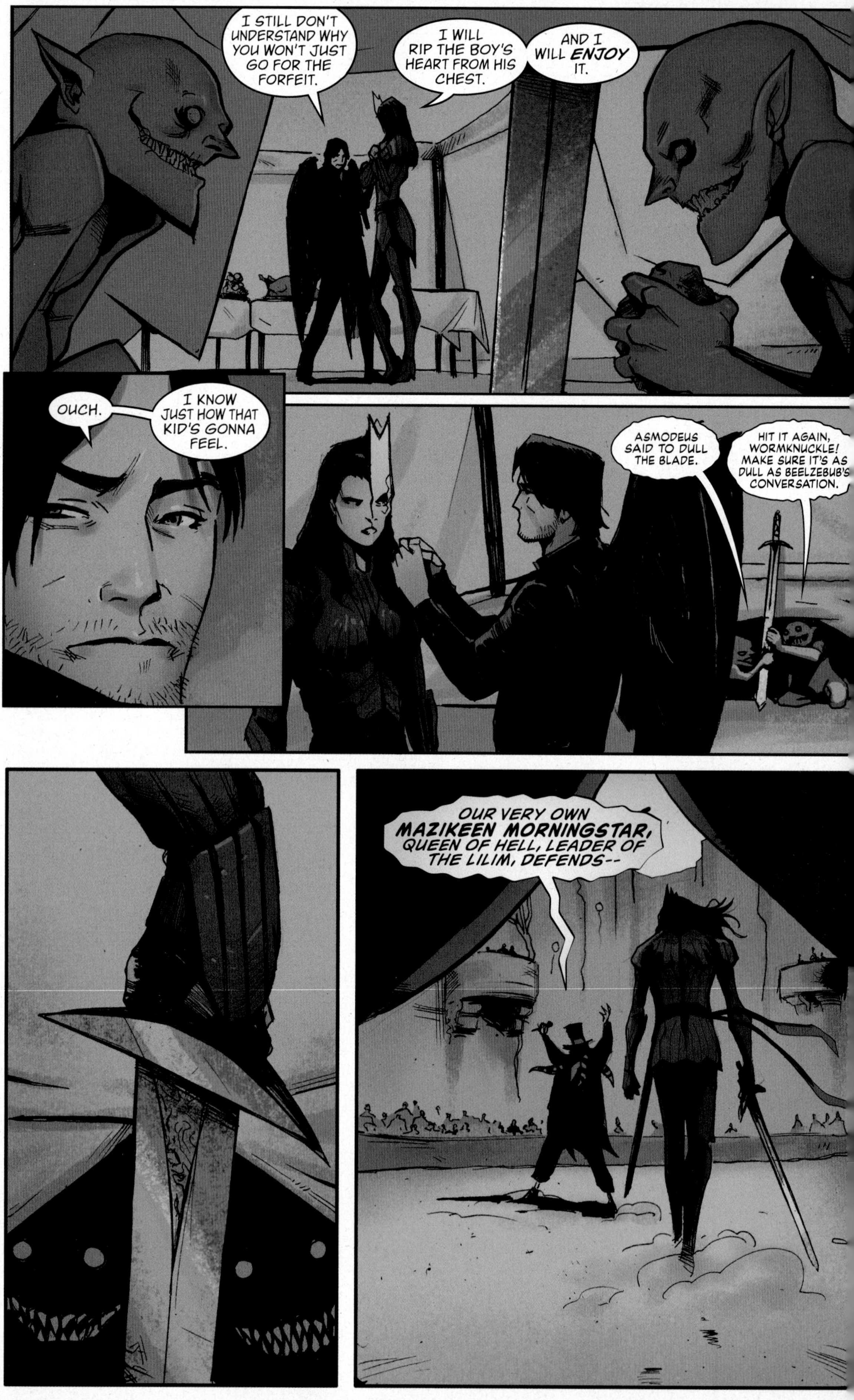

I STILL DON'T UNDERSTAND WHY YOU WON'T JUST GO FOR THE FORFEIT.
I WILL RIP THE BOY'S HEART FROM HIS CHEST.
AND I WILL ENJOY IT.
OUCH.
I KNOW JUST HOW THAT KID'S GONNA FEEL.
ASMODEUS SAID TO DULL THE BLADE.
HIT IT AGAIN, WORMKNUCKLE! MAKE SURE IT'S AS DULL AS BEELZEBUB'S CONVERSATION.
OUR VERY OWN MAZIKEEN MORNINGSTAR, QUEEN OF HELL, LEADER OF THE LILIM, DEFENDS--

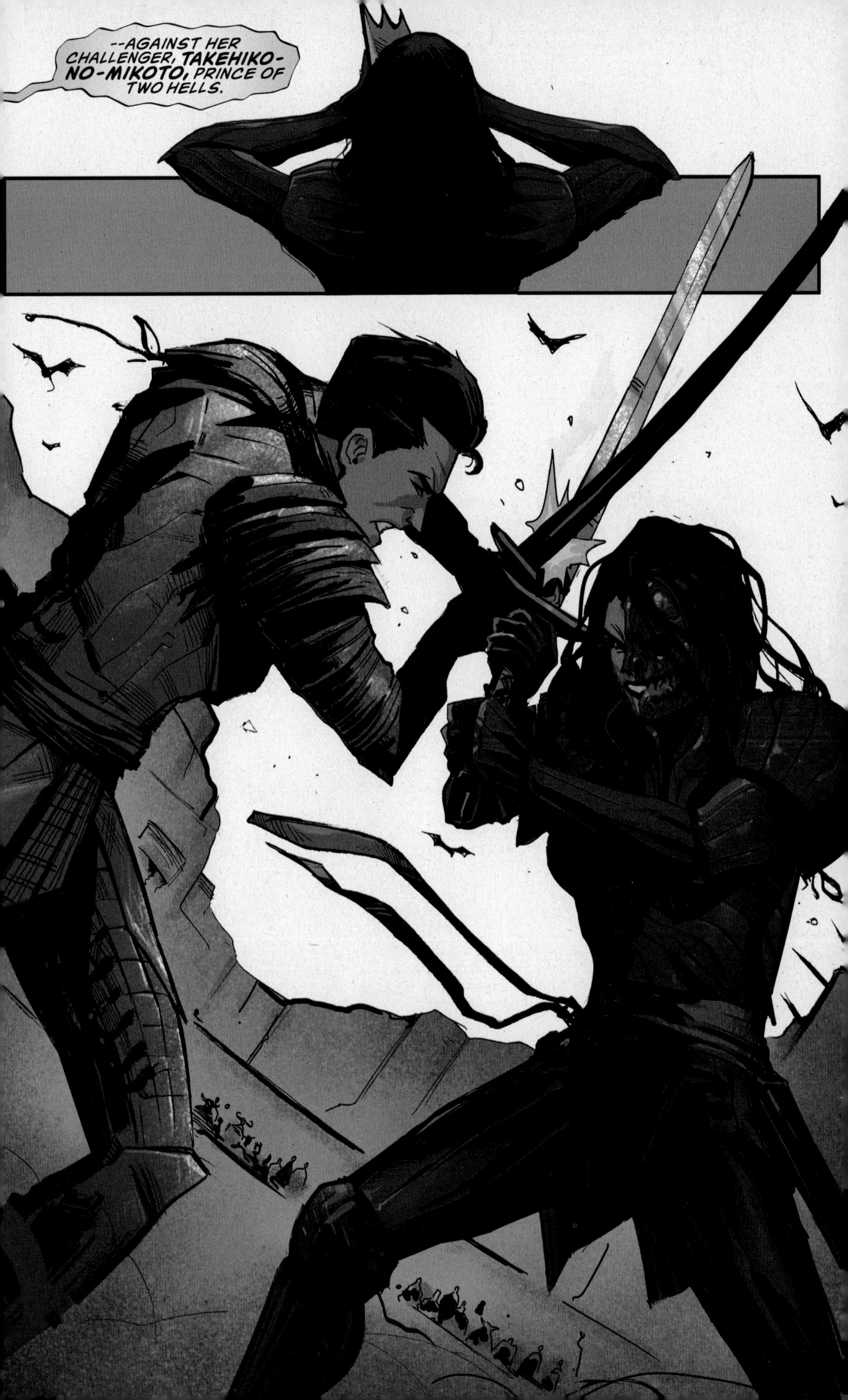
--AGAINST HER CHALLENGER, TAKEHIKO-NO-MIKOTO, PRINCE OF TWO HELLS.

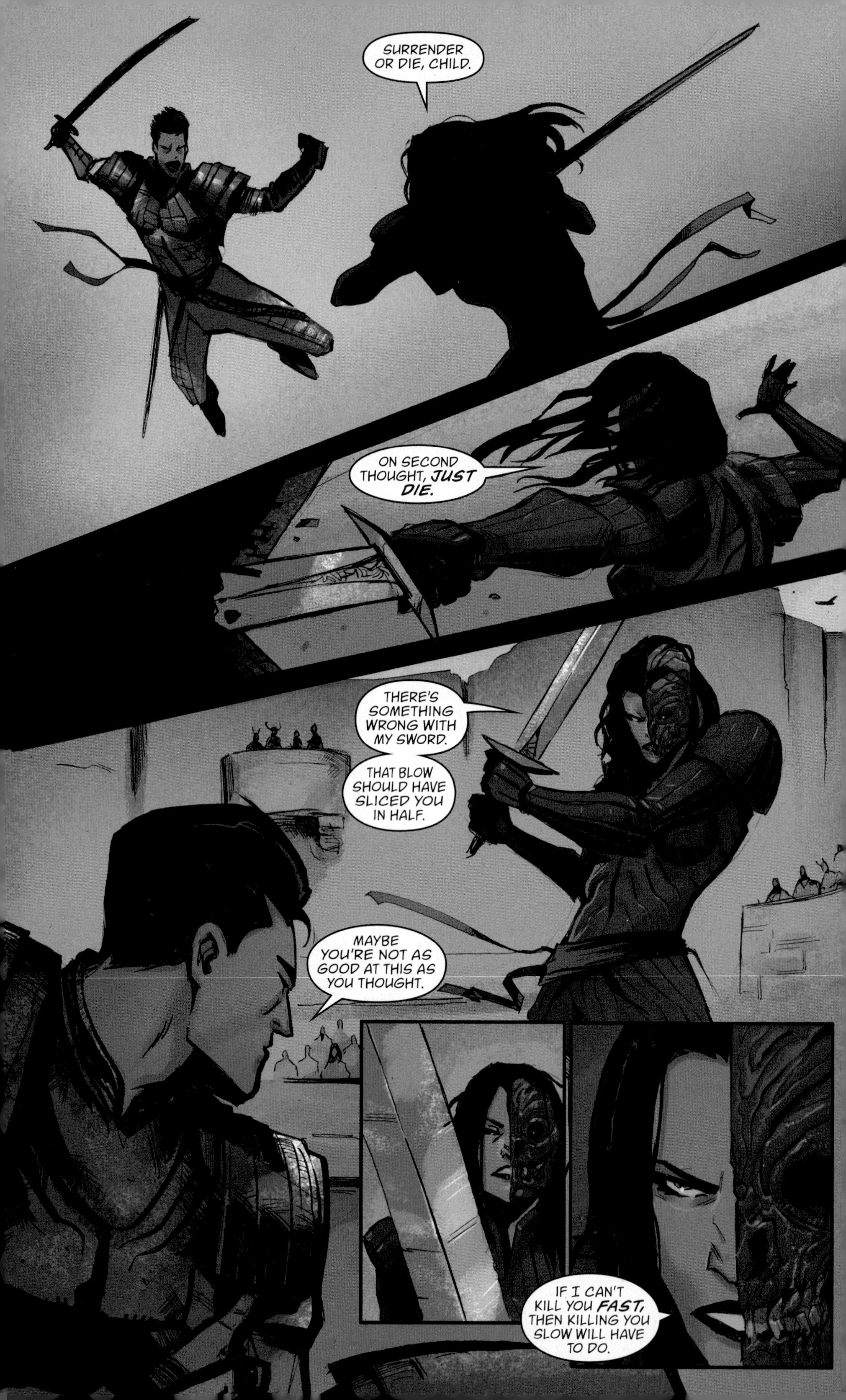
SURRENDER OR DIE, CHILD.
ON SECOND THOUGHT, JUST DIE.
THERE'S SOMETHING WRONG WITH MY SWORD.
THAT BLOW SHOULD HAVE SLICED YOU IN HALF.
MAYBE YOU'RE NOT AS GOOD AT THIS AS YOU THOUGHT.
IF I CAN'T KILL YOU FAST, THEN KILLING YOU SLOW WILL HAVE TO DO.

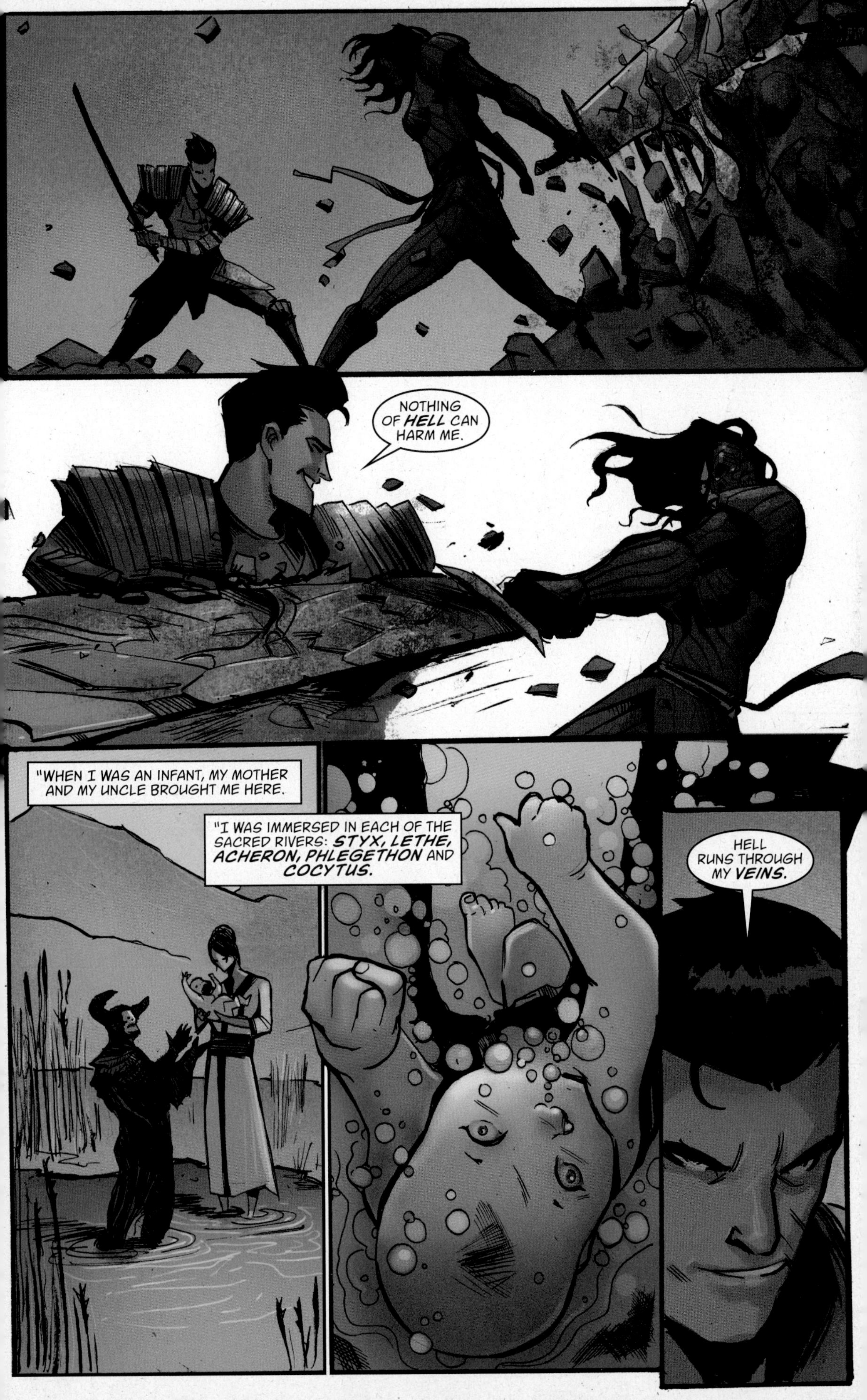
NOTHING OF **HELL** CAN HARM ME.
"WHEN I WAS AN INFANT, MY MOTHER AND MY UNCLE BROUGHT ME HERE.
"I WAS IMMERSED IN EACH OF THE SACRED RIVERS: ***STYX, LETHE, ACHERON, PHLEGETHON*** AND ***COCYTUS.***
HELL RUNS THROUGH MY ***VEINS.***

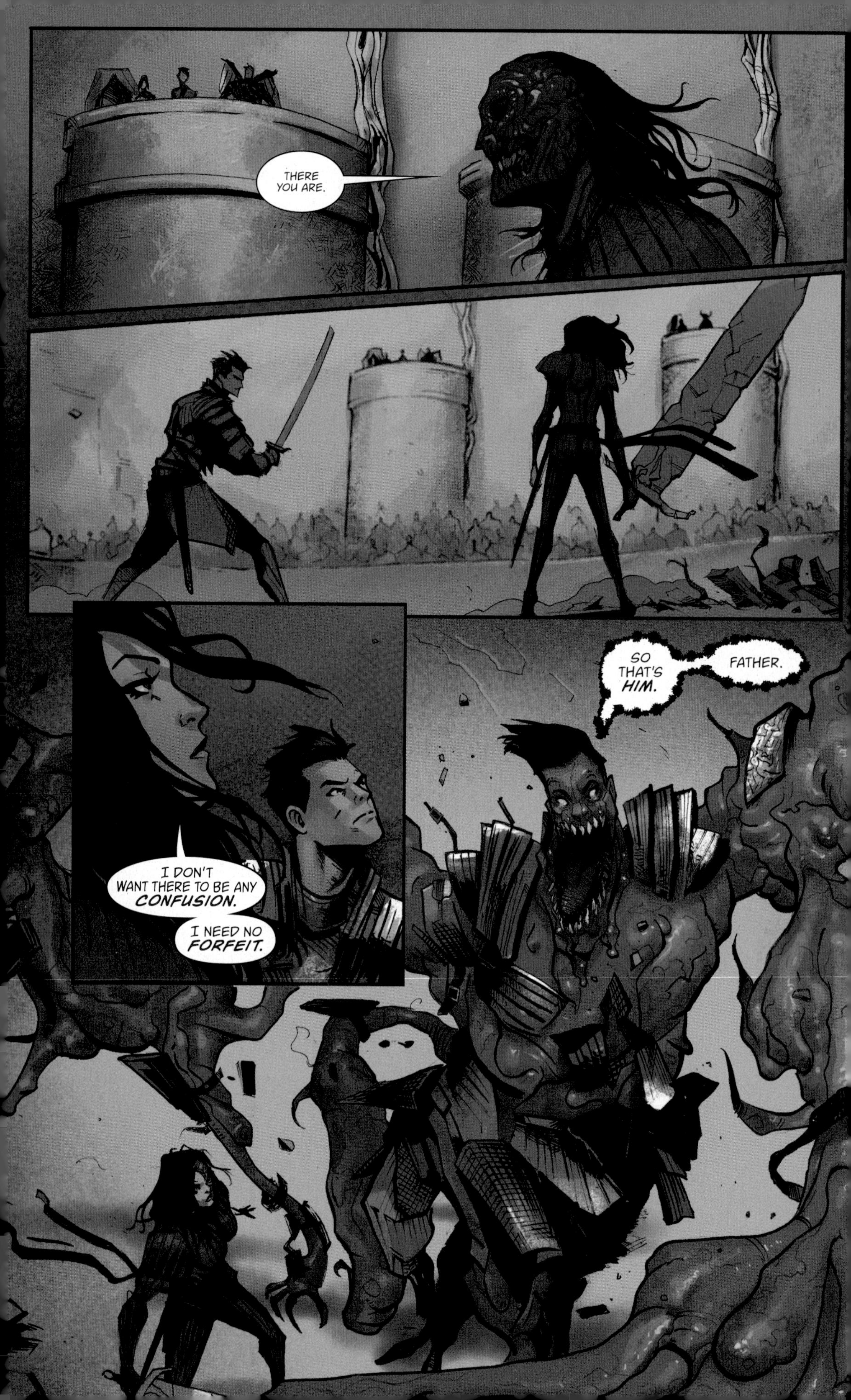
THERE YOU ARE.
SO THAT'S HIM.
FATHER.
I DON'T WANT THERE TO BE ANY CONFUSION.
I NEED NO FORFEIT.

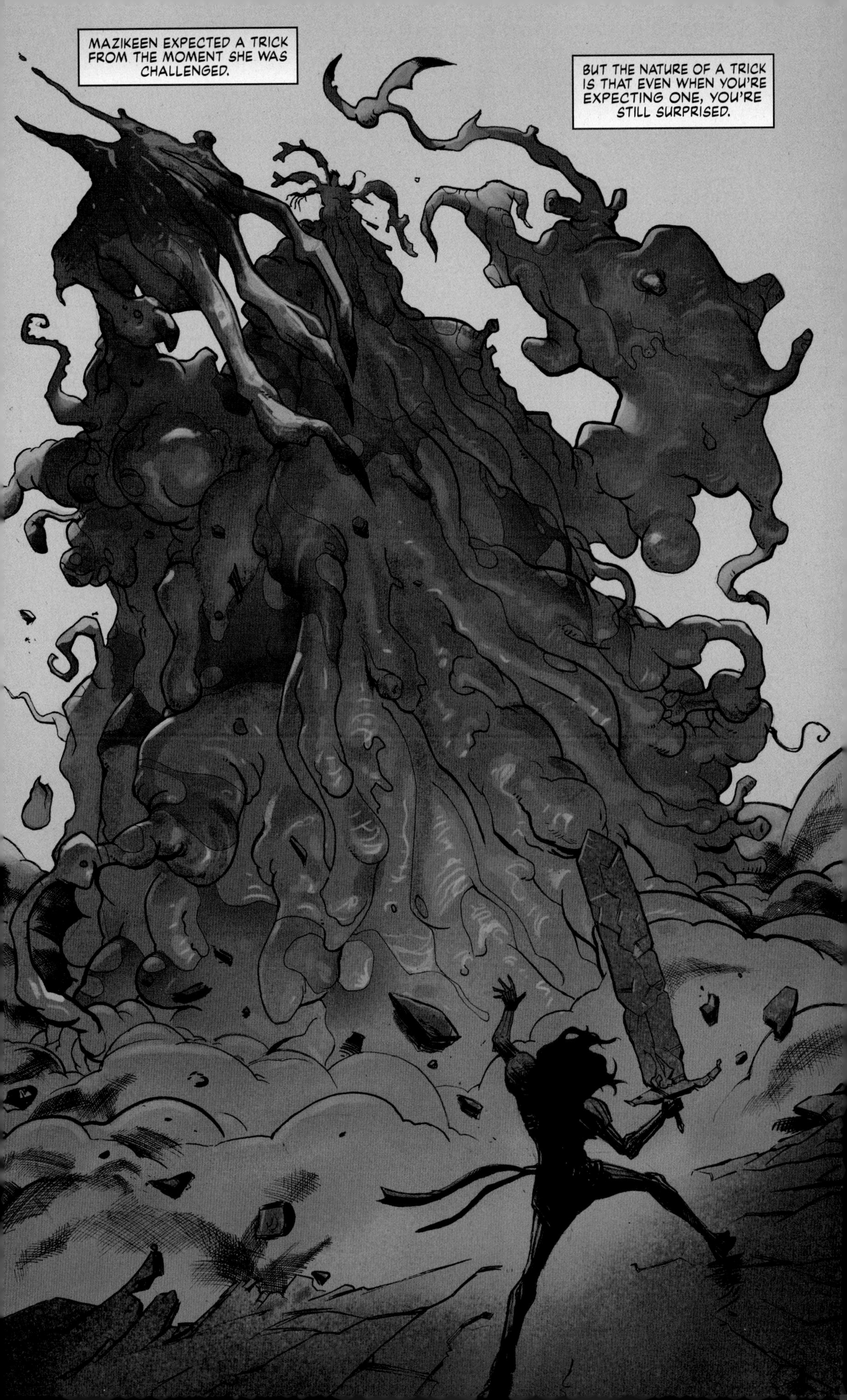
MAZIKEEN EXPECTED A TRICK FROM THE MOMENT SHE WAS CHALLENGED.
BUT THE NATURE OF A TRICK IS THAT EVEN WHEN YOU'RE EXPECTING ONE, YOU'RE STILL SURPRISED.

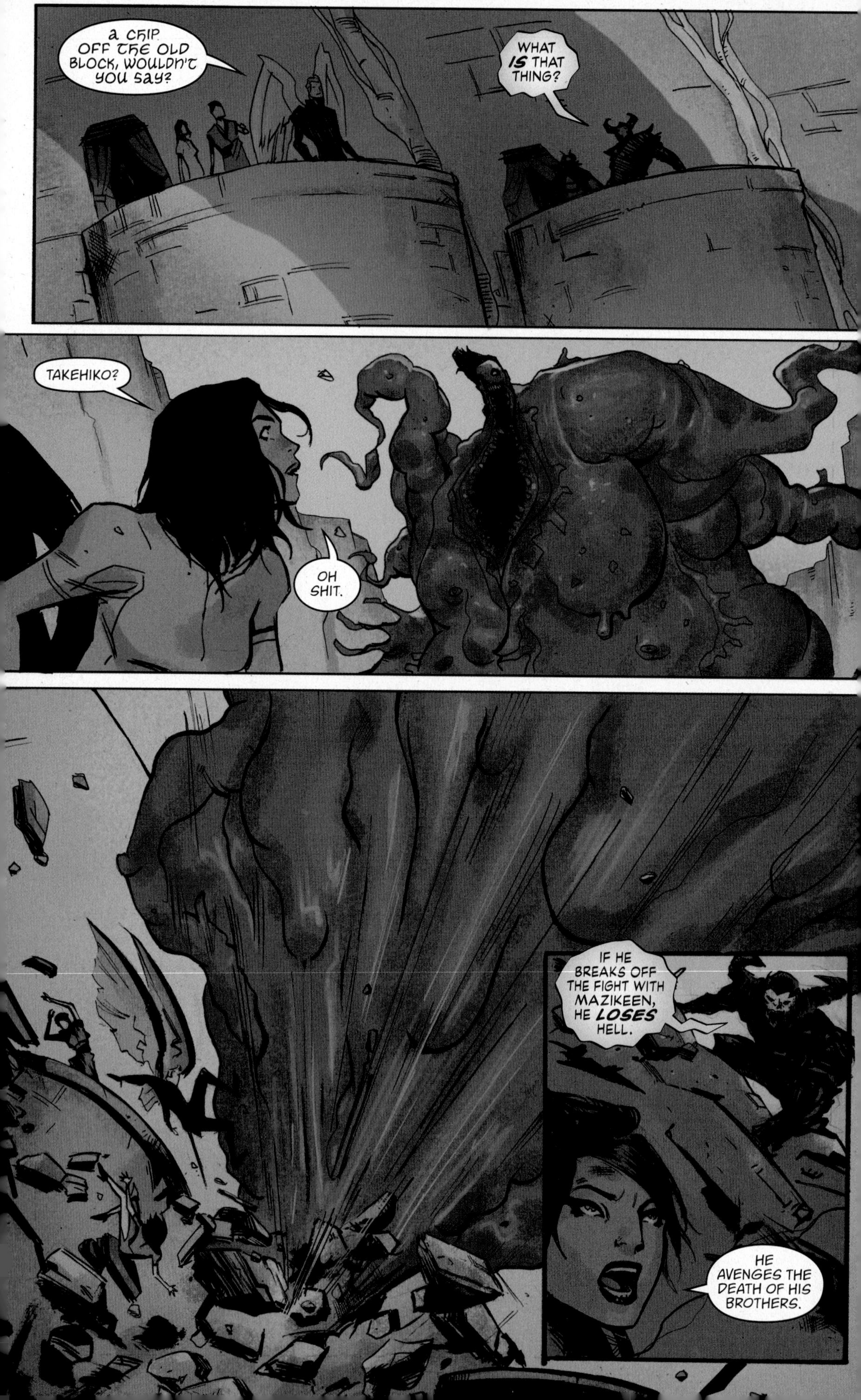
A CHIP OFF THE OLD BLOCK, WOULDN'T YOU SAY?
WHAT *IS* THAT THING?
TAKEHIKO?
OH SHIT.
IF HE BREAKS OFF THE FIGHT WITH MAZIKEEN, HE *LOSES* HELL.
HE AVENGES THE DEATH OF HIS BROTHERS.

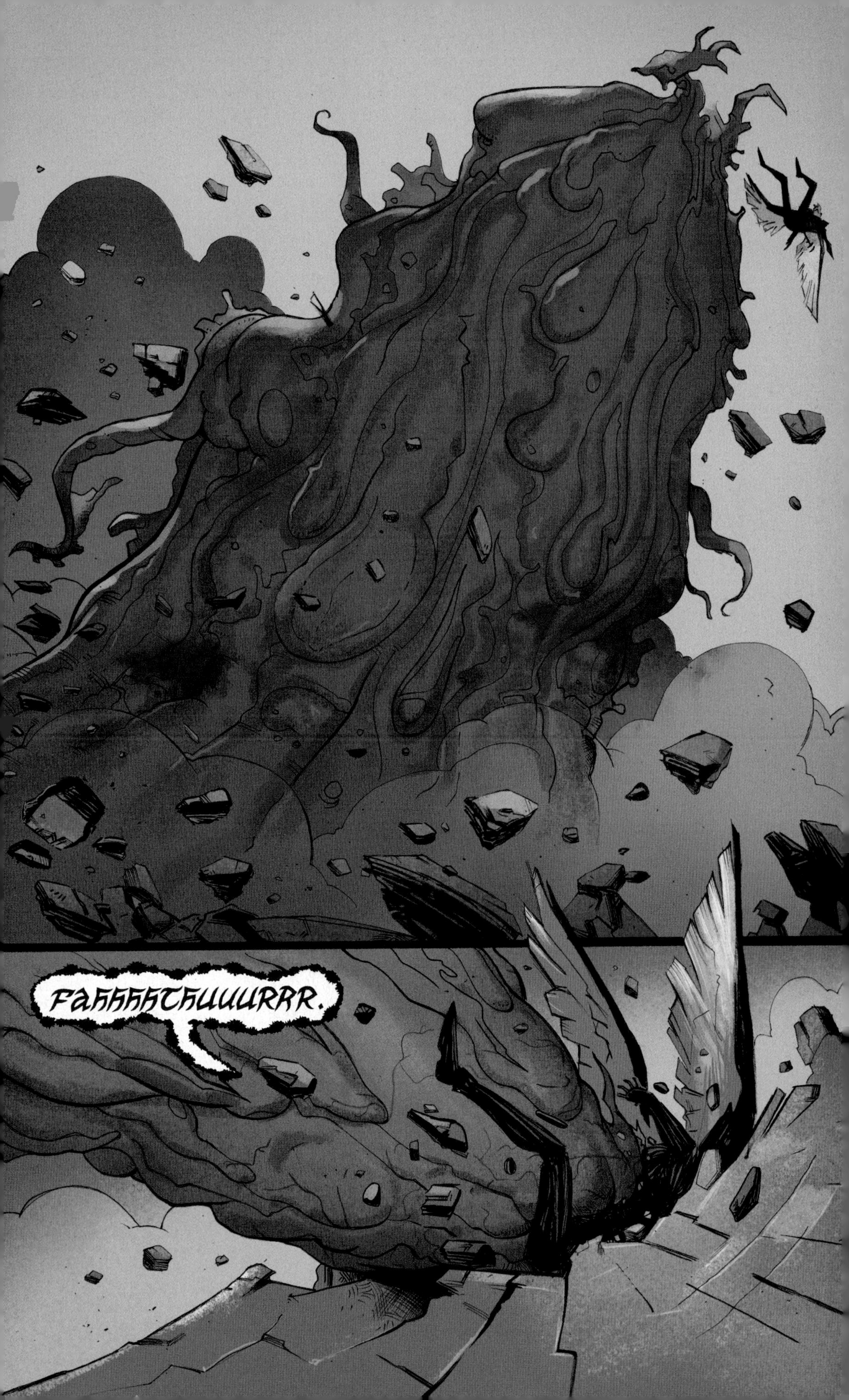
FAHHHHTHUUURRR.

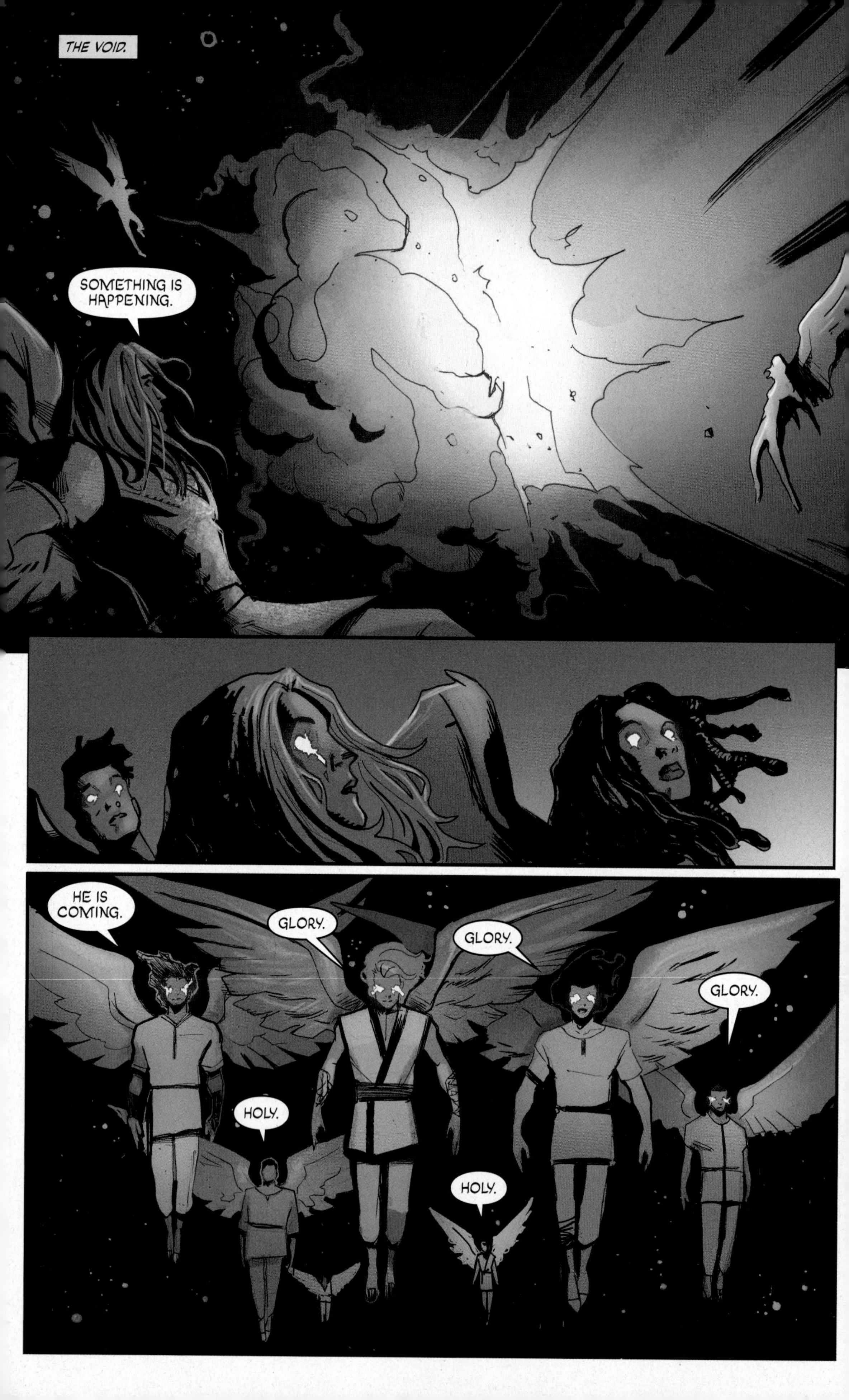
THE VOID.
SOMETHING IS HAPPENING.
HE IS COMING.
GLORY.
GLORY.
GLORY.
HOLY.
HOLY.

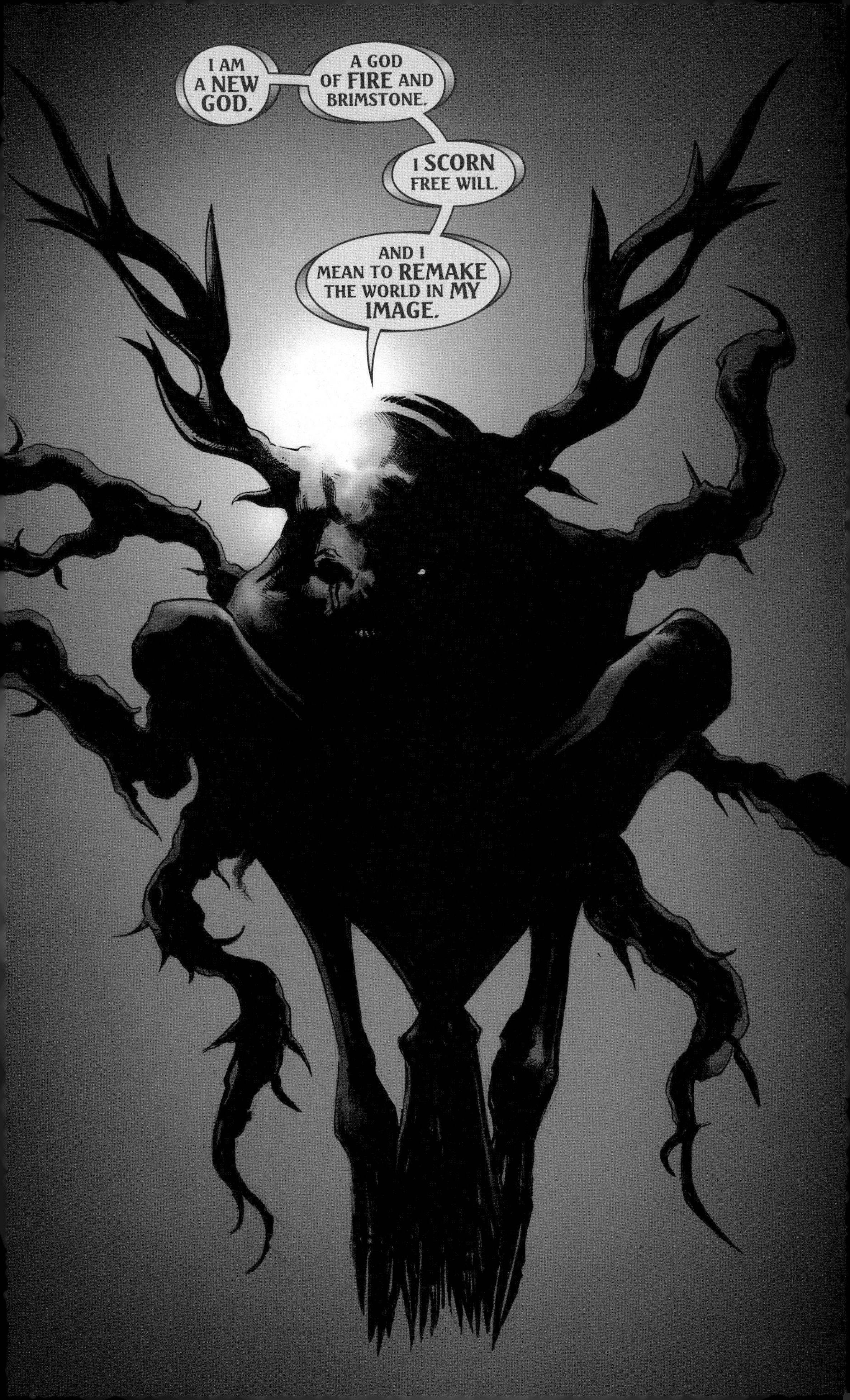
I AM A NEW GOD.
A GOD OF FIRE AND BRIMSTONE.
I SCORN FREE WILL.
AND I MEAN TO REMAKE THE WORLD IN MY IMAGE.

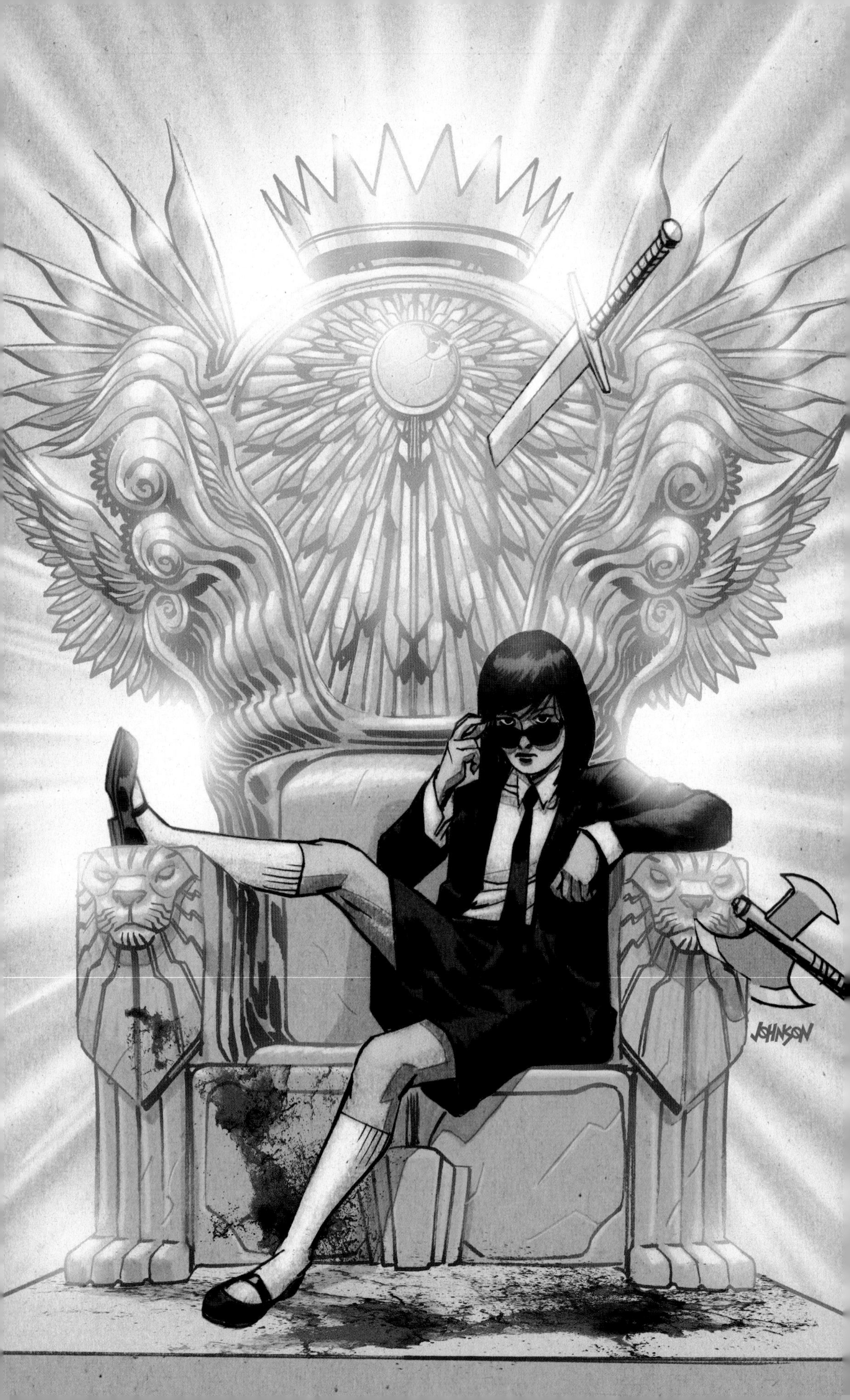
JOHNSON

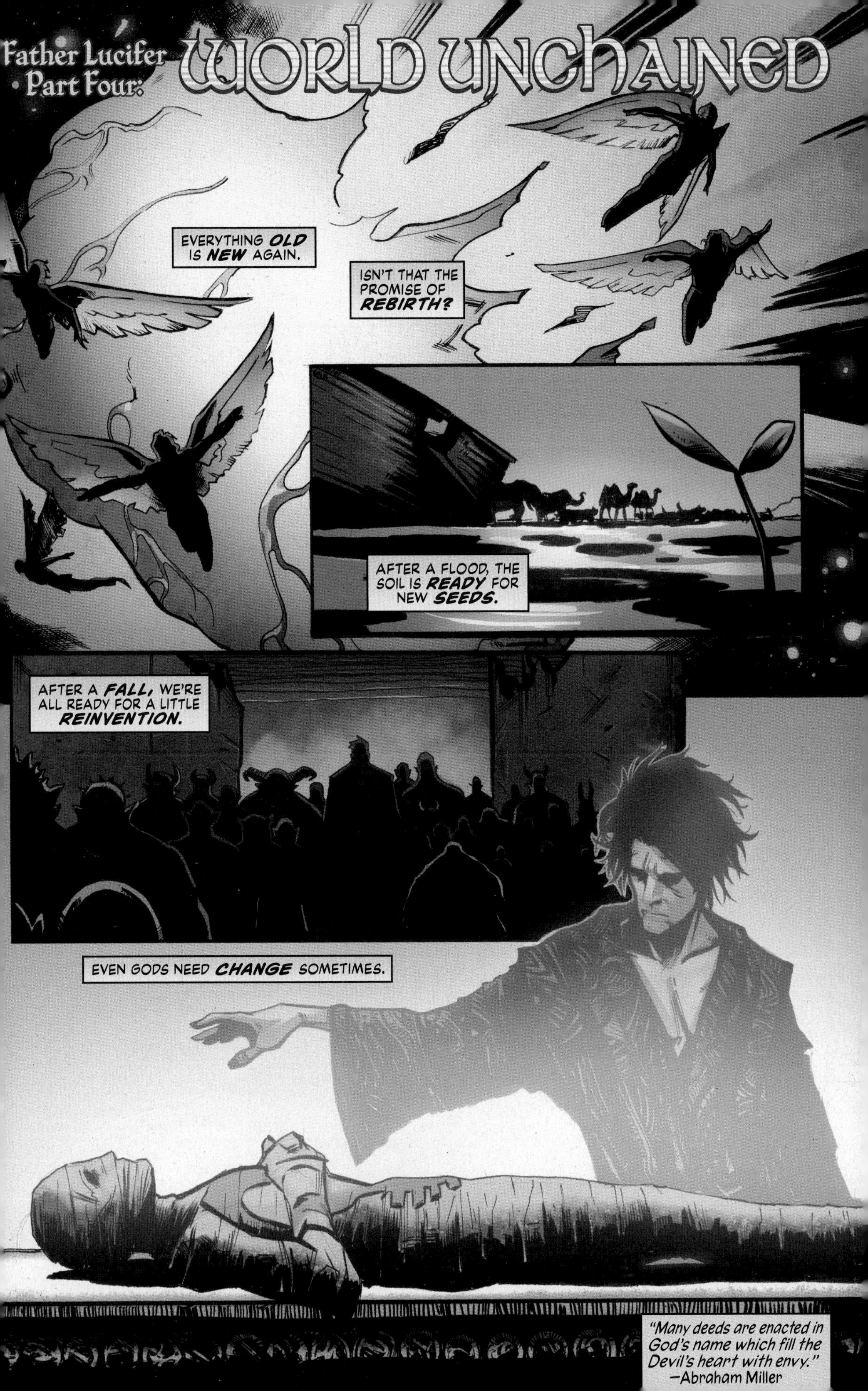
Father Lucifer • Part Four:
WORLD UNCHAINED
EVERYTHING OLD IS NEW AGAIN.
ISN'T THAT THE PROMISE OF REBIRTH?
AFTER A FLOOD, THE SOIL IS READY FOR NEW SEEDS.
AFTER A FALL, WE'RE ALL READY FOR A LITTLE REINVENTION.
EVEN GODS NEED CHANGE SOMETIMES.
"Many deeds are enacted in God's name which fill the Devil's heart with envy."
—Abraham Miller

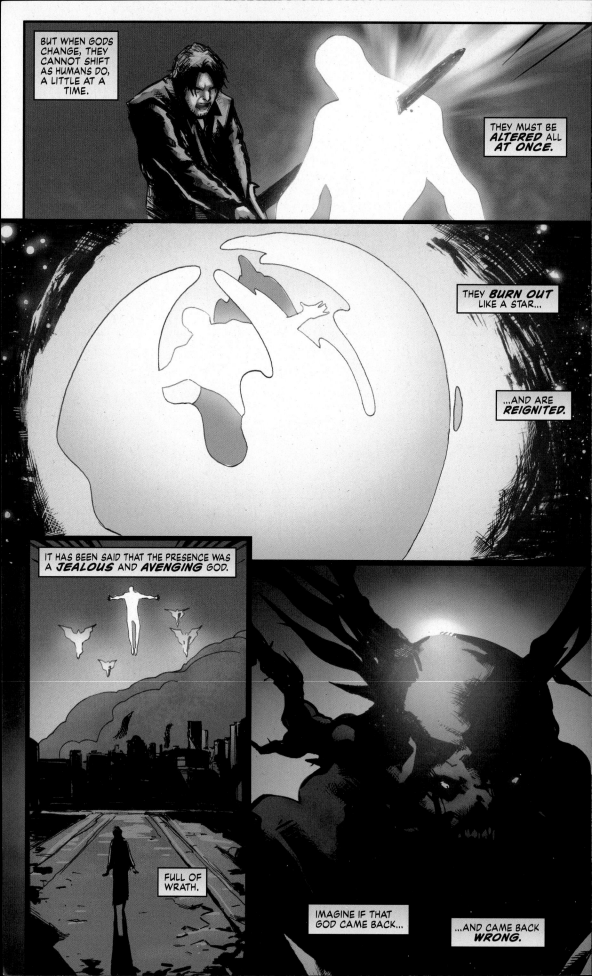

BUT WHEN GODS CHANGE, THEY CANNOT SHIFT AS HUMANS DO, A LITTLE AT A TIME.

THEY MUST BE *ALTERED* ALL *AT ONCE.*

THEY *BURN OUT* LIKE A STAR...

...AND ARE *REIGNITED.*

IT HAS BEEN SAID THAT THE PRESENCE WAS A *JEALOUS* AND *AVENGING* GOD.

FULL OF WRATH.

IMAGINE IF THAT GOD CAME BACK...

...AND CAME BACK *WRONG.*

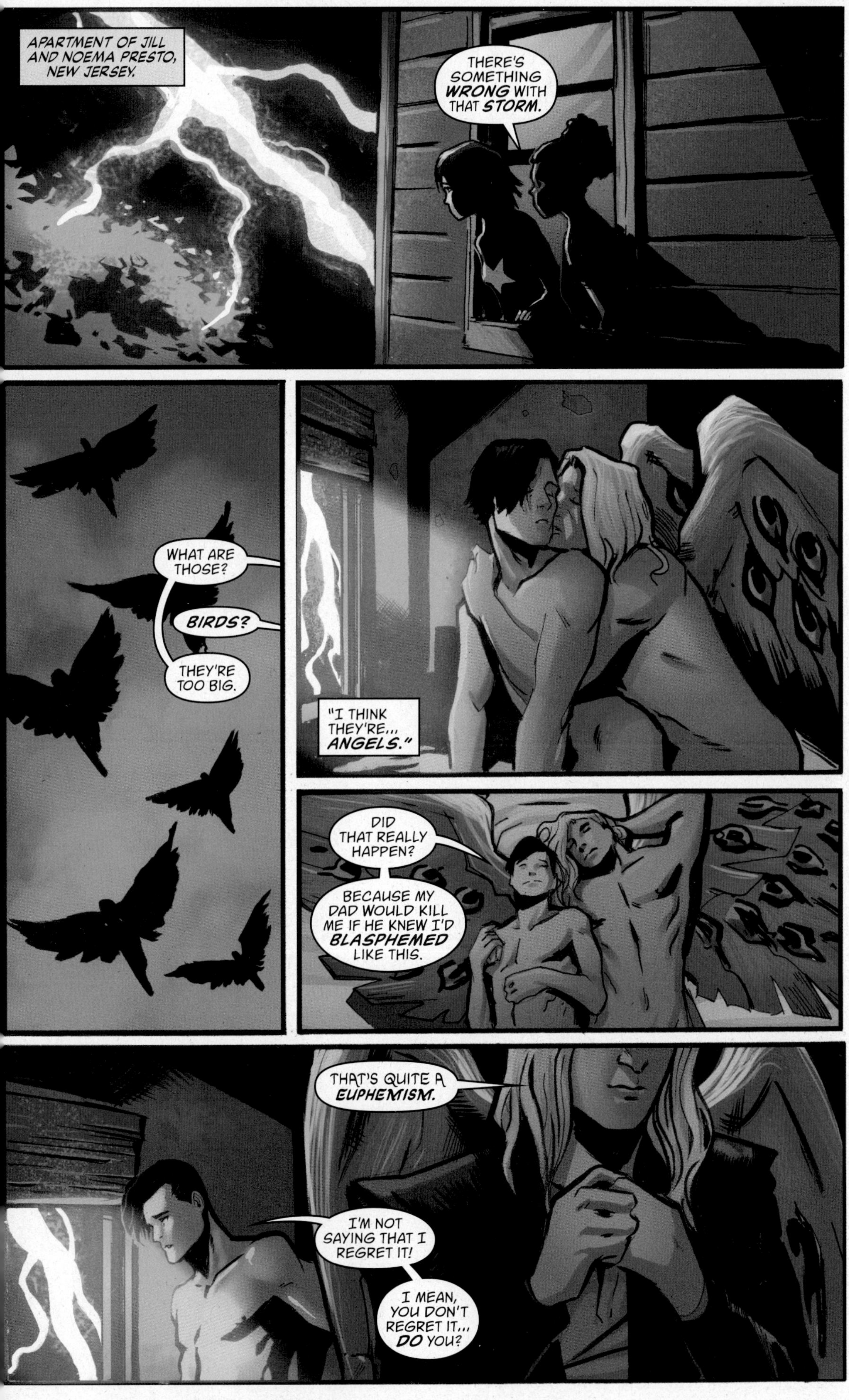

APARTMENT OF JILL AND NOEMA PRESTO, NEW JERSEY.
THERE'S SOMETHING WRONG WITH THAT STORM.
WHAT ARE THOSE?
BIRDS?
THEY'RE TOO BIG.
"I THINK THEY'RE... ANGELS."
DID THAT REALLY HAPPEN?
BECAUSE MY DAD WOULD KILL ME IF HE KNEW I'D BLASPHEMED LIKE THIS.
THAT'S QUITE A EUPHEMISM.
I'M NOT SAYING THAT I REGRET IT!
I MEAN, YOU DON'T REGRET IT... DO YOU?

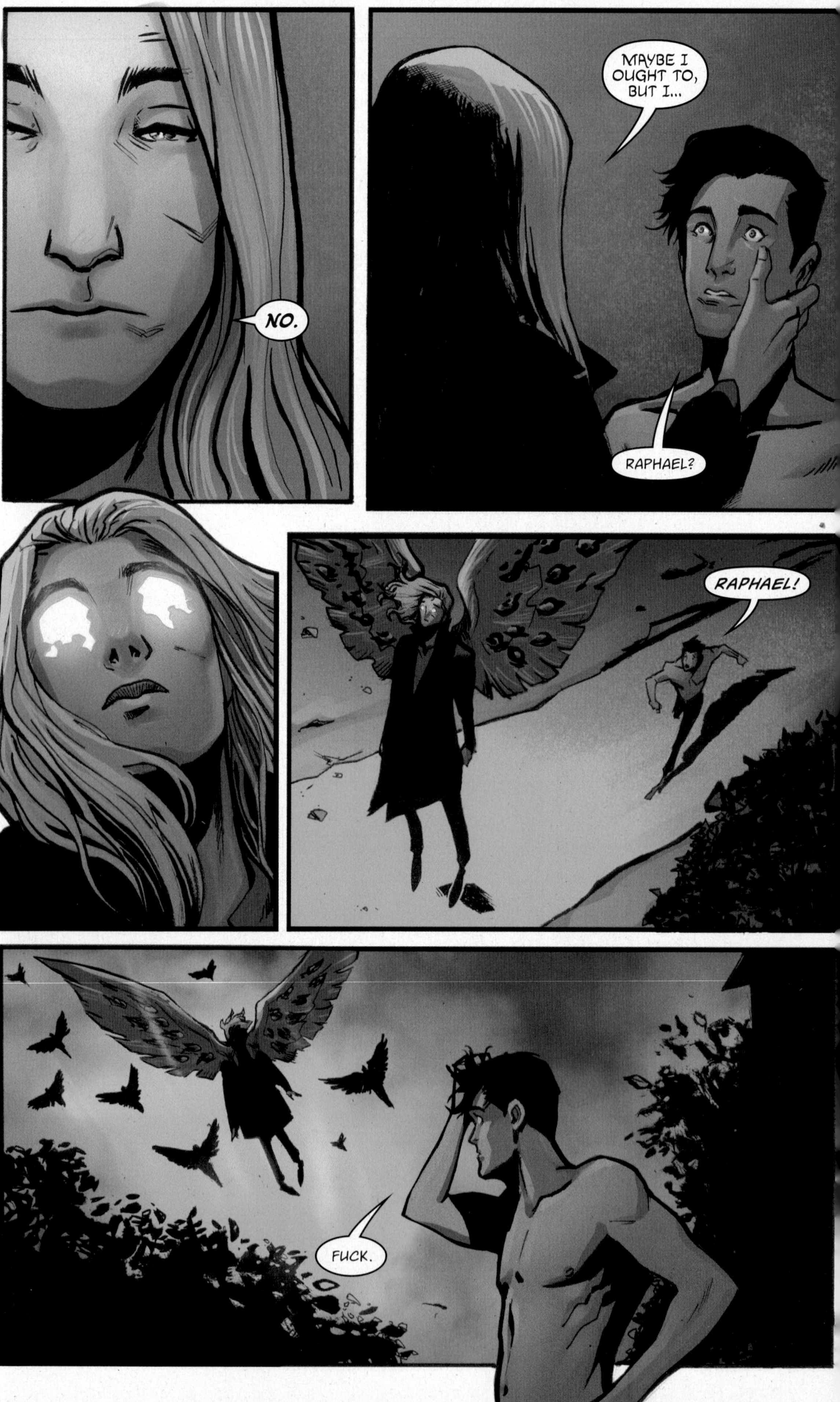
NO.
MAYBE I OUGHT TO, BUT I...
RAPHAEL?
RAPHAEL!
FUCK.

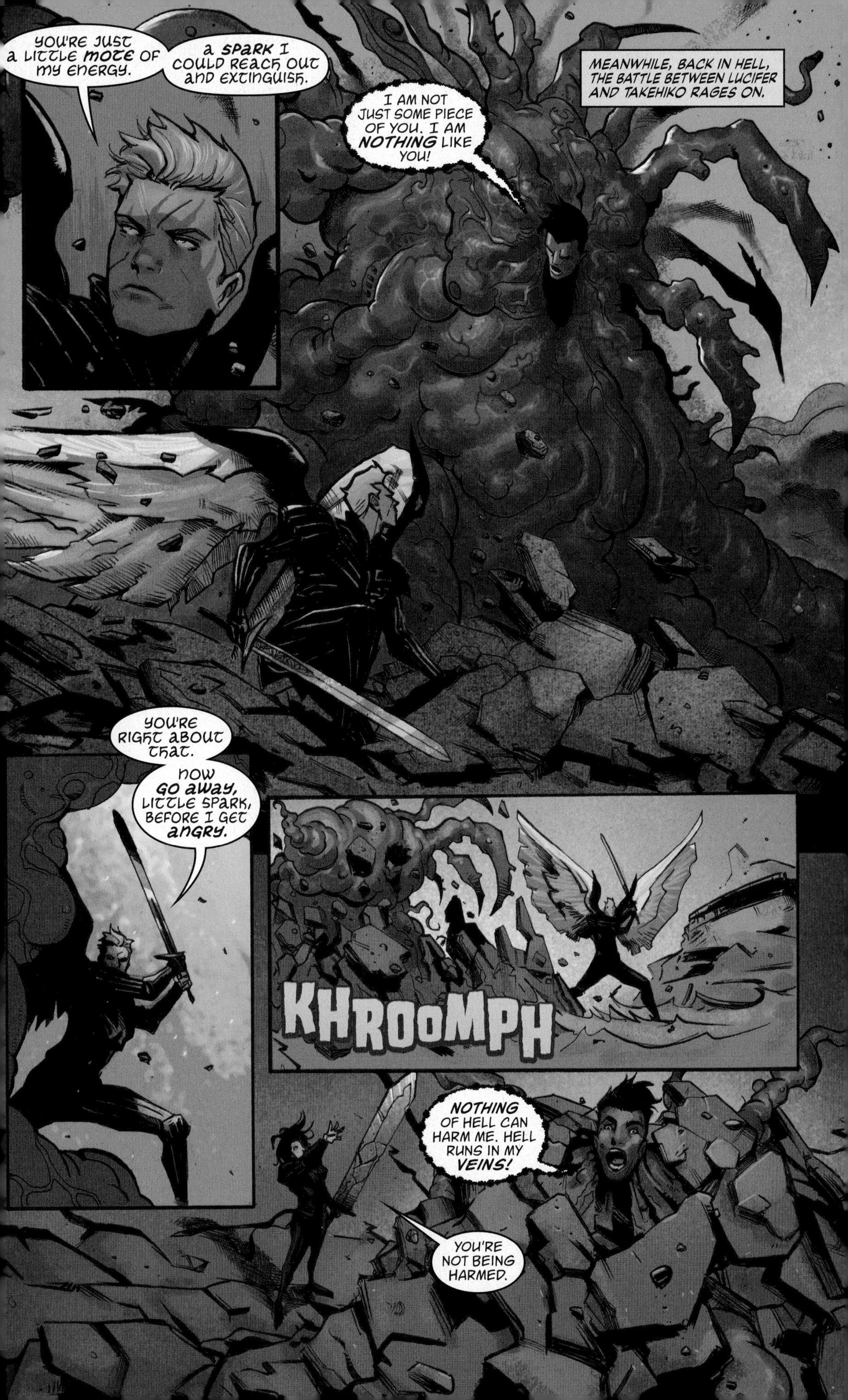
YOU'RE JUST A LITTLE MOTE OF MY ENERGY.
A SPARK I COULD REACH OUT AND EXTINGUISH.
MEANWHILE, BACK IN HELL, THE BATTLE BETWEEN LUCIFER AND TAKEHIKO RAGES ON.
I AM NOT JUST SOME PIECE OF YOU. I AM NOTHING LIKE YOU!
YOU'RE RIGHT ABOUT THAT.
NOW GO AWAY, LITTLE SPARK, BEFORE I GET ANGRY.
KHROOMPH
NOTHING OF HELL CAN HARM ME. HELL RUNS IN MY VEINS!
YOU'RE NOT BEING HARMED.

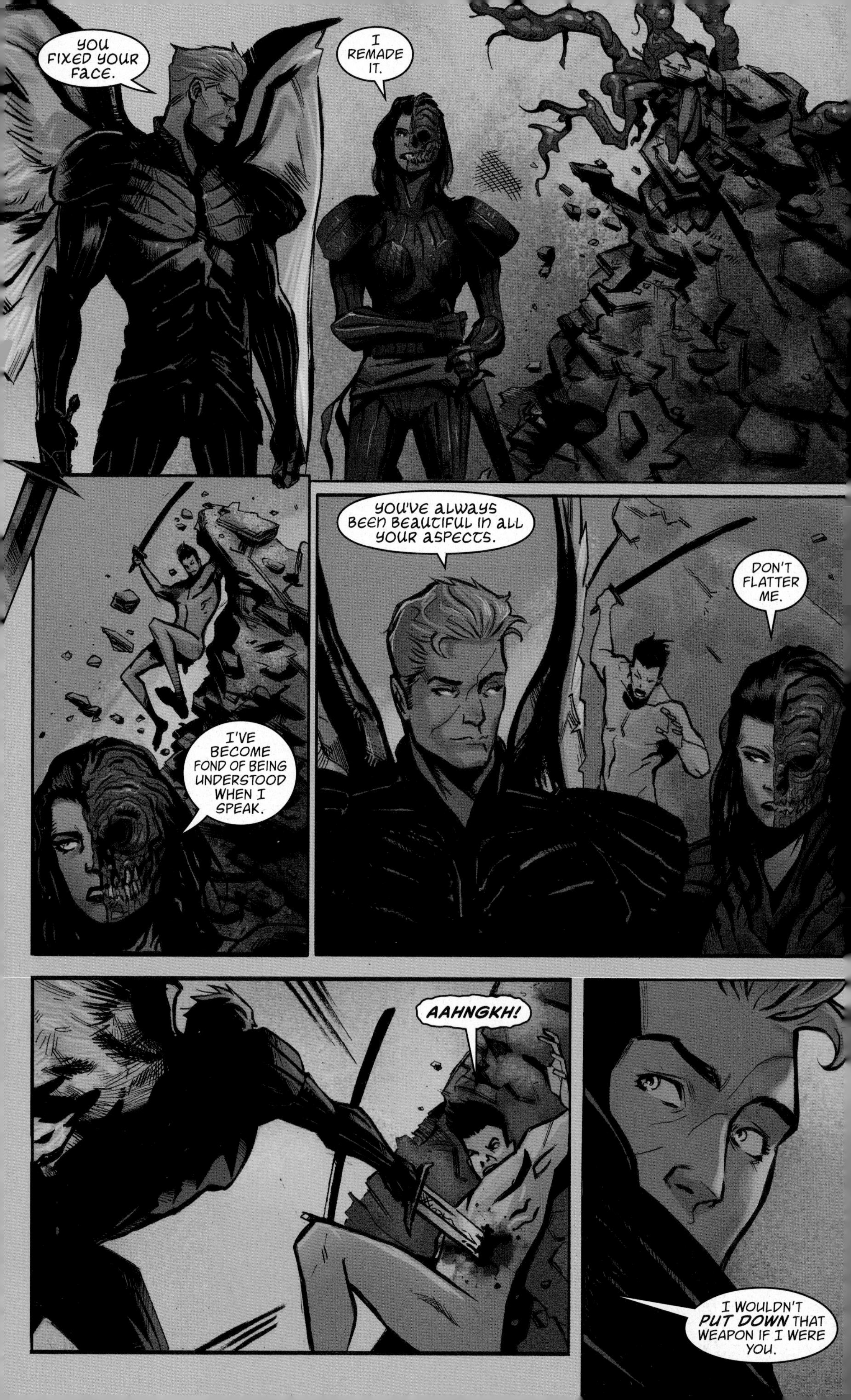
YOU FIXED YOUR FACE.
I REMADE IT.
I'VE BECOME FOND OF BEING UNDERSTOOD WHEN I SPEAK.
YOU'VE ALWAYS BEEN BEAUTIFUL IN ALL YOUR ASPECTS.
DON'T FLATTER ME.
AAHNGKH!
I WOULDN'T PUT DOWN THAT WEAPON IF I WERE YOU.

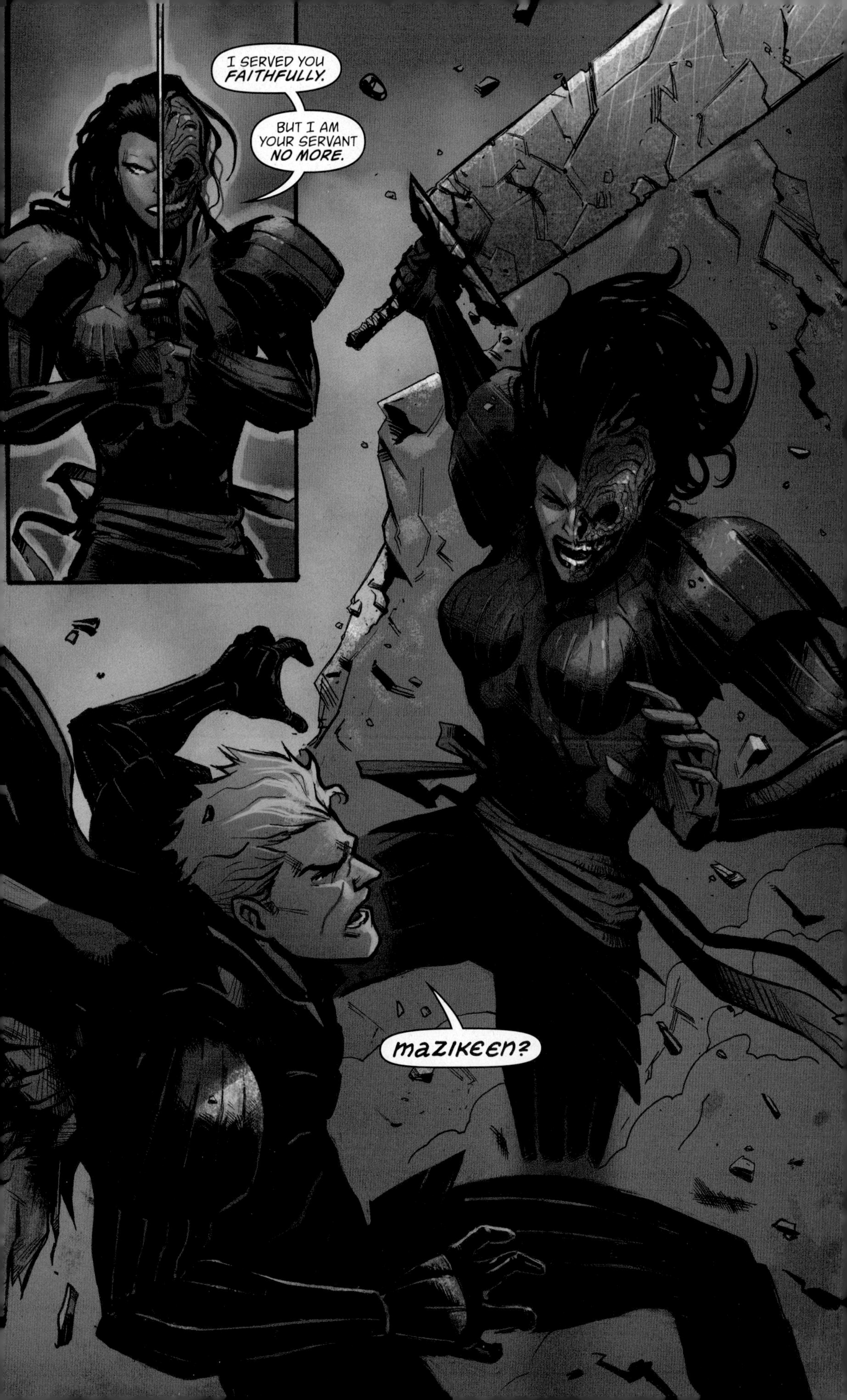
I SERVED YOU FAITHFULLY.
BUT I AM YOUR SERVANT NO MORE.
MAZIKEEN?

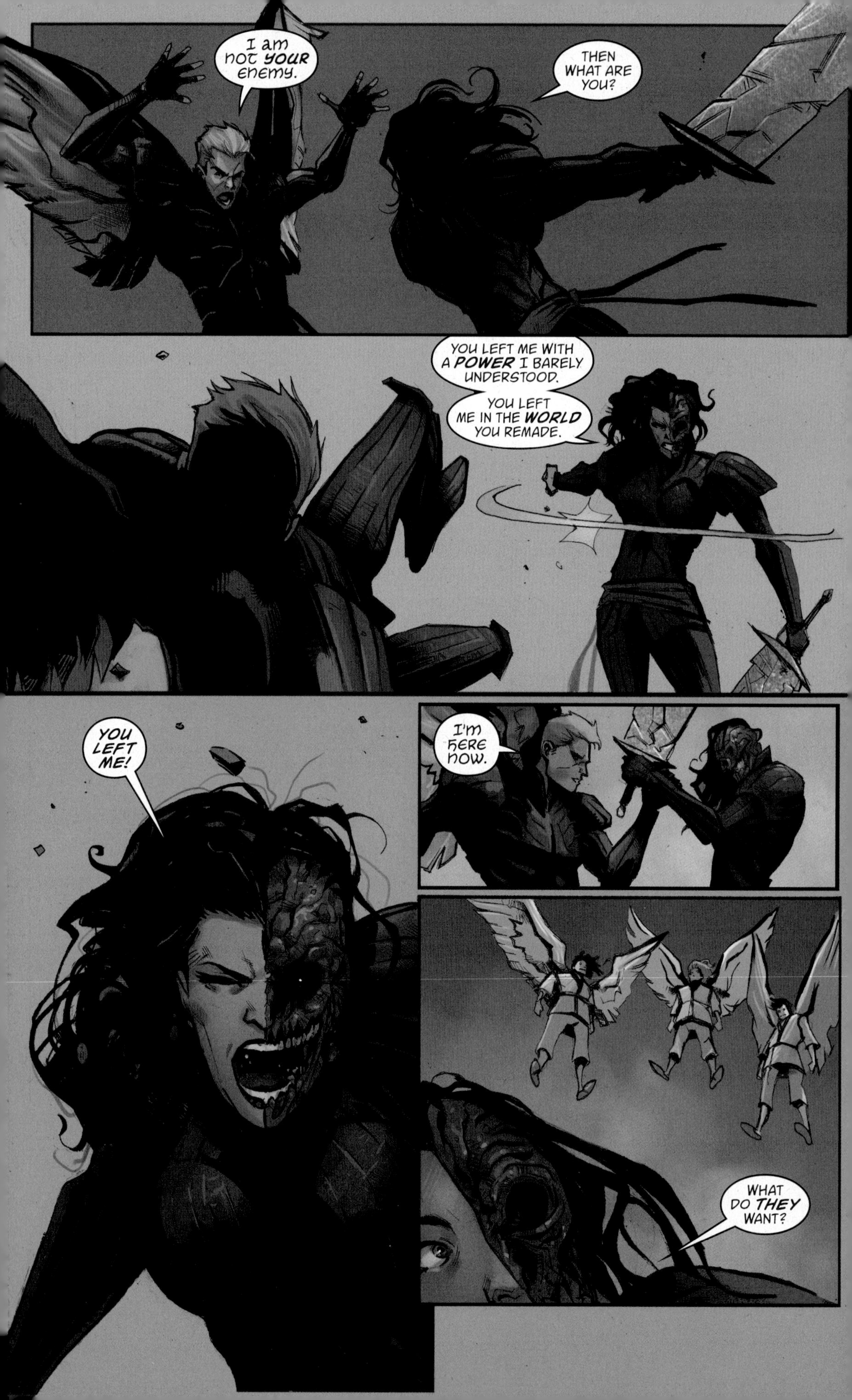
I am not YOUR enemy.
THEN WHAT ARE YOU?
YOU LEFT ME WITH A POWER I BARELY UNDERSTOOD.
YOU LEFT ME IN THE WORLD YOU REMADE.
YOU LEFT ME!
I'm here now.
WHAT DO THEY WANT?

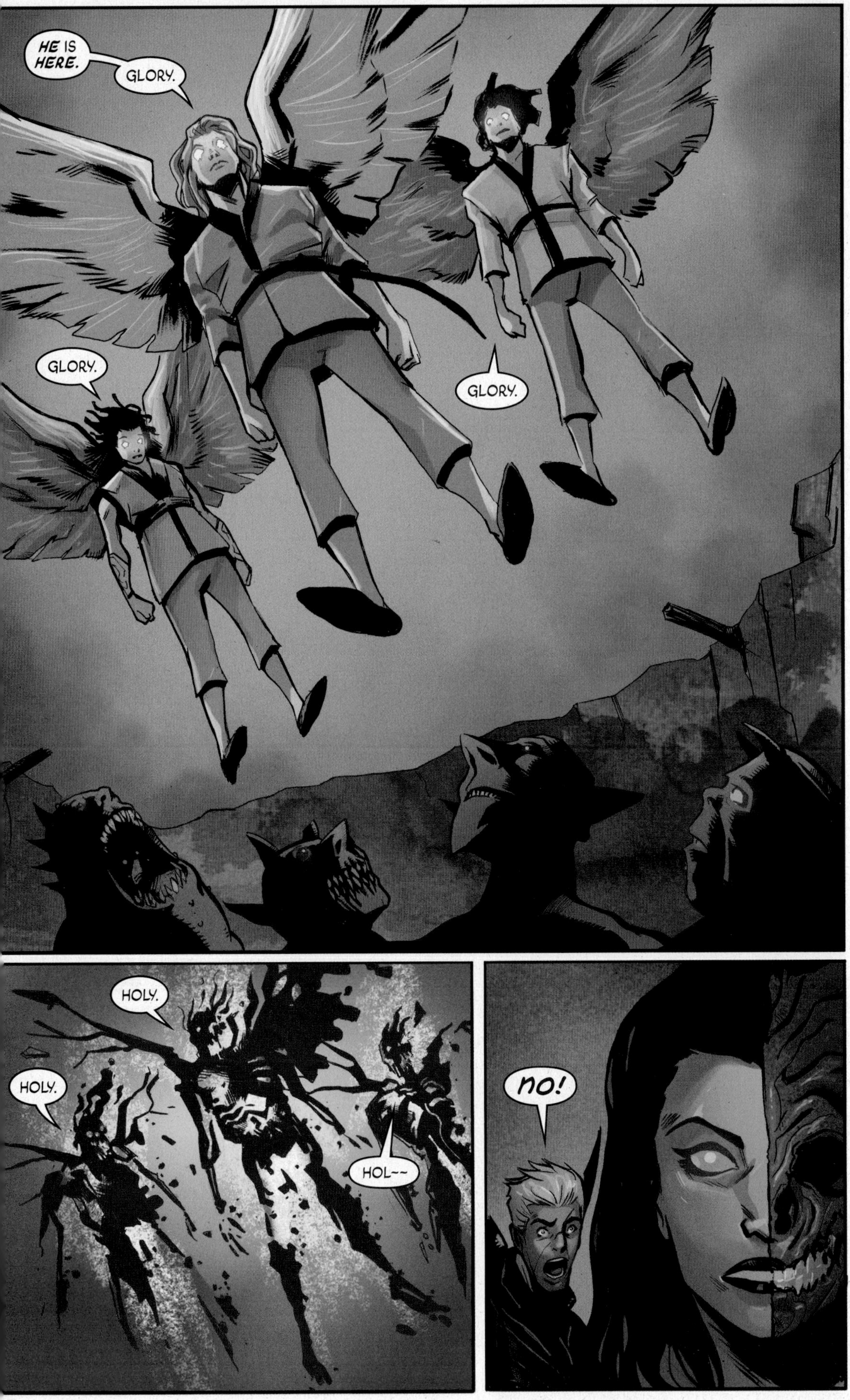
HE IS HERE.
GLORY.
GLORY.
GLORY.
HOLY.
HOLY.
HOL--
NO!

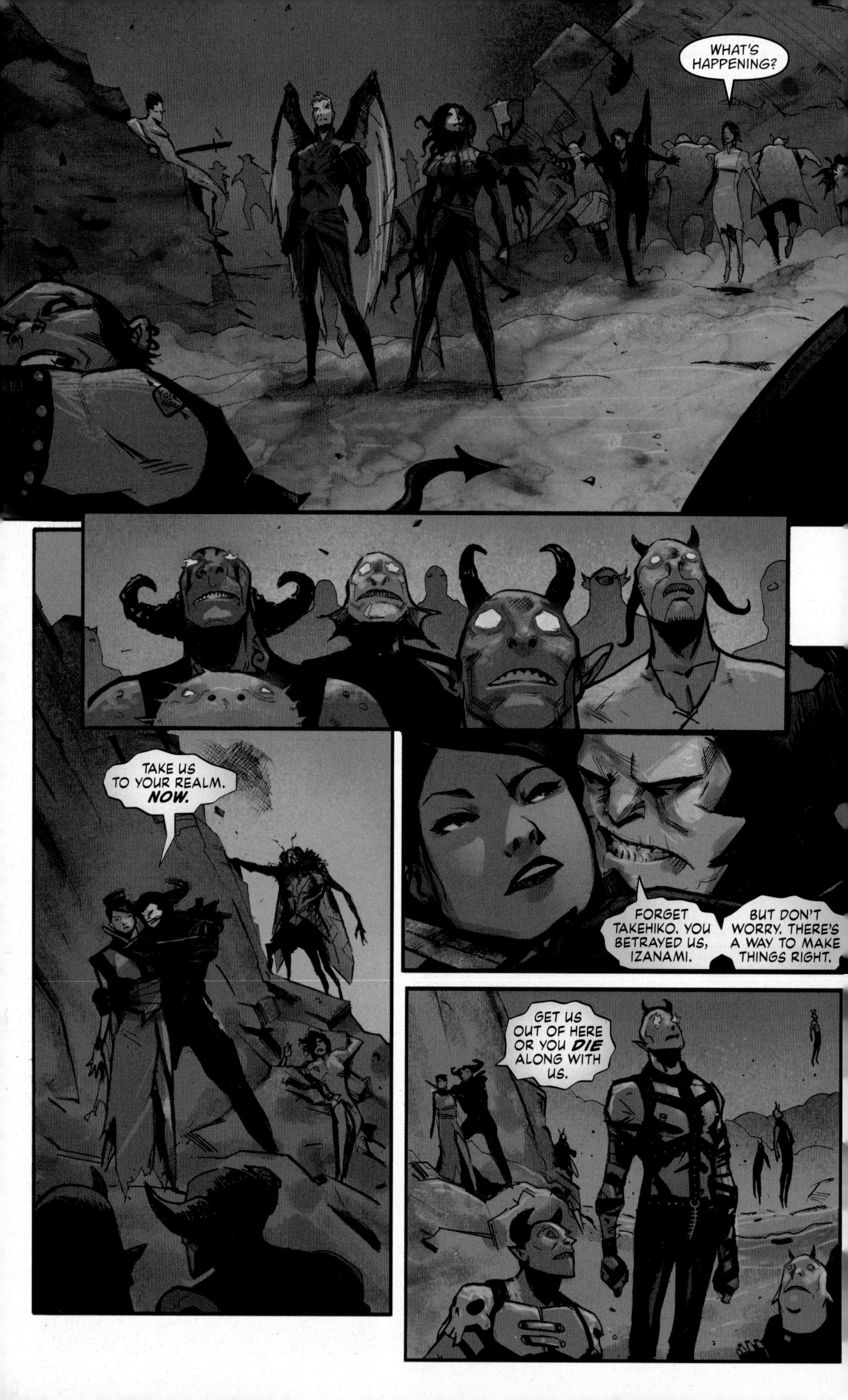
WHAT'S HAPPENING?
TAKE US TO YOUR REALM. NOW.
FORGET TAKEHIKO. YOU BETRAYED US, IZANAMI.
BUT DON'T WORRY. THERE'S A WAY TO MAKE THINGS RIGHT.
GET US OUT OF HERE OR YOU DIE ALONG WITH US.

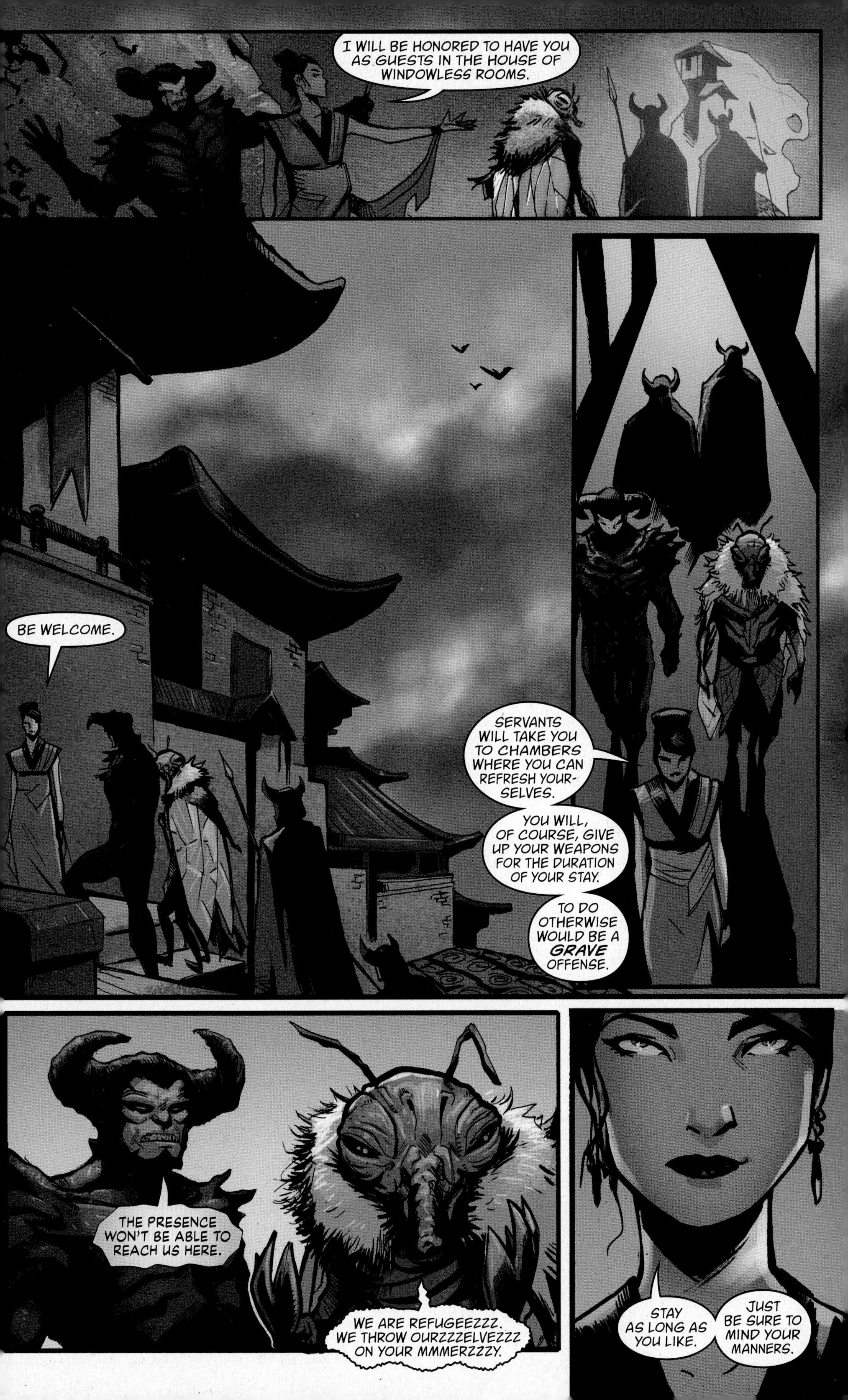
I WILL BE HONORED TO HAVE YOU AS GUESTS IN THE HOUSE OF WINDOWLESS ROOMS.
BE WELCOME.
SERVANTS WILL TAKE YOU TO CHAMBERS WHERE YOU CAN REFRESH YOUR-SELVES.
YOU WILL, OF COURSE, GIVE UP YOUR WEAPONS FOR THE DURATION OF YOUR STAY.
TO DO OTHERWISE WOULD BE A GRAVE OFFENSE.
THE PRESENCE WON'T BE ABLE TO REACH US HERE.
WE ARE REFUGEEZZZ. WE THROW OURZZZELVEZZZ ON YOUR MMMERZZZY.
STAY AS LONG AS YOU LIKE.
JUST BE SURE TO MIND YOUR MANNERS.

YOU ARE **NO** ONE'S SERVANT, YOU SAID SO YOURSELF. DO NOT **LET HIM** DO THIS TO YOU.

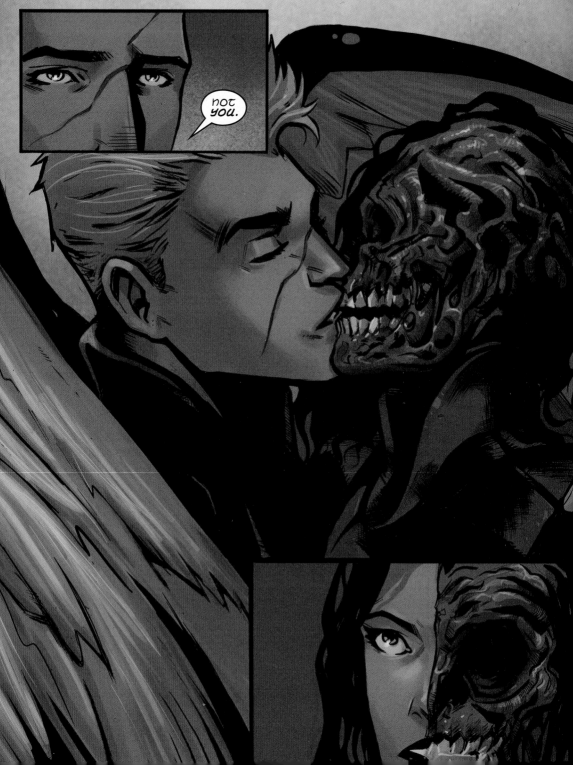

NOT YOU.

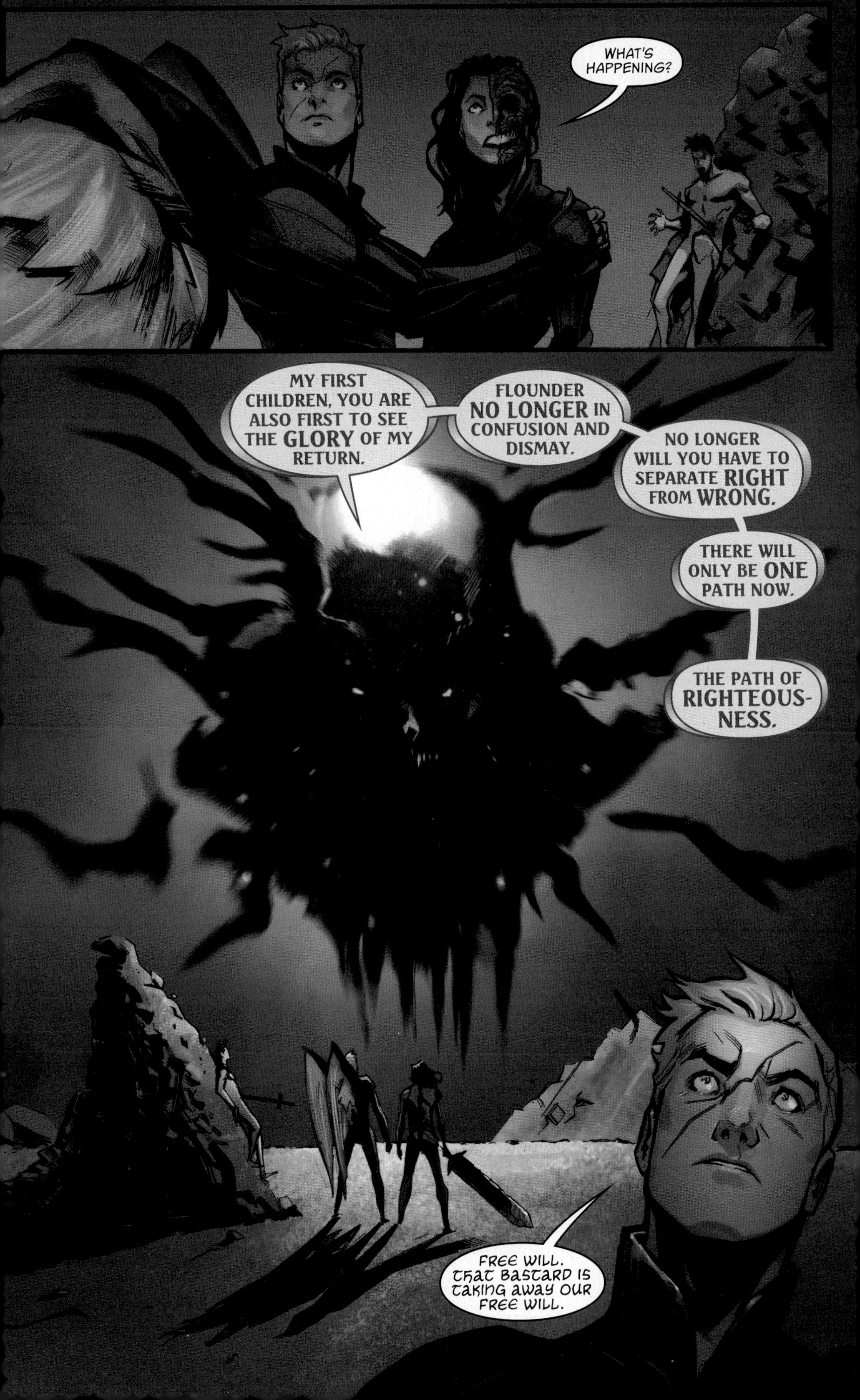
WHAT'S HAPPENING?
MY FIRST CHILDREN, YOU ARE ALSO FIRST TO SEE THE GLORY OF MY RETURN.
FLOUNDER NO LONGER IN CONFUSION AND DISMAY.
NO LONGER WILL YOU HAVE TO SEPARATE RIGHT FROM WRONG.
THERE WILL ONLY BE ONE PATH NOW.
THE PATH OF RIGHTEOUS-NESS.
FREE WILL. THAT BASTARD IS TAKING AWAY OUR FREE WILL.

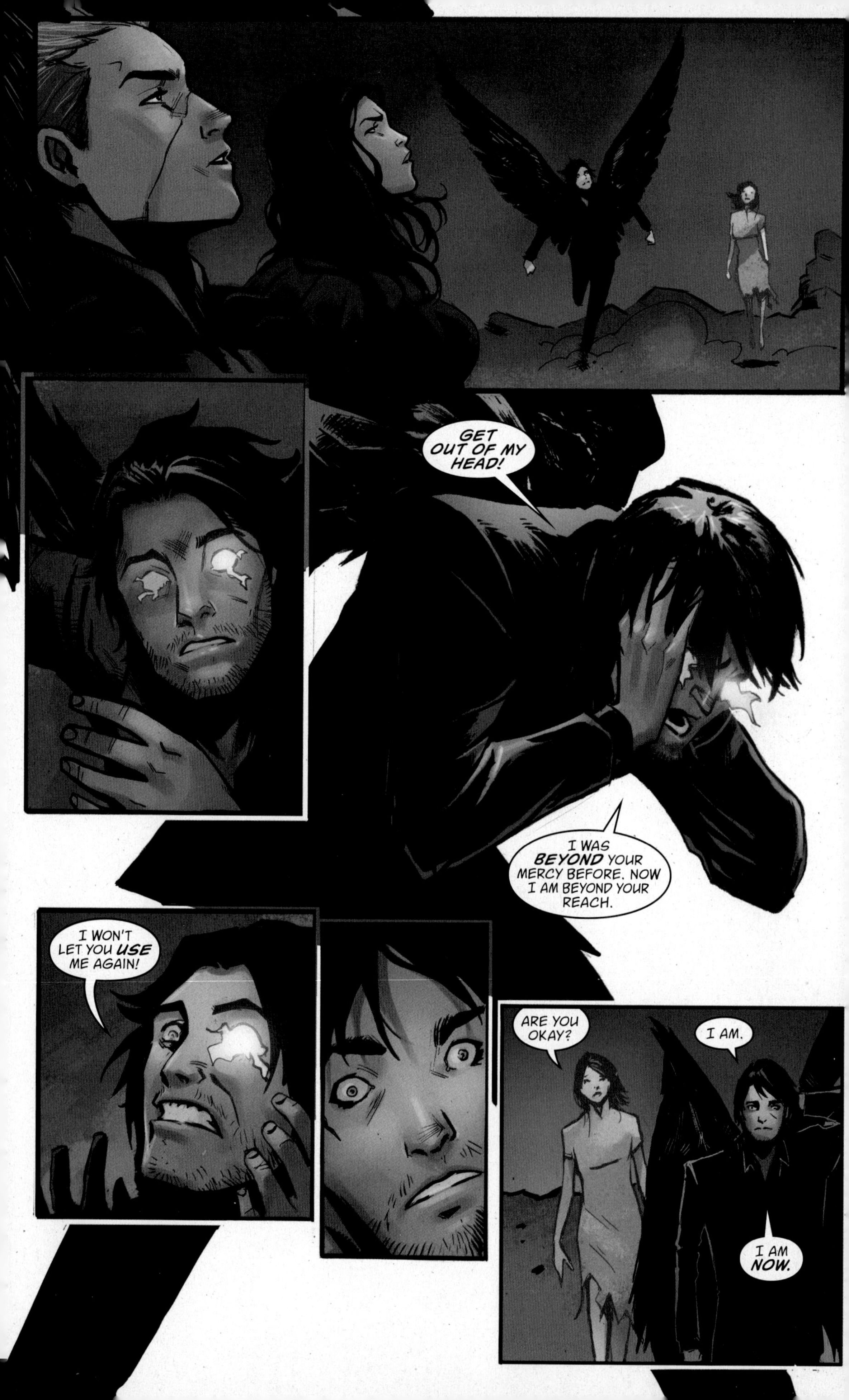
GET OUT OF MY HEAD!
I WAS BEYOND YOUR MERCY BEFORE. NOW I AM BEYOND YOUR REACH.
I WON'T LET YOU USE ME AGAIN!
ARE YOU OKAY?
I AM.
I AM NOW.

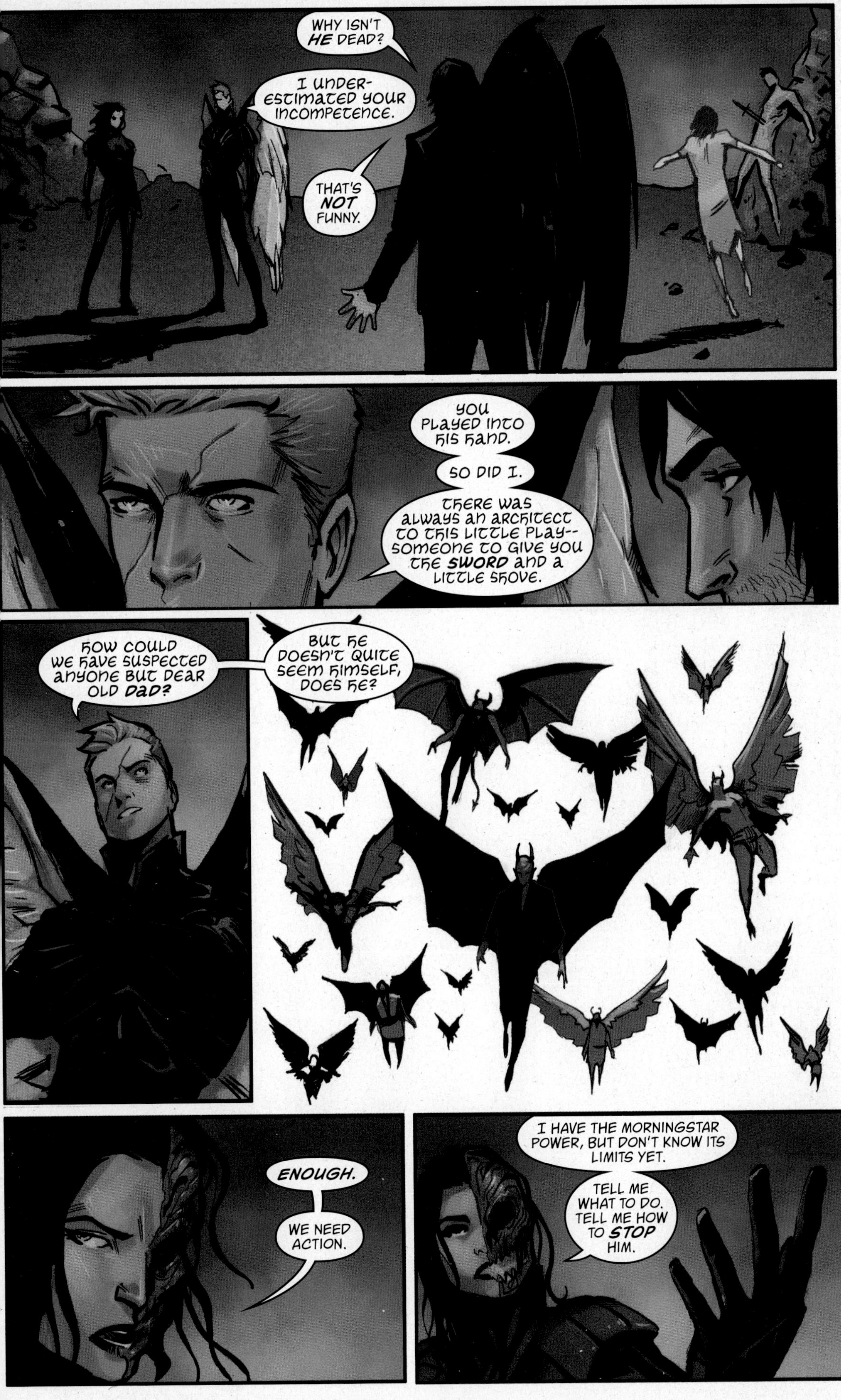
WHY ISN'T HE DEAD?
I UNDER-ESTIMATED YOUR INCOMPETENCE.
THAT'S NOT FUNNY.
YOU PLAYED INTO HIS HAND.
SO DID I.
THERE WAS ALWAYS AN ARCHITECT TO THIS LITTLE PLAY--SOMEONE TO GIVE YOU THE SWORD AND A LITTLE SHOVE.
HOW COULD WE HAVE SUSPECTED ANYONE BUT DEAR OLD DAD?
BUT HE DOESN'T QUITE SEEM HIMSELF, DOES HE?
ENOUGH.
WE NEED ACTION.
I HAVE THE MORNINGSTAR POWER, BUT DON'T KNOW ITS LIMITS YET.
TELL ME WHAT TO DO. TELL ME HOW TO STOP HIM.

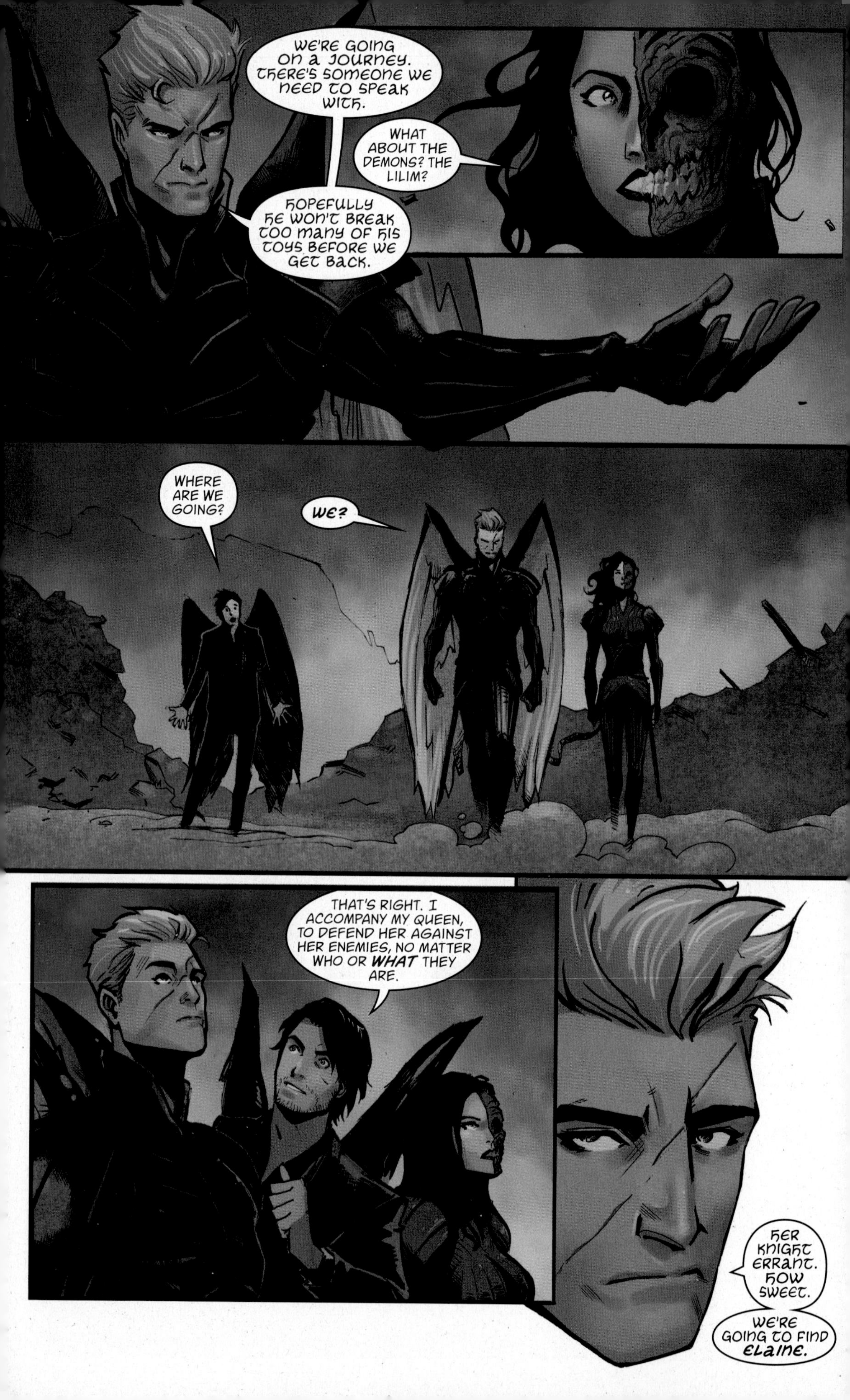
WE'RE GOING ON A JOURNEY. THERE'S SOMEONE WE NEED TO SPEAK WITH.
WHAT ABOUT THE DEMONS? THE LILIM?
HOPEFULLY HE WON'T BREAK TOO MANY OF HIS TOYS BEFORE WE GET BACK.
WHERE ARE WE GOING?
WE?
THAT'S RIGHT. I ACCOMPANY MY QUEEN, TO DEFEND HER AGAINST HER ENEMIES, NO MATTER WHO OR WHAT THEY ARE.
HER KNIGHT ERRANT. HOW SWEET.
WE'RE GOING TO FIND ELAINE.

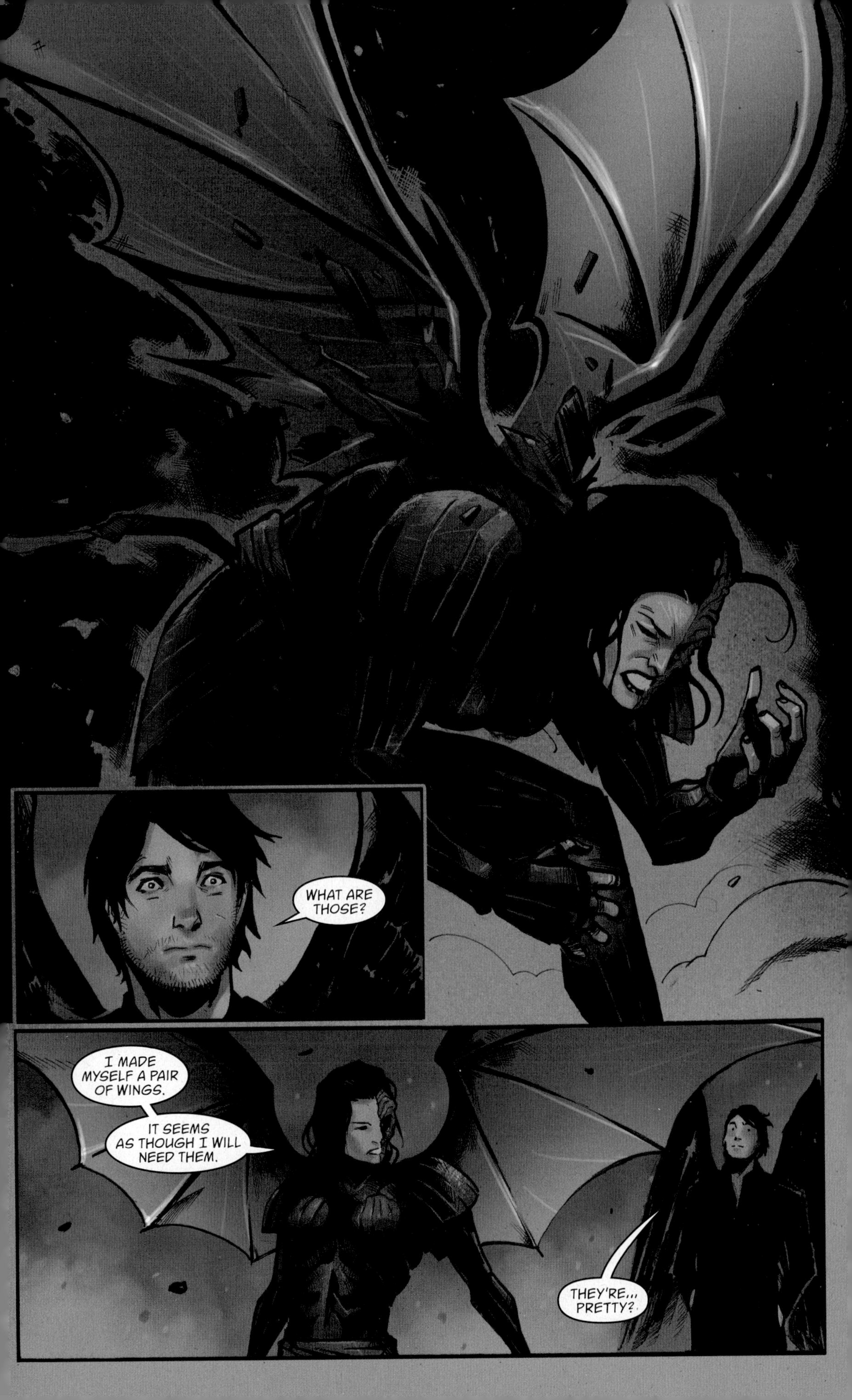
WHAT ARE THOSE?
I MADE MYSELF A PAIR OF WINGS.
IT SEEMS AS THOUGH I WILL NEED THEM.
THEY'RE... PRETTY?

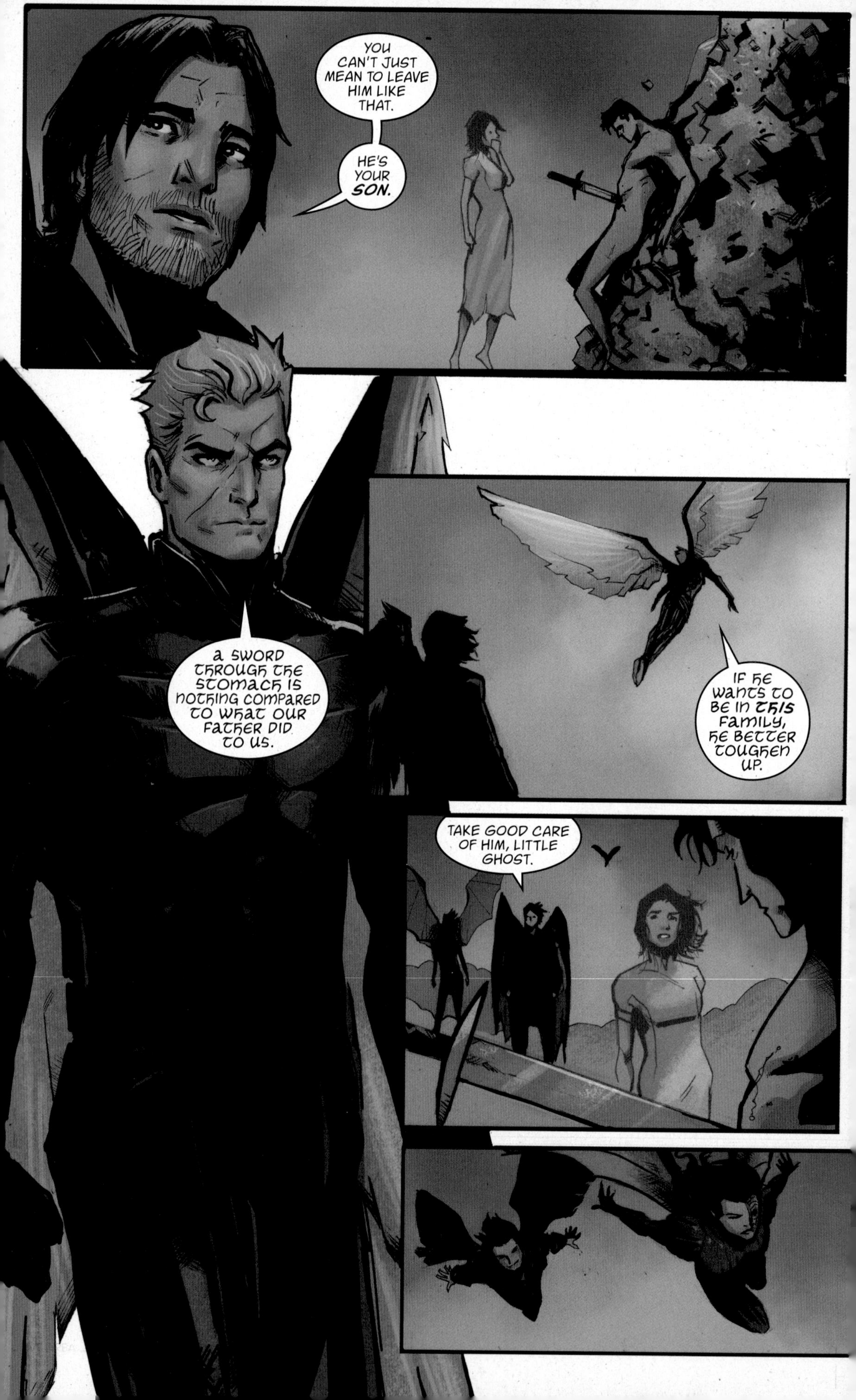

YOU CAN'T JUST MEAN TO LEAVE HIM LIKE THAT.
HE'S YOUR SON.
A SWORD THROUGH THE STOMACH IS NOTHING COMPARED TO WHAT OUR FATHER DID TO US.
IF HE WANTS TO BE IN THIS FAMILY, HE BETTER TOUGHEN UP.
TAKE GOOD CARE OF HIM, LITTLE GHOST.

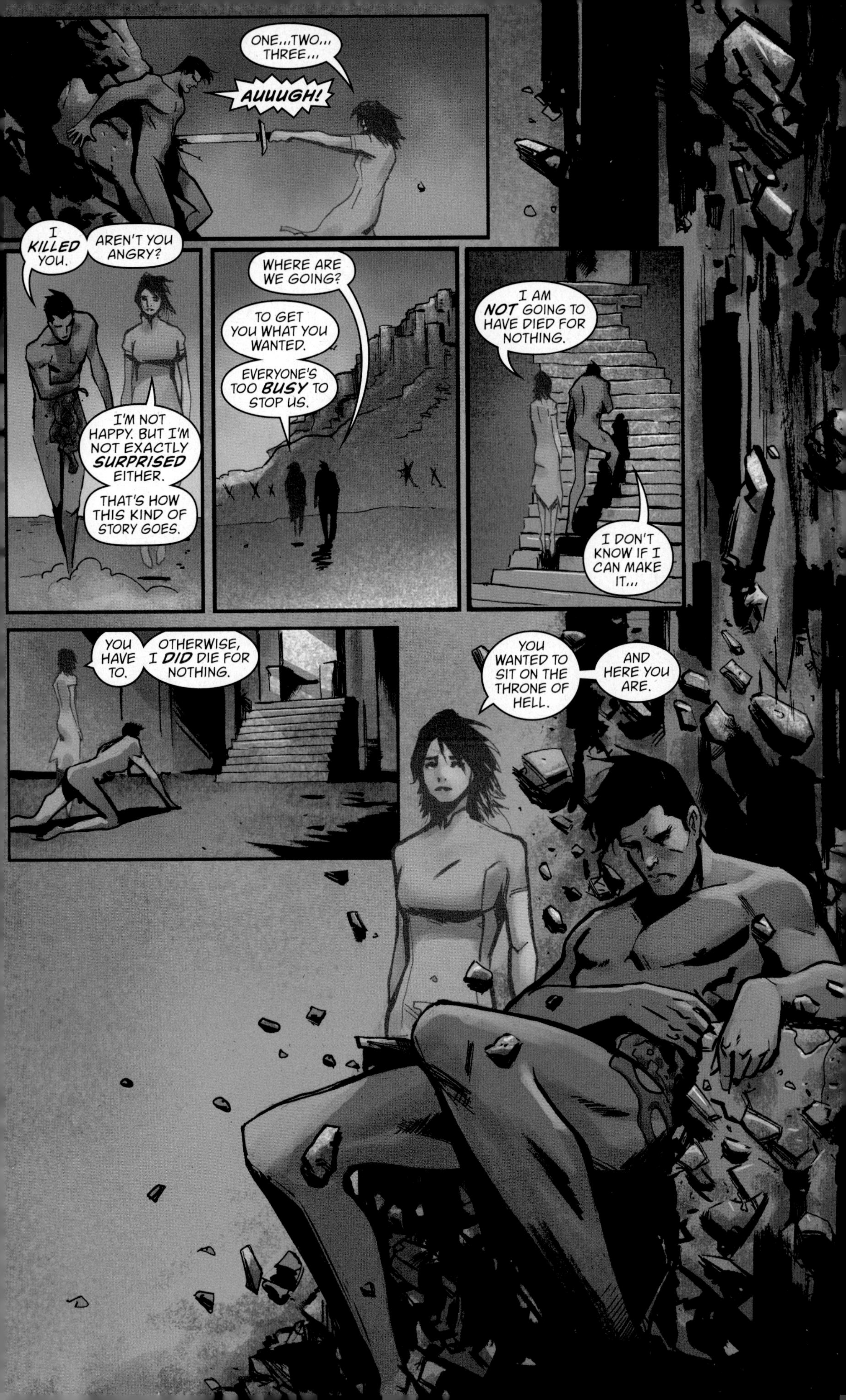
ONE...TWO... THREE...
AUUUGH!
I KILLED YOU.
AREN'T YOU ANGRY?
I'M NOT HAPPY. BUT I'M NOT EXACTLY SURPRISED EITHER.
THAT'S HOW THIS KIND OF STORY GOES.
WHERE ARE WE GOING?
TO GET YOU WHAT YOU WANTED.
EVERYONE'S TOO BUSY TO STOP US.
I AM NOT GOING TO HAVE DIED FOR NOTHING.
I DON'T KNOW IF I CAN MAKE IT...
YOU HAVE TO.
OTHERWISE, I DID DIE FOR NOTHING.
YOU WANTED TO SIT ON THE THRONE OF HELL.
AND HERE YOU ARE.

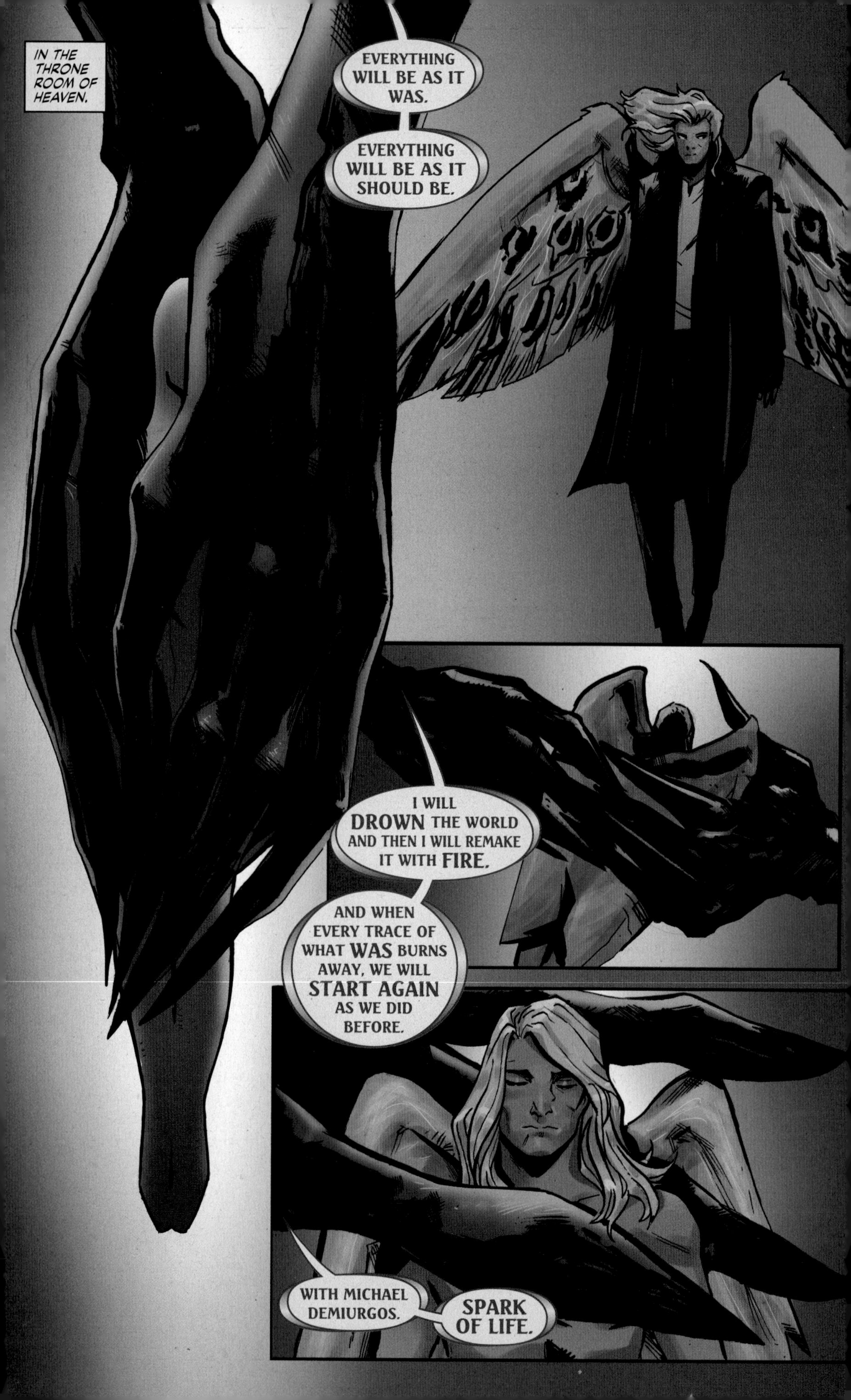
IN THE THRONE ROOM OF HEAVEN.
EVERYTHING WILL BE AS IT WAS.
EVERYTHING WILL BE AS IT SHOULD BE.
I WILL DROWN THE WORLD AND THEN I WILL REMAKE IT WITH FIRE.
AND WHEN EVERY TRACE OF WHAT WAS BURNS AWAY, WE WILL START AGAIN AS WE DID BEFORE.
WITH MICHAEL DEMIURGOS.
SPARK OF LIFE.

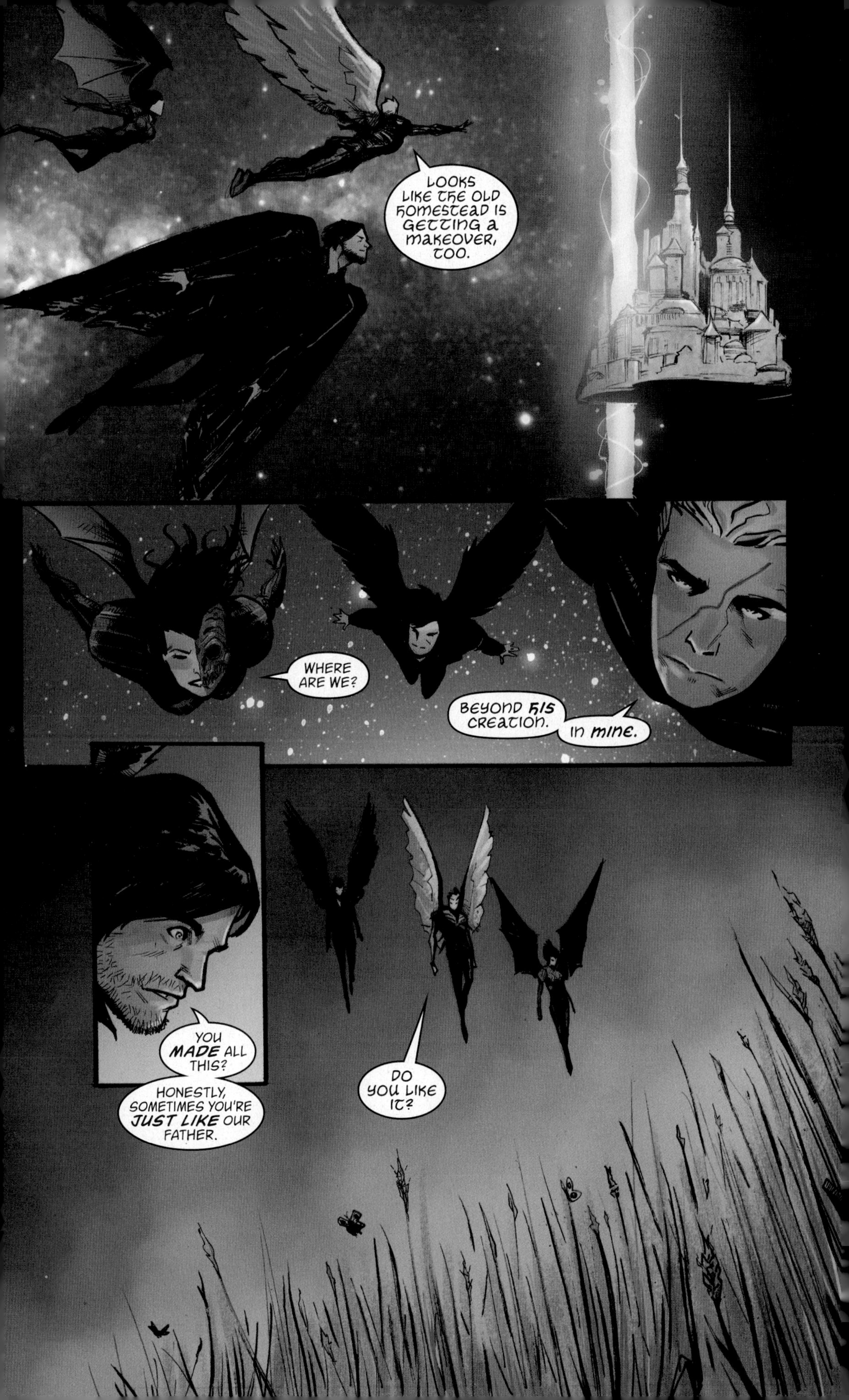

LOOKS LIKE THE OLD HOMESTEAD IS GETTING A MAKEOVER, TOO.
WHERE ARE WE?
BEYOND HIS CREATION.
IN MINE.
YOU MADE ALL THIS?
HONESTLY, SOMETIMES YOU'RE JUST LIKE OUR FATHER.
DO YOU LIKE IT?

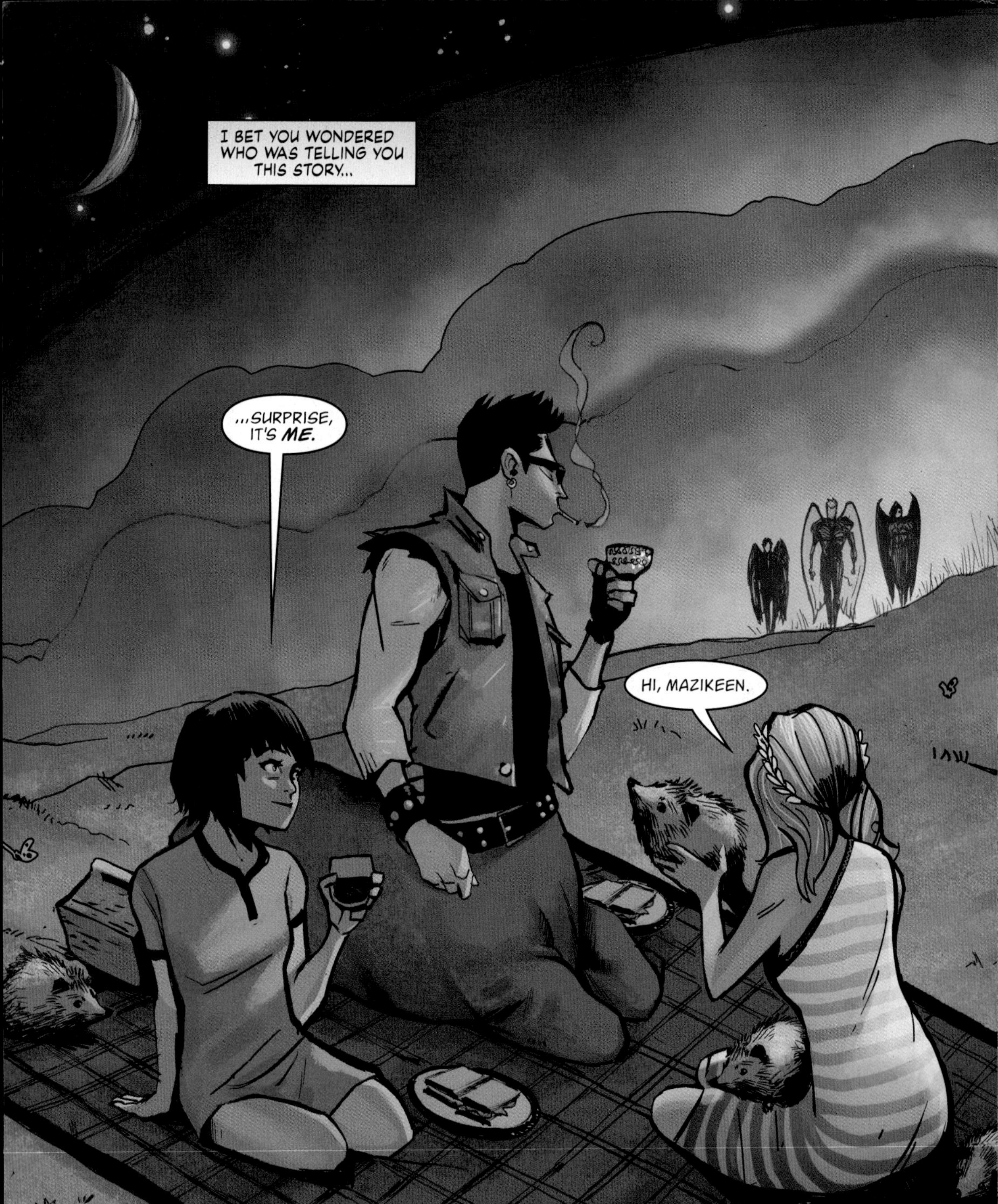
I BET YOU WONDERED WHO WAS TELLING YOU THIS STORY...
...SURPRISE, IT'S **ME.**
HI, MAZIKEEN.

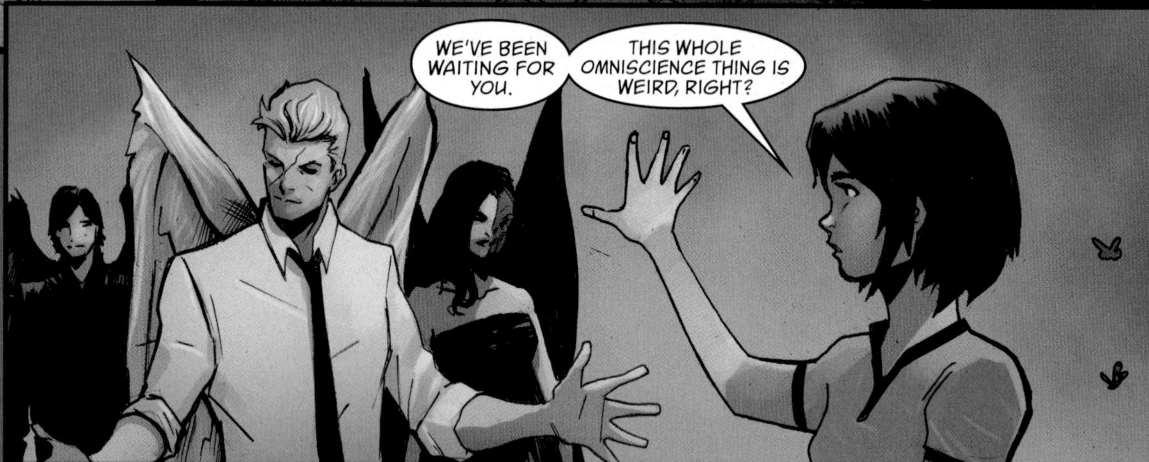
WE'VE BEEN WAITING FOR YOU.
THIS WHOLE OMNISCIENCE THING IS WEIRD, RIGHT?

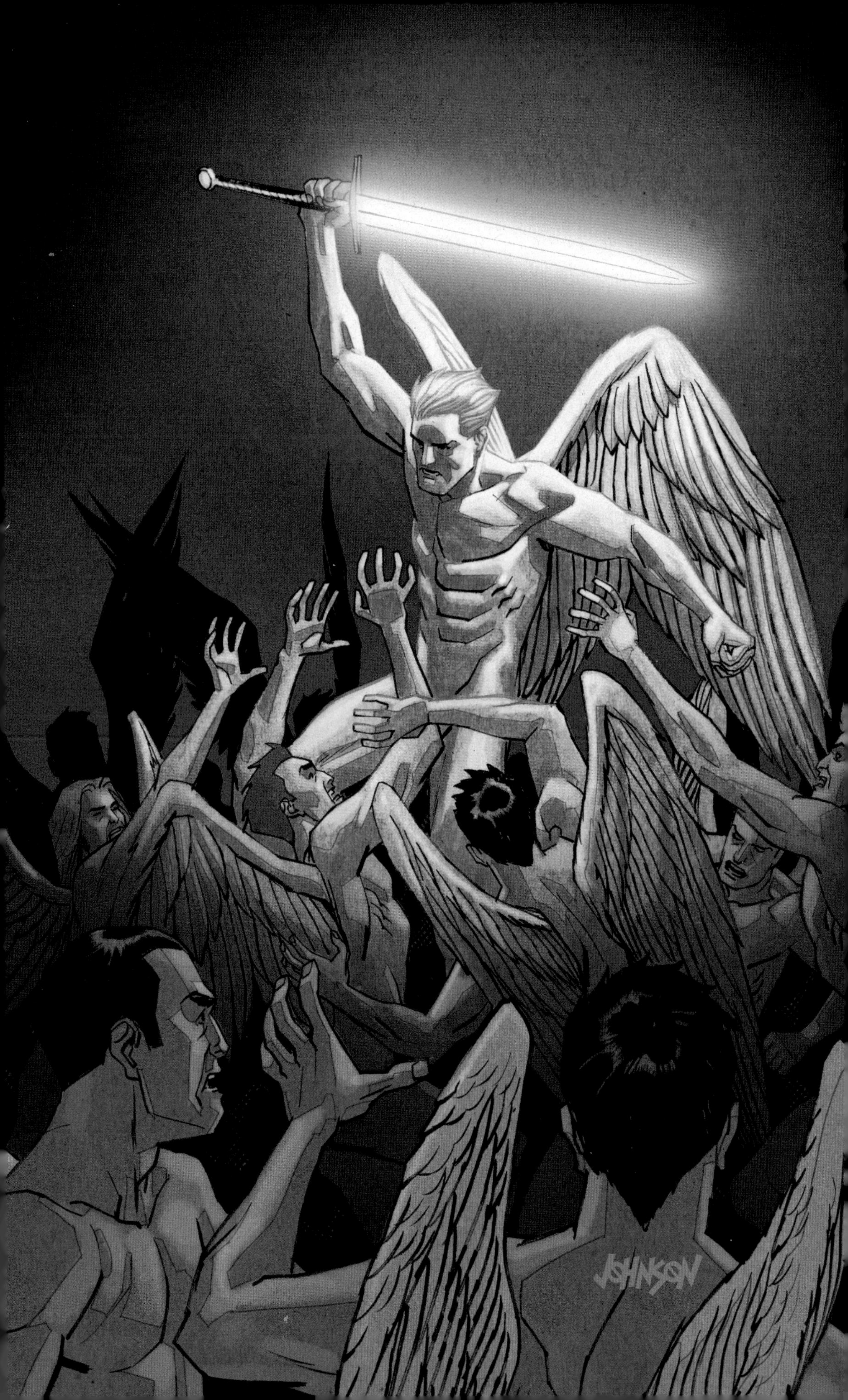
JOHNSON

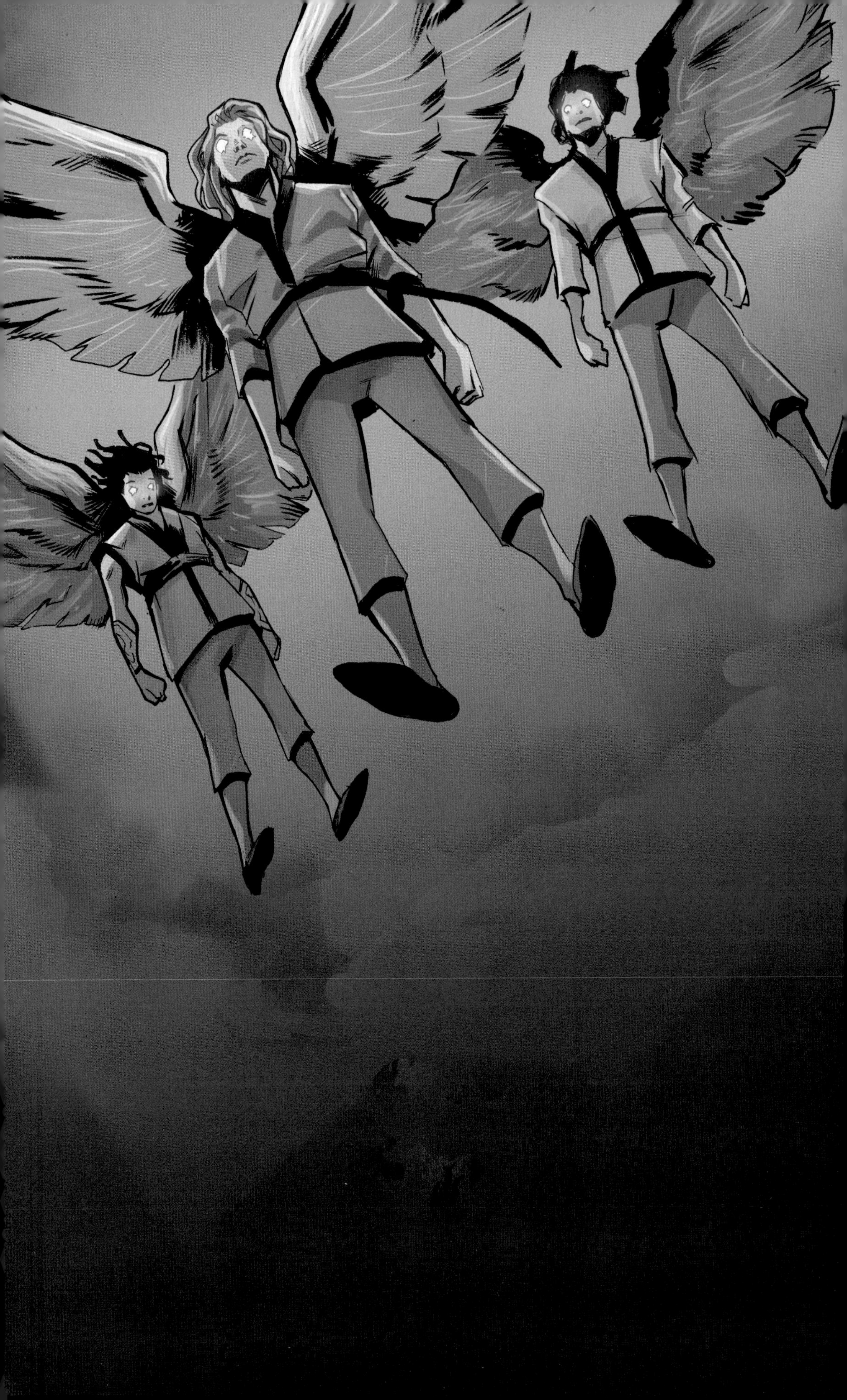

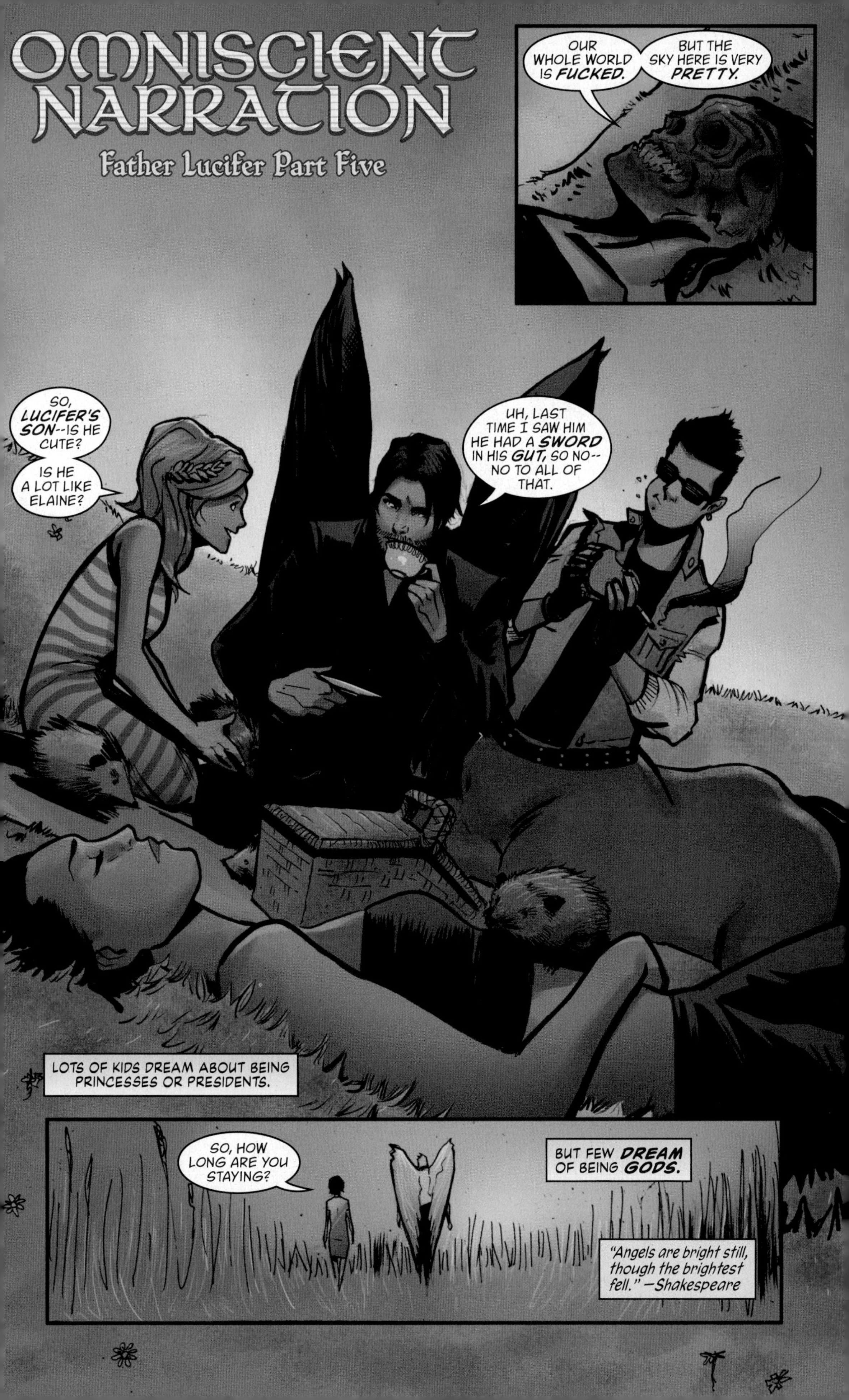
OMNISCIENT NARRATION
Father Lucifer Part Five
OUR WHOLE WORLD IS FUCKED.
BUT THE SKY HERE IS VERY PRETTY.
SO, LUCIFER'S SON--IS HE CUTE?
IS HE A LOT LIKE ELAINE?
UH, LAST TIME I SAW HIM HE HAD A SWORD IN HIS GUT, SO NO--NO TO ALL OF THAT.
LOTS OF KIDS DREAM ABOUT BEING PRINCESSES OR PRESIDENTS.
SO, HOW LONG ARE YOU STAYING?
BUT FEW DREAM OF BEING GODS.
"Angels are bright still, though the brightest fell." —Shakespeare

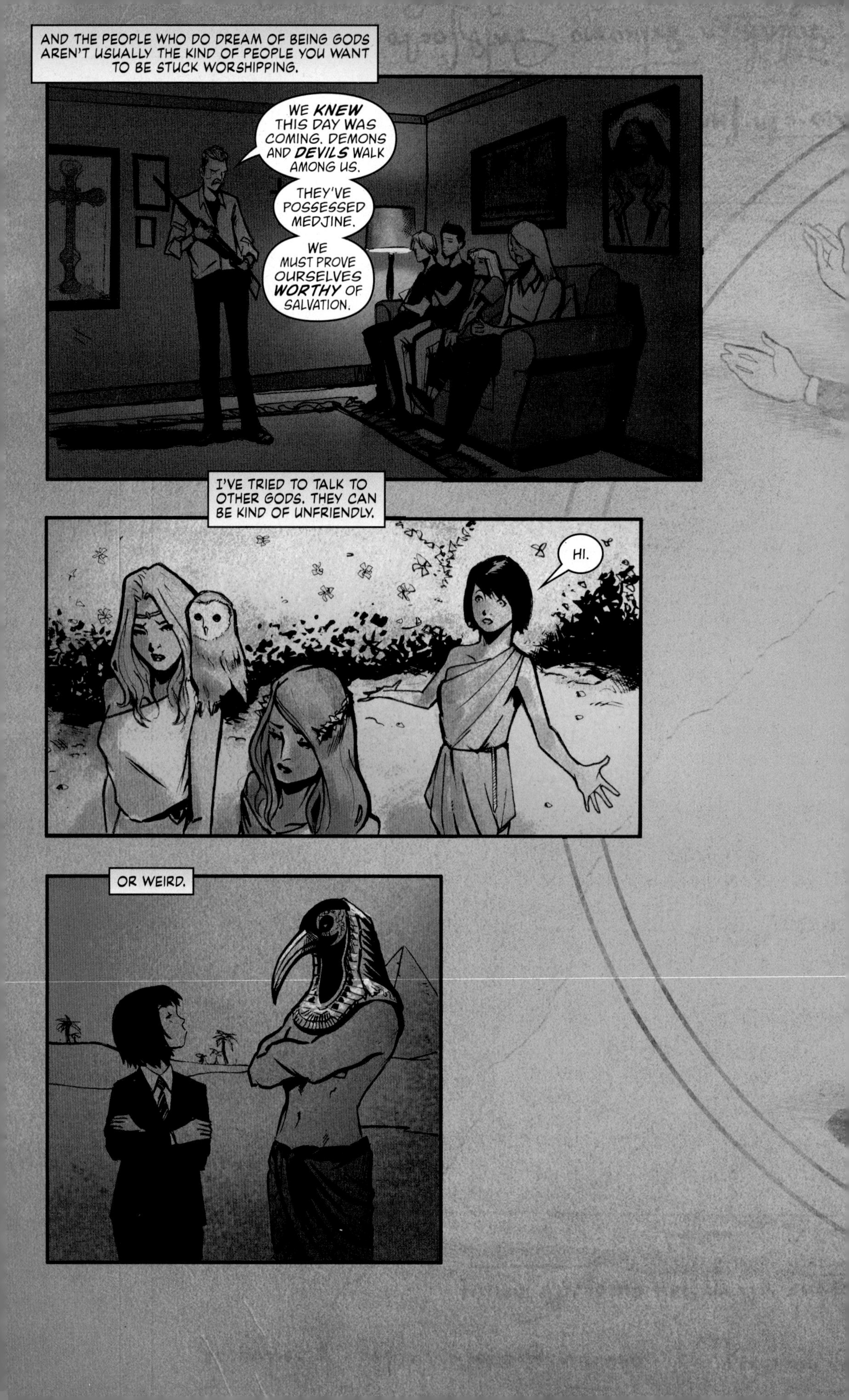
AND THE PEOPLE WHO DO DREAM OF BEING GODS AREN'T USUALLY THE KIND OF PEOPLE YOU WANT TO BE STUCK WORSHIPPING.
WE KNEW THIS DAY WAS COMING. DEMONS AND DEVILS WALK AMONG US.
THEY'VE POSSESSED MEDJINE.
WE MUST PROVE OURSELVES WORTHY OF SALVATION.
I'VE TRIED TO TALK TO OTHER GODS. THEY CAN BE KIND OF UNFRIENDLY.
HI.
OR WEIRD.

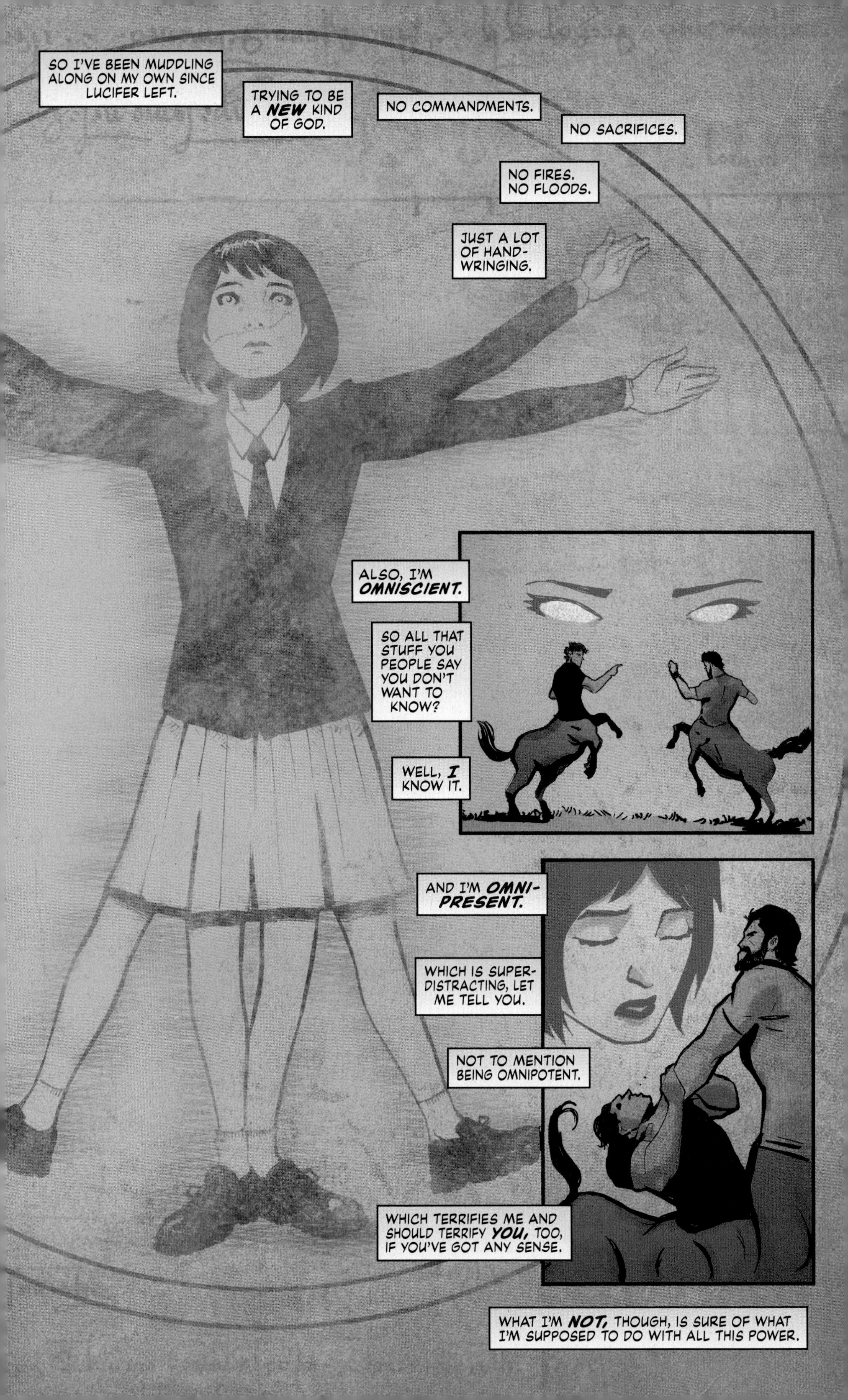
SO I'VE BEEN MUDDLING ALONG ON MY OWN SINCE LUCIFER LEFT.
TRYING TO BE A NEW KIND OF GOD.
NO COMMANDMENTS.
NO SACRIFICES.
NO FIRES. NO FLOODS.
JUST A LOT OF HAND-WRINGING.
ALSO, I'M OMNISCIENT.
SO ALL THAT STUFF YOU PEOPLE SAY YOU DON'T WANT TO KNOW?
WELL, I KNOW IT.
AND I'M OMNI-PRESENT.
WHICH IS SUPER-DISTRACTING, LET ME TELL YOU.
NOT TO MENTION BEING OMNIPOTENT.
WHICH TERRIFIES ME AND SHOULD TERRIFY YOU, TOO, IF YOU'VE GOT ANY SENSE.
WHAT I'M NOT, THOUGH, IS SURE OF WHAT I'M SUPPOSED TO DO WITH ALL THIS POWER.

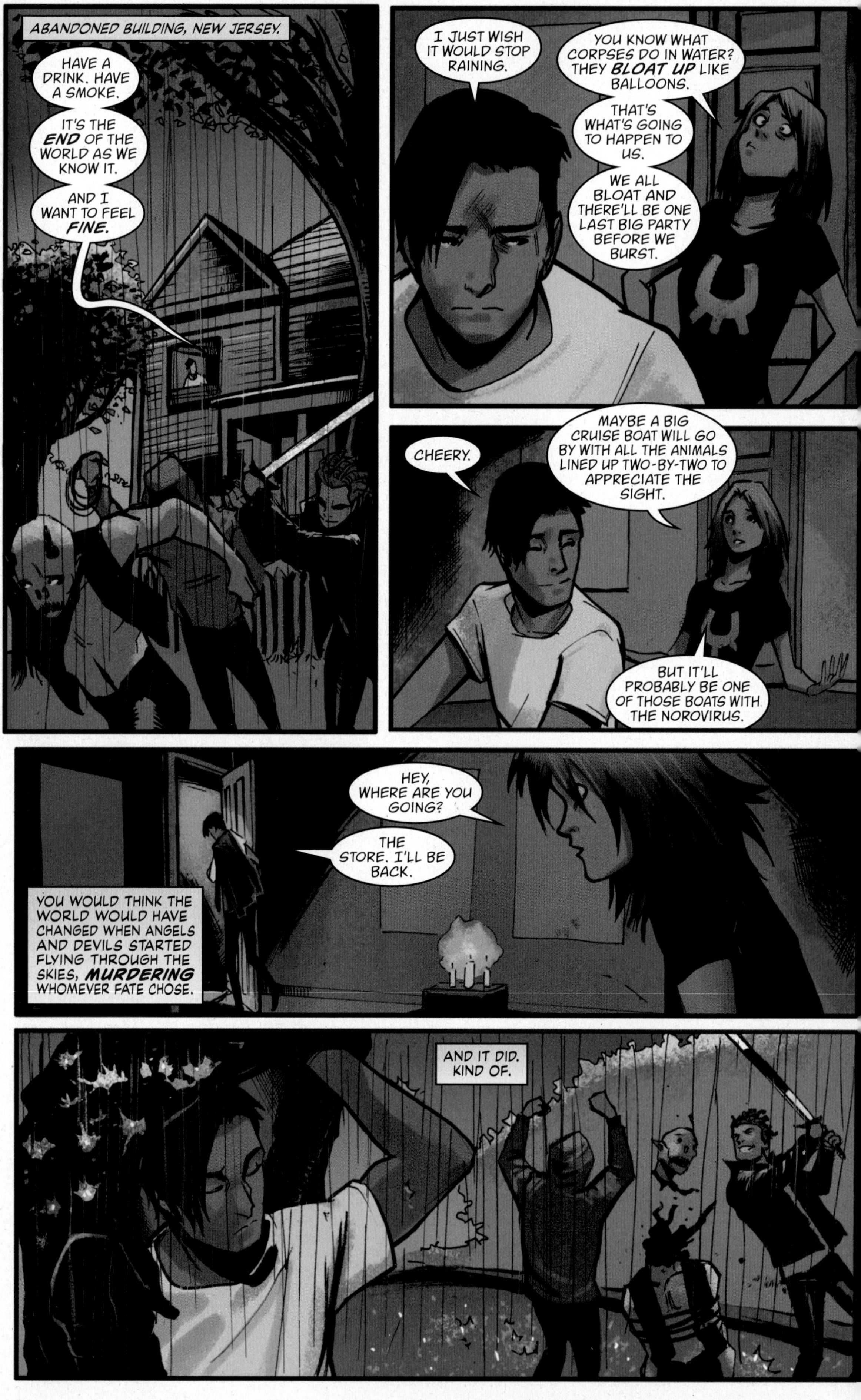
ABANDONED BUILDING, NEW JERSEY.
HAVE A DRINK. HAVE A SMOKE.
IT'S THE END OF THE WORLD AS WE KNOW IT.
AND I WANT TO FEEL FINE.
I JUST WISH IT WOULD STOP RAINING.
YOU KNOW WHAT CORPSES DO IN WATER? THEY BLOAT UP LIKE BALLOONS.
THAT'S WHAT'S GOING TO HAPPEN TO US.
WE ALL BLOAT AND THERE'LL BE ONE LAST BIG PARTY BEFORE WE BURST.
CHEERY.
MAYBE A BIG CRUISE BOAT WILL GO BY WITH ALL THE ANIMALS LINED UP TWO-BY-TWO TO APPRECIATE THE SIGHT.
BUT IT'LL PROBABLY BE ONE OF THOSE BOATS WITH THE NOROVIRUS.
HEY, WHERE ARE YOU GOING?
THE STORE. I'LL BE BACK.
YOU WOULD THINK THE WORLD WOULD HAVE CHANGED WHEN ANGELS AND DEVILS STARTED FLYING THROUGH THE SKIES, MURDERING WHOMEVER FATE CHOSE.
AND IT DID. KIND OF.

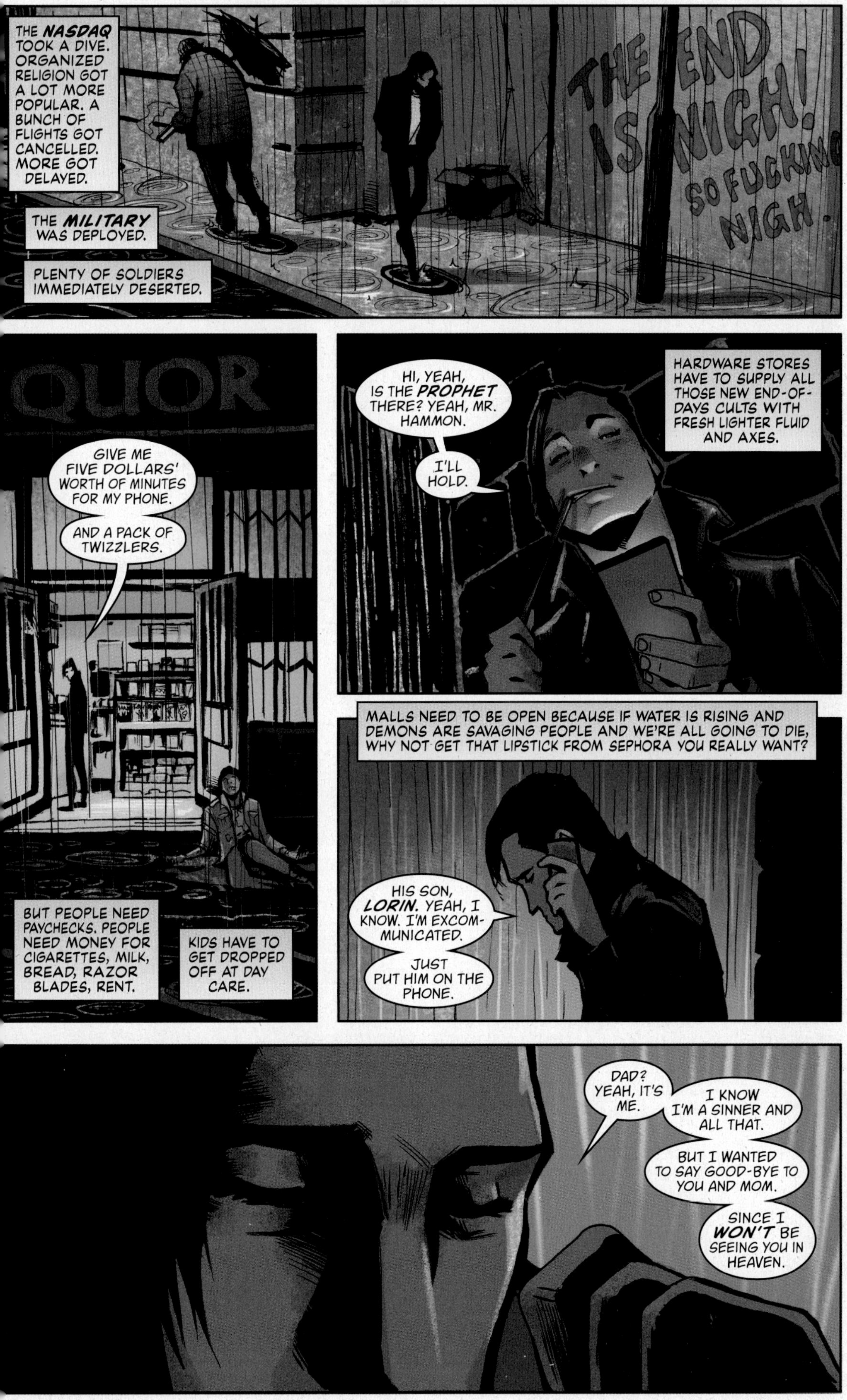
THE NASDAQ TOOK A DIVE. ORGANIZED RELIGION GOT A LOT MORE POPULAR. A BUNCH OF FLIGHTS GOT CANCELLED. MORE GOT DELAYED.
THE MILITARY WAS DEPLOYED.
PLENTY OF SOLDIERS IMMEDIATELY DESERTED.
THE END IS NIGH! SO FUCKING NIGH.
QUOR
GIVE ME FIVE DOLLARS' WORTH OF MINUTES FOR MY PHONE.
AND A PACK OF TWIZZLERS.
BUT PEOPLE NEED PAYCHECKS. PEOPLE NEED MONEY FOR CIGARETTES, MILK, BREAD, RAZOR BLADES, RENT.
KIDS HAVE TO GET DROPPED OFF AT DAY CARE.
HI, YEAH, IS THE PROPHET THERE? YEAH, MR. HAMMON.
I'LL HOLD.
HARDWARE STORES HAVE TO SUPPLY ALL THOSE NEW END-OF-DAYS CULTS WITH FRESH LIGHTER FLUID AND AXES.
MALLS NEED TO BE OPEN BECAUSE IF WATER IS RISING AND DEMONS ARE SAVAGING PEOPLE AND WE'RE ALL GOING TO DIE, WHY NOT GET THAT LIPSTICK FROM SEPHORA YOU REALLY WANT?
HIS SON, LORIN. YEAH, I KNOW. I'M EXCOMMUNICATED.
JUST PUT HIM ON THE PHONE.
DAD? YEAH, IT'S ME.
I KNOW I'M A SINNER AND ALL THAT.
BUT I WANTED TO SAY GOOD-BYE TO YOU AND MOM.
SINCE I WON'T BE SEEING YOU IN HEAVEN.

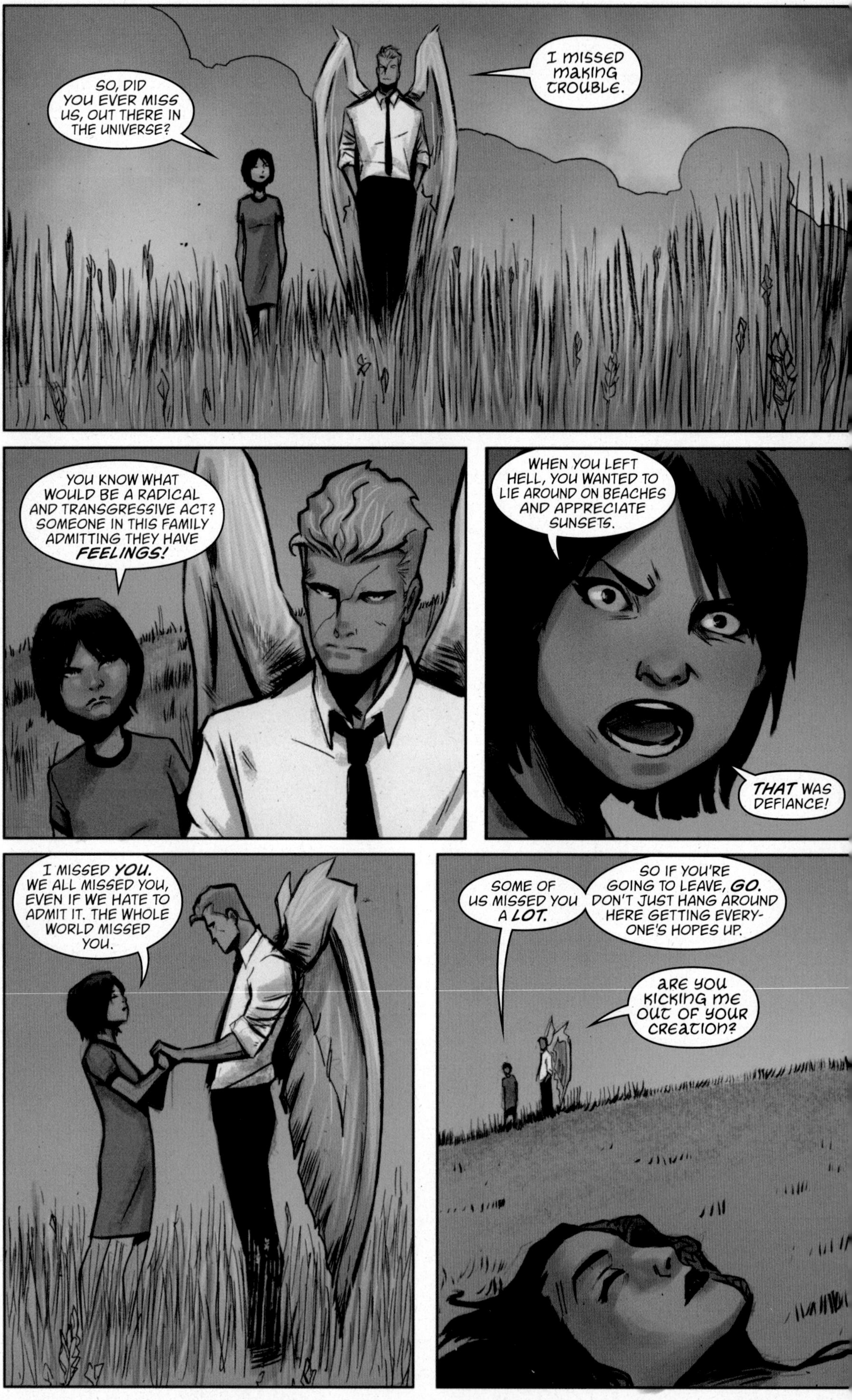
SO, DID YOU EVER MISS US, OUT THERE IN THE UNIVERSE?
I MISSED MAKING TROUBLE.
YOU KNOW WHAT WOULD BE A RADICAL AND TRANSGRESSIVE ACT? SOMEONE IN THIS FAMILY ADMITTING THEY HAVE FEELINGS!
WHEN YOU LEFT HELL, YOU WANTED TO LIE AROUND ON BEACHES AND APPRECIATE SUNSETS.
THAT WAS DEFIANCE!
I MISSED YOU. WE ALL MISSED YOU, EVEN IF WE HATE TO ADMIT IT. THE WHOLE WORLD MISSED YOU.
SOME OF US MISSED YOU A LOT.
SO IF YOU'RE GOING TO LEAVE, GO. DON'T JUST HANG AROUND HERE GETTING EVERY-ONE'S HOPES UP.
ARE YOU KICKING ME OUT OF YOUR CREATION?

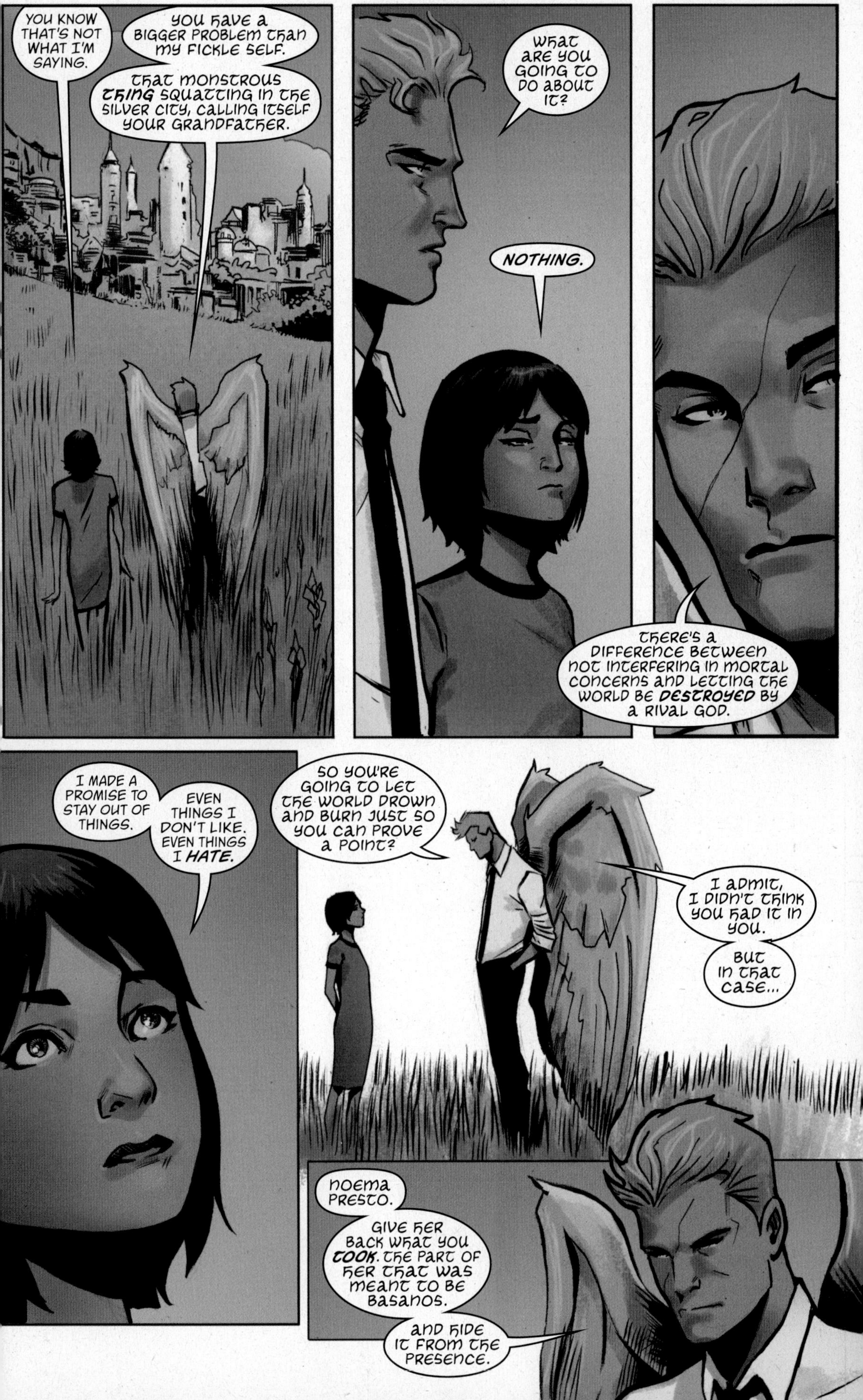
YOU KNOW THAT'S NOT WHAT I'M SAYING.
YOU HAVE A BIGGER PROBLEM THAN MY FICKLE SELF.
THAT MONSTROUS THING SQUATTING IN THE SILVER CITY, CALLING ITSELF YOUR GRANDFATHER.
WHAT ARE YOU GOING TO DO ABOUT IT?
NOTHING.
THERE'S A DIFFERENCE BETWEEN NOT INTERFERING IN MORTAL CONCERNS AND LETTING THE WORLD BE DESTROYED BY A RIVAL GOD.
I MADE A PROMISE TO STAY OUT OF THINGS.
EVEN THINGS I DON'T LIKE. EVEN THINGS I HATE.
SO YOU'RE GOING TO LET THE WORLD DROWN AND BURN JUST SO YOU CAN PROVE A POINT?
I ADMIT, I DIDN'T THINK YOU HAD IT IN YOU.
BUT IN THAT CASE...
NOEMA PRESTO.
GIVE HER BACK WHAT YOU TOOK. THE PART OF HER THAT WAS MEANT TO BE BASANOS.
AND HIDE IT FROM THE PRESENCE.

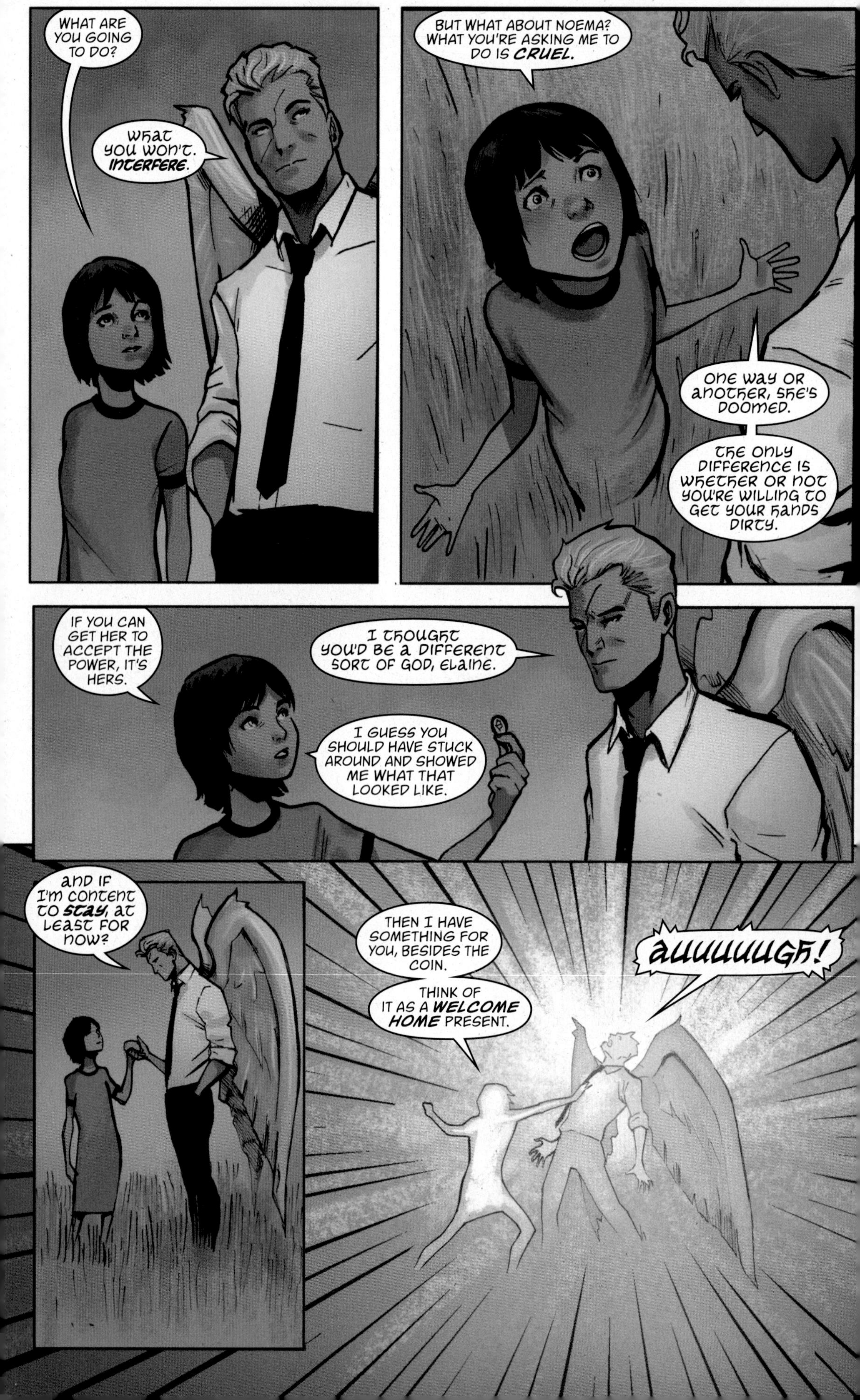
WHAT ARE YOU GOING TO DO?
WHAT YOU WON'T. INTERFERE.
BUT WHAT ABOUT NOEMA? WHAT YOU'RE ASKING ME TO DO IS CRUEL.
ONE WAY OR ANOTHER, SHE'S DOOMED.
THE ONLY DIFFERENCE IS WHETHER OR NOT YOU'RE WILLING TO GET YOUR HANDS DIRTY.
IF YOU CAN GET HER TO ACCEPT THE POWER, IT'S HERS.
I THOUGHT YOU'D BE A DIFFERENT SORT OF GOD, ELAINE.
I GUESS YOU SHOULD HAVE STUCK AROUND AND SHOWED ME WHAT THAT LOOKED LIKE.
AND IF I'M CONTENT TO STAY, AT LEAST FOR NOW?
THEN I HAVE SOMETHING FOR YOU, BESIDES THE COIN.
THINK OF IT AS A WELCOME HOME PRESENT.
AUUUUUGH!

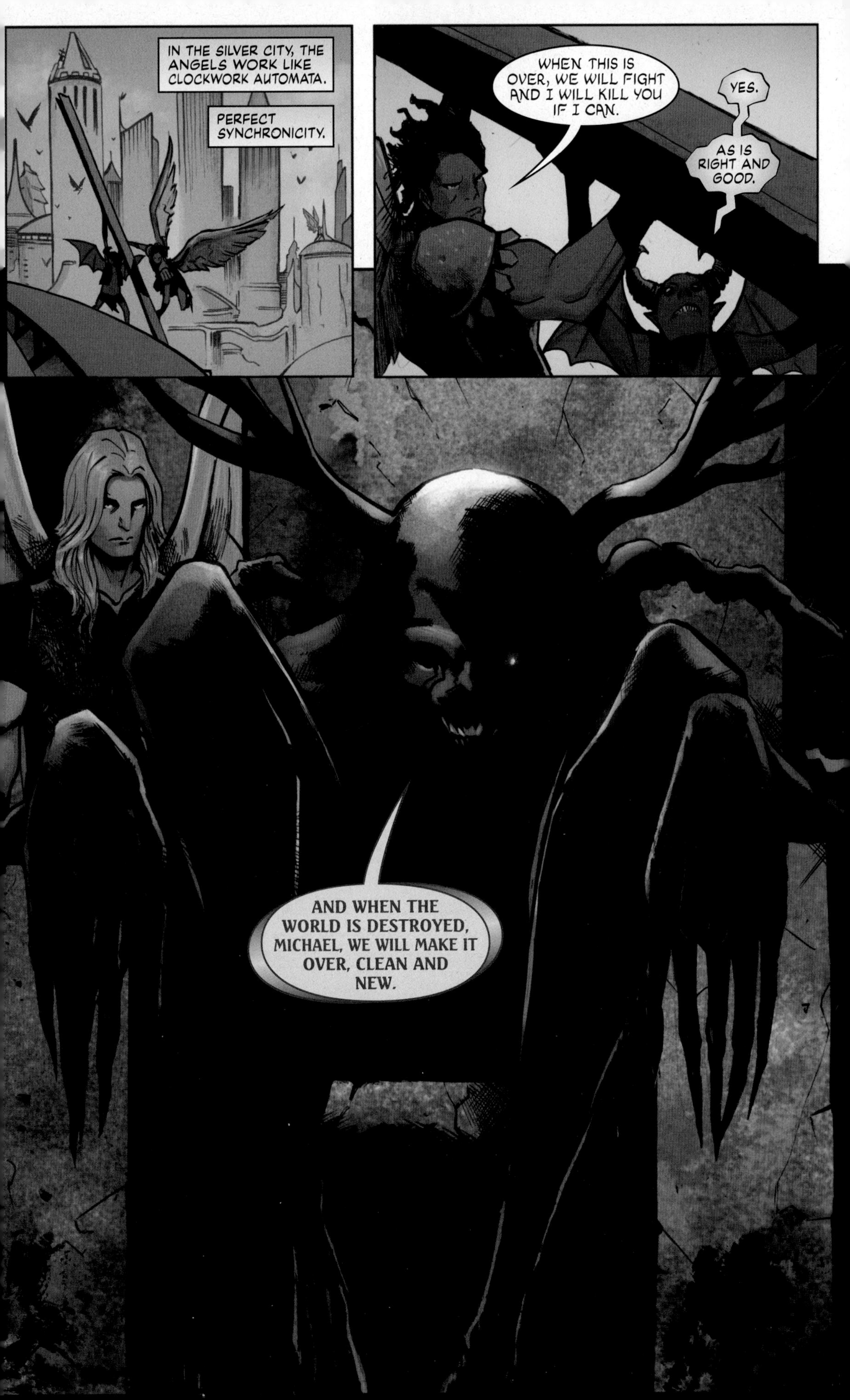
IN THE SILVER CITY, THE ANGELS WORK LIKE CLOCKWORK AUTOMATA.
PERFECT SYNCHRONICITY.
WHEN THIS IS OVER, WE WILL FIGHT AND I WILL KILL YOU IF I CAN.
YES.
AS IS RIGHT AND GOOD.
AND WHEN THE WORLD IS DESTROYED, MICHAEL, WE WILL MAKE IT OVER, CLEAN AND NEW.

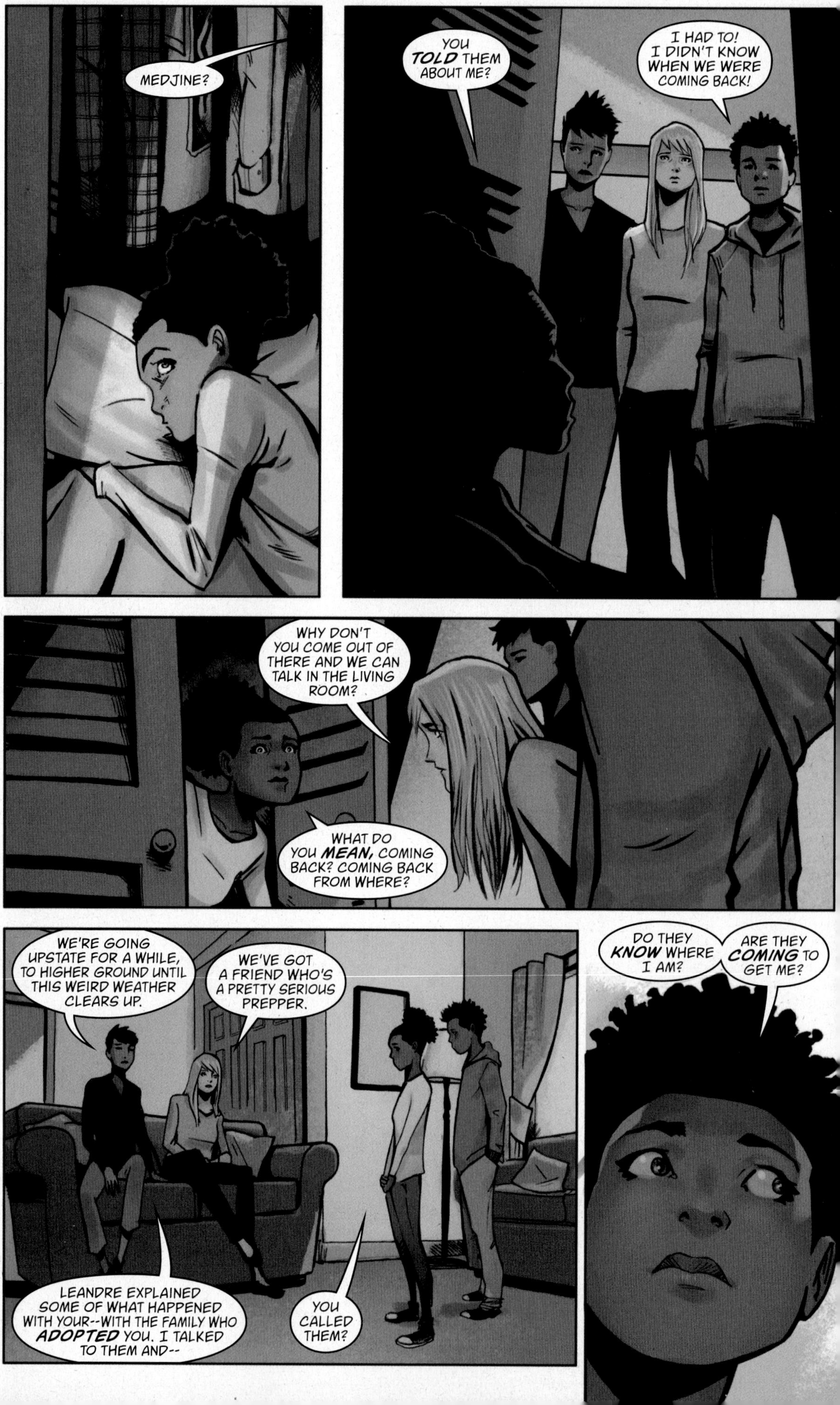
MEDJINE?
YOU TOLD THEM ABOUT ME?
I HAD TO! I DIDN'T KNOW WHEN WE WERE COMING BACK!
WHY DON'T YOU COME OUT OF THERE AND WE CAN TALK IN THE LIVING ROOM?
WHAT DO YOU MEAN, COMING BACK? COMING BACK FROM WHERE?
WE'RE GOING UPSTATE FOR A WHILE, TO HIGHER GROUND UNTIL THIS WEIRD WEATHER CLEARS UP.
WE'VE GOT A FRIEND WHO'S A PRETTY SERIOUS PREPPER.
LEANDRE EXPLAINED SOME OF WHAT HAPPENED WITH YOUR--WITH THE FAMILY WHO ADOPTED YOU. I TALKED TO THEM AND--
YOU CALLED THEM?
DO THEY KNOW WHERE I AM?
ARE THEY COMING TO GET ME?

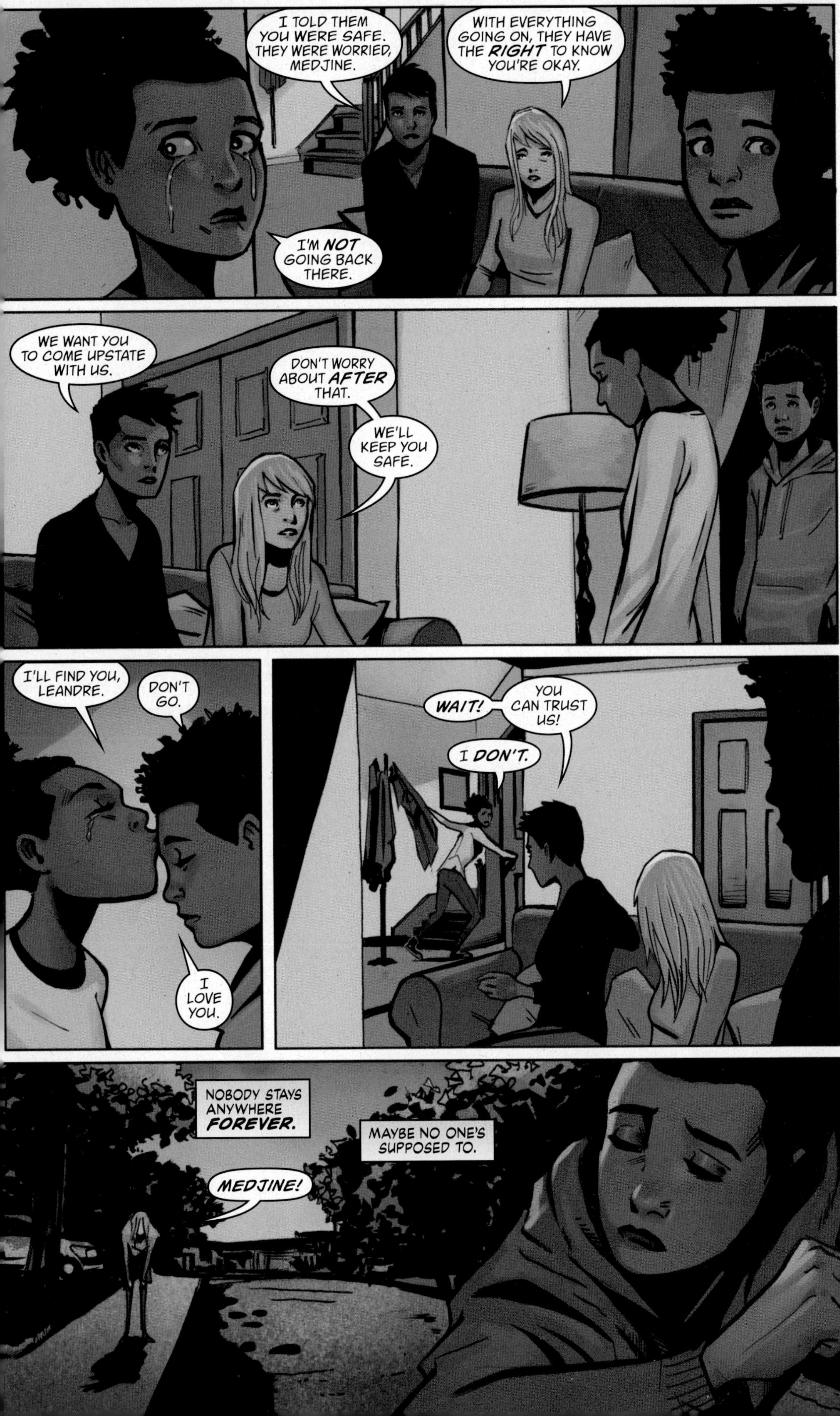
I TOLD THEM YOU WERE SAFE. THEY WERE WORRIED, MEDJINE.
WITH EVERYTHING GOING ON, THEY HAVE THE RIGHT TO KNOW YOU'RE OKAY.
I'M NOT GOING BACK THERE.
WE WANT YOU TO COME UPSTATE WITH US.
DON'T WORRY ABOUT AFTER THAT.
WE'LL KEEP YOU SAFE.
I'LL FIND YOU, LEANDRE.
DON'T GO.
I LOVE YOU.
WAIT!
YOU CAN TRUST US!
I DON'T.
NOBODY STAYS ANYWHERE FOREVER.
MAYBE NO ONE'S SUPPOSED TO.
MEDJINE!

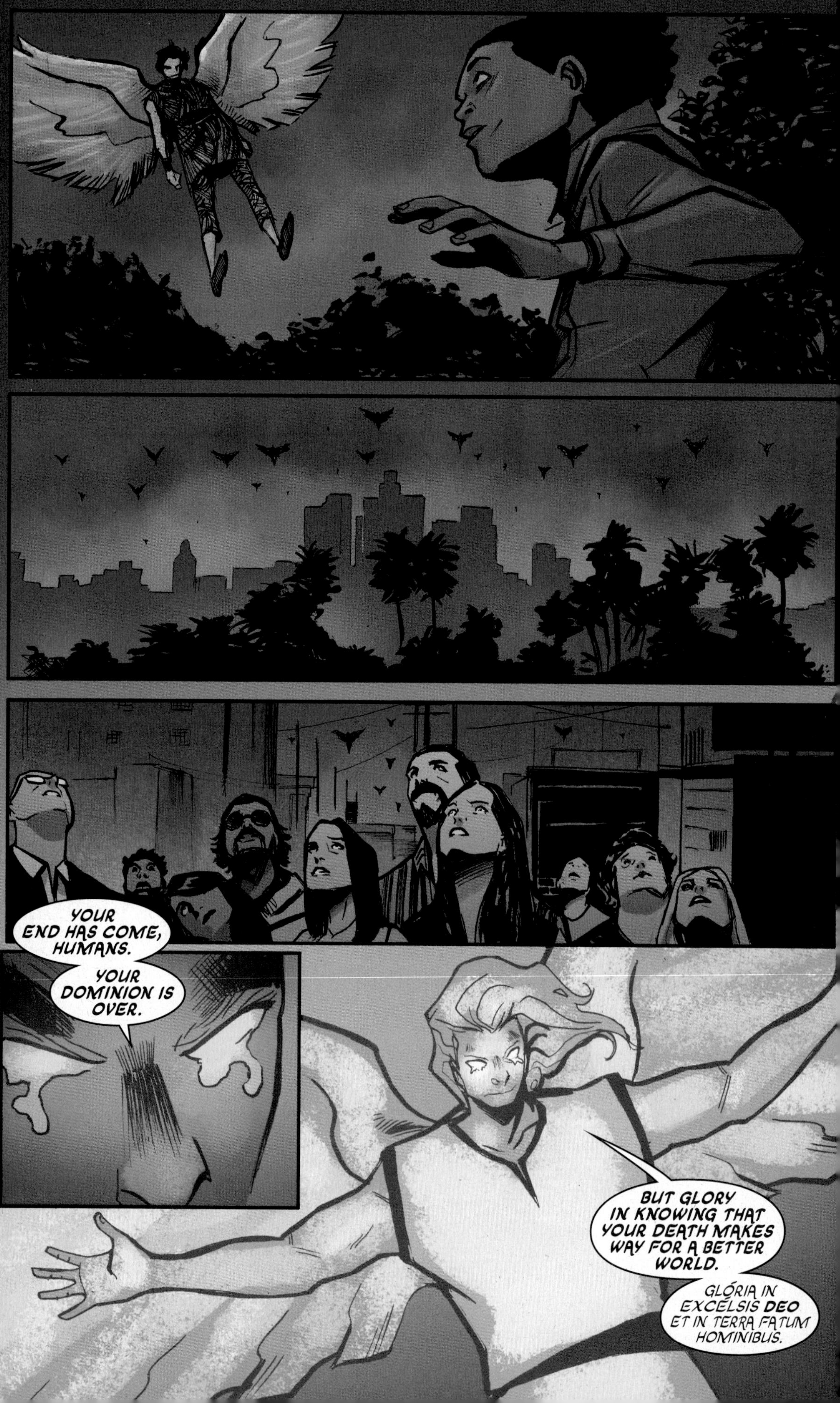
YOUR END HAS COME, HUMANS.
YOUR DOMINION IS OVER.
BUT GLORY IN KNOWING THAT YOUR DEATH MAKES WAY FOR A BETTER WORLD.
GLÓRIA IN EXCELSIS **DEO** ET IN TERRA FATUM HOMINIBUS.

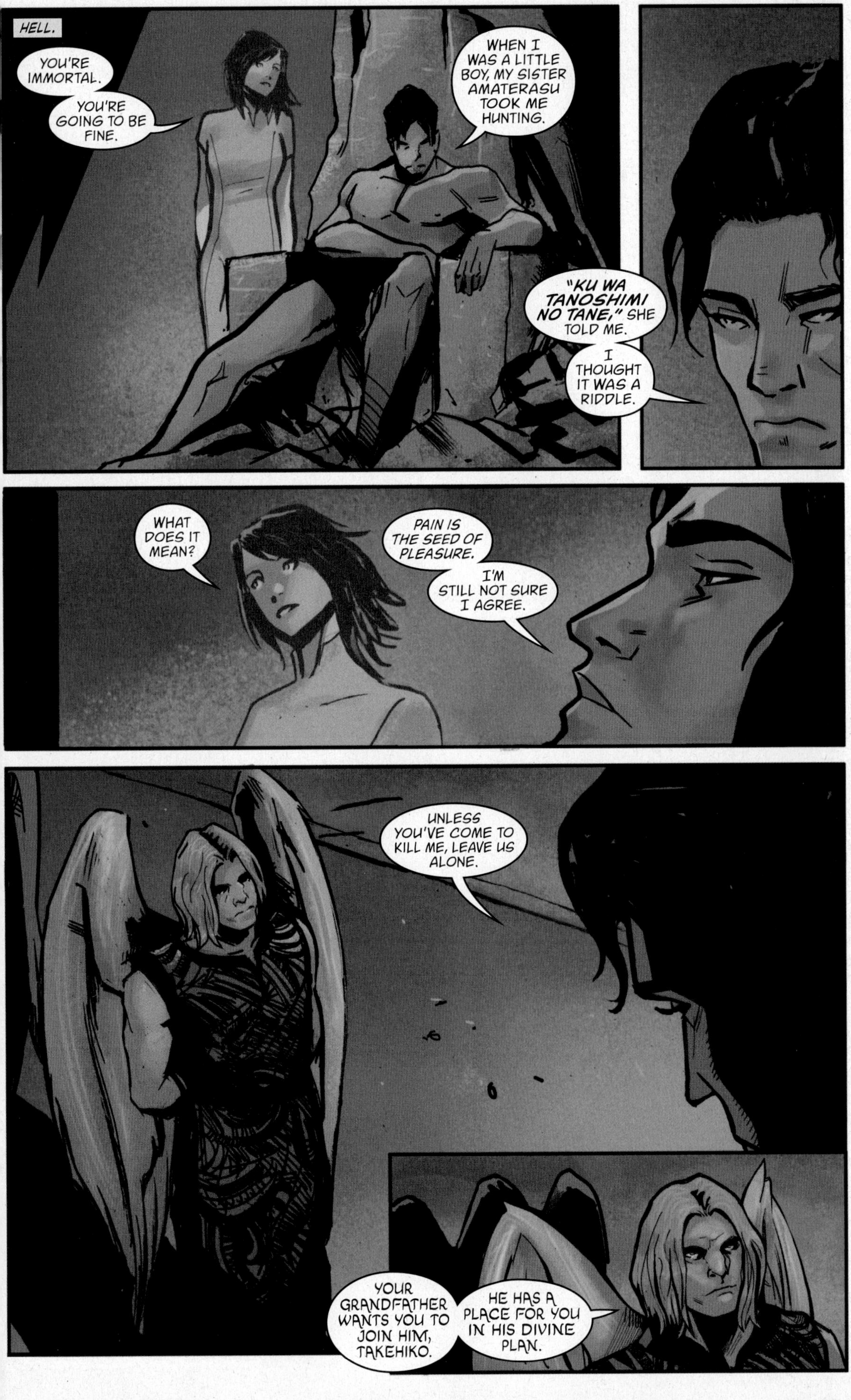
HELL.
YOU'RE IMMORTAL.
YOU'RE GOING TO BE FINE.
WHEN I WAS A LITTLE BOY, MY SISTER AMATERASU TOOK ME HUNTING.
"KU WA TANOSHIMI NO TANE," SHE TOLD ME.
I THOUGHT IT WAS A RIDDLE.
WHAT DOES IT MEAN?
PAIN IS THE SEED OF PLEASURE.
I'M STILL NOT SURE I AGREE.
UNLESS YOU'VE COME TO KILL ME, LEAVE US ALONE.
YOUR GRANDFATHER WANTS YOU TO JOIN HIM, TAKEHIKO.
HE HAS A PLACE FOR YOU IN HIS DIVINE PLAN.

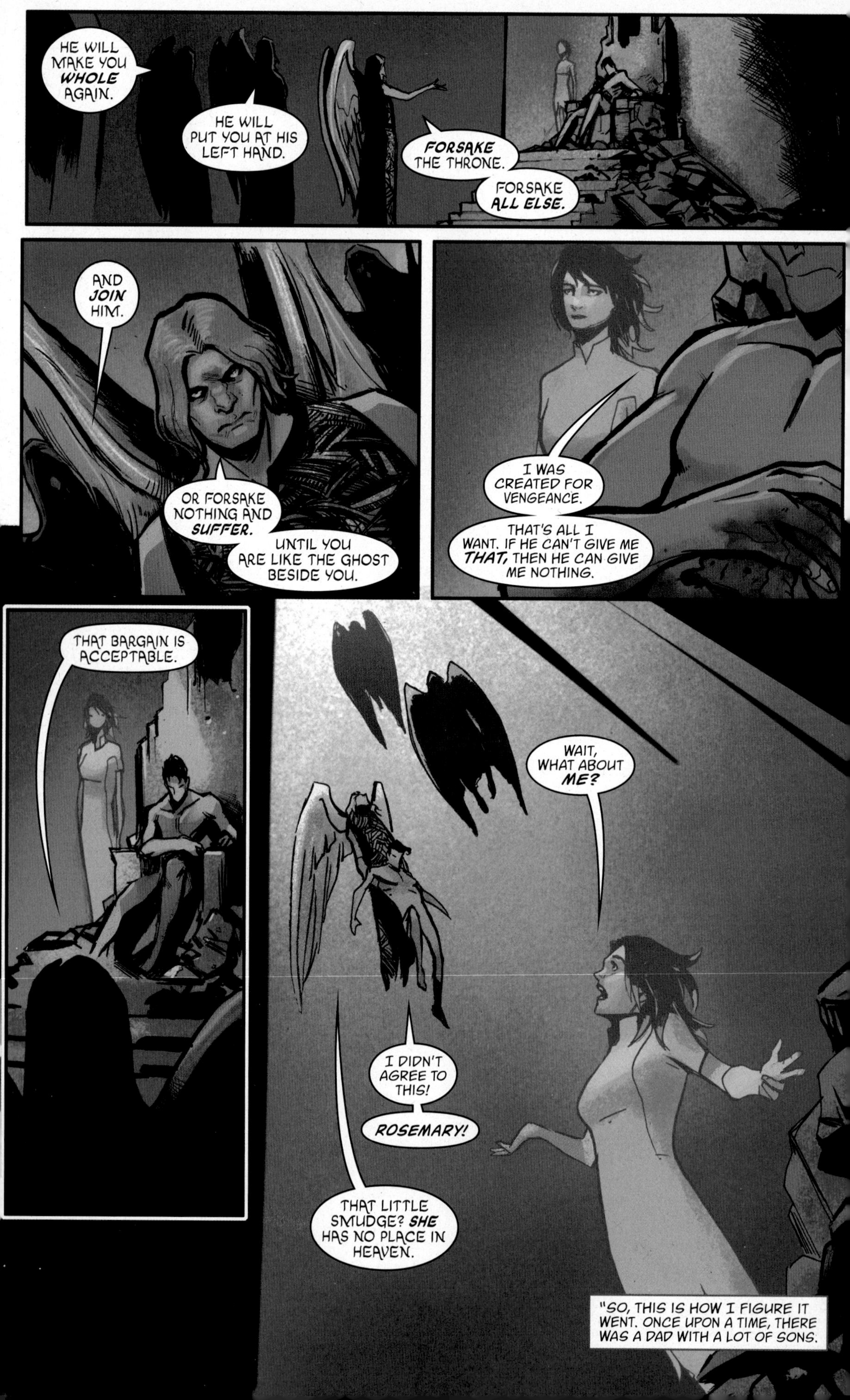
HE WILL MAKE YOU WHOLE AGAIN.
HE WILL PUT YOU AT HIS LEFT HAND.
FORSAKE THE THRONE.
FORSAKE ALL ELSE.
AND JOIN HIM.
OR FORSAKE NOTHING AND SUFFER.
UNTIL YOU ARE LIKE THE GHOST BESIDE YOU.
I WAS CREATED FOR VENGEANCE.
THAT'S ALL I WANT. IF HE CAN'T GIVE ME THAT, THEN HE CAN GIVE ME NOTHING.
THAT BARGAIN IS ACCEPTABLE.
WAIT, WHAT ABOUT ME?
I DIDN'T AGREE TO THIS!
ROSEMARY!
THAT LITTLE SMUDGE? SHE HAS NO PLACE IN HEAVEN.
"SO, THIS IS HOW I FIGURE IT WENT. ONCE UPON A TIME, THERE WAS A DAD WITH A LOT OF SONS.

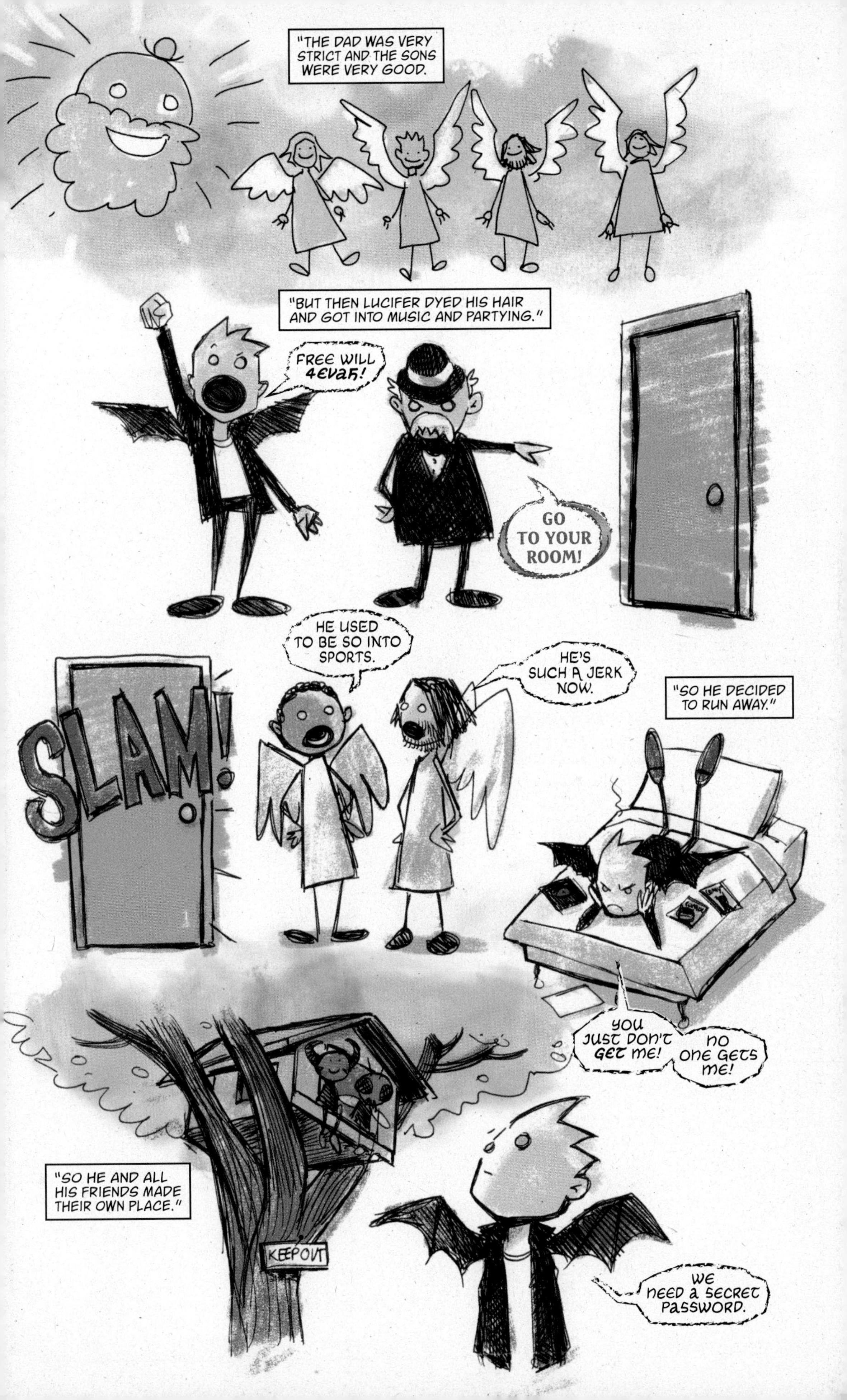
"THE DAD WAS VERY STRICT AND THE SONS WERE VERY GOOD.
"BUT THEN LUCIFER DYED HIS HAIR AND GOT INTO MUSIC AND PARTYING."
FREE WILL 4EVAH!
GO TO YOUR ROOM!
SLAM!
HE USED TO BE SO INTO SPORTS.
HE'S SUCH A JERK NOW.
"SO HE DECIDED TO RUN AWAY."
YOU JUST DON'T GET ME!
NO ONE GETS ME!
"SO HE AND ALL HIS FRIENDS MADE THEIR OWN PLACE."
KEEPOUT
WE NEED A SECRET PASSWORD.

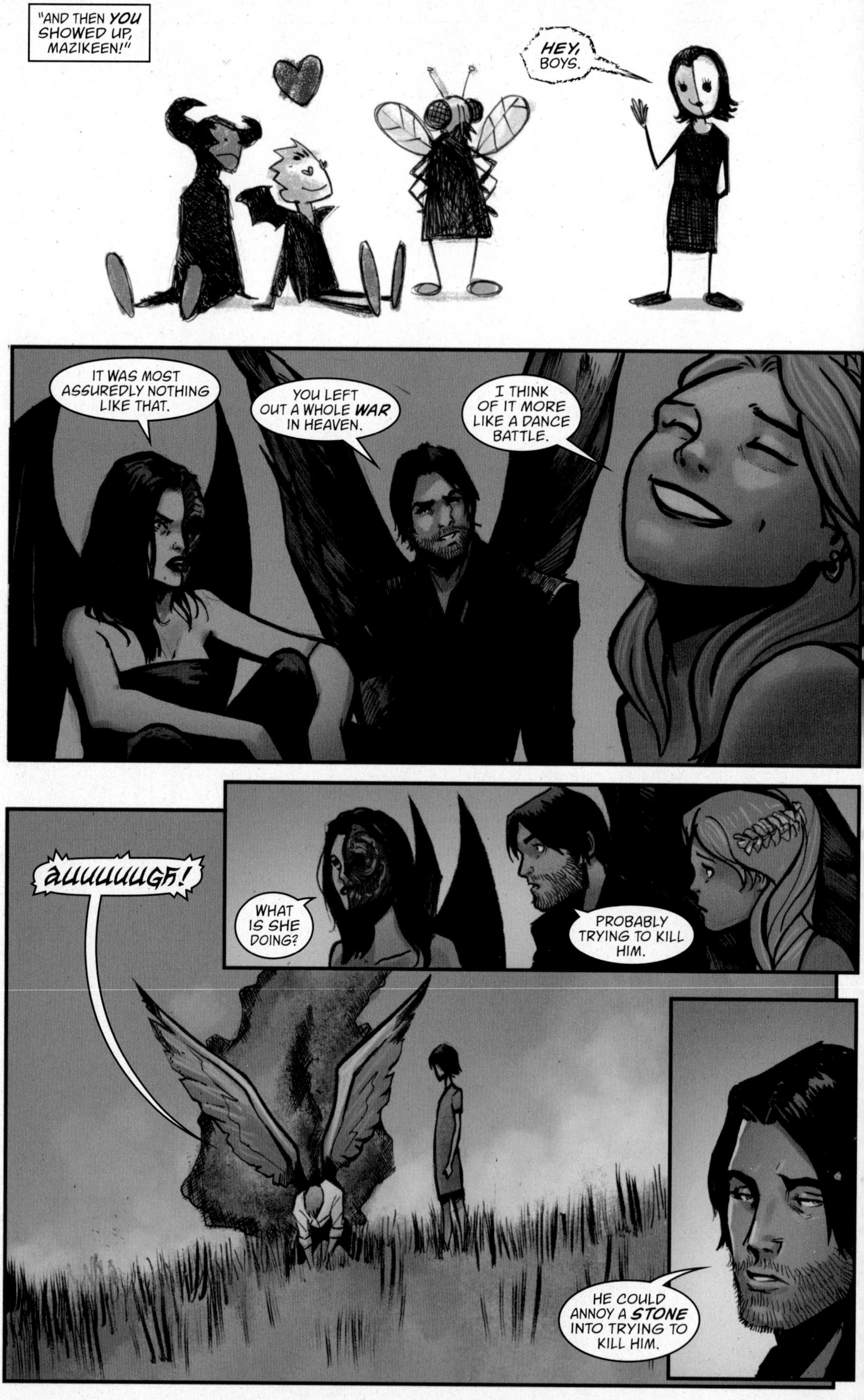
"AND THEN YOU SHOWED UP, MAZIKEEN!"
HEY, BOYS.
IT WAS MOST ASSUREDLY NOTHING LIKE THAT.
YOU LEFT OUT A WHOLE WAR IN HEAVEN.
I THINK OF IT MORE LIKE A DANCE BATTLE.
AUUUUUGH!
WHAT IS SHE DOING?
PROBABLY TRYING TO KILL HIM.
HE COULD ANNOY A STONE INTO TRYING TO KILL HIM.

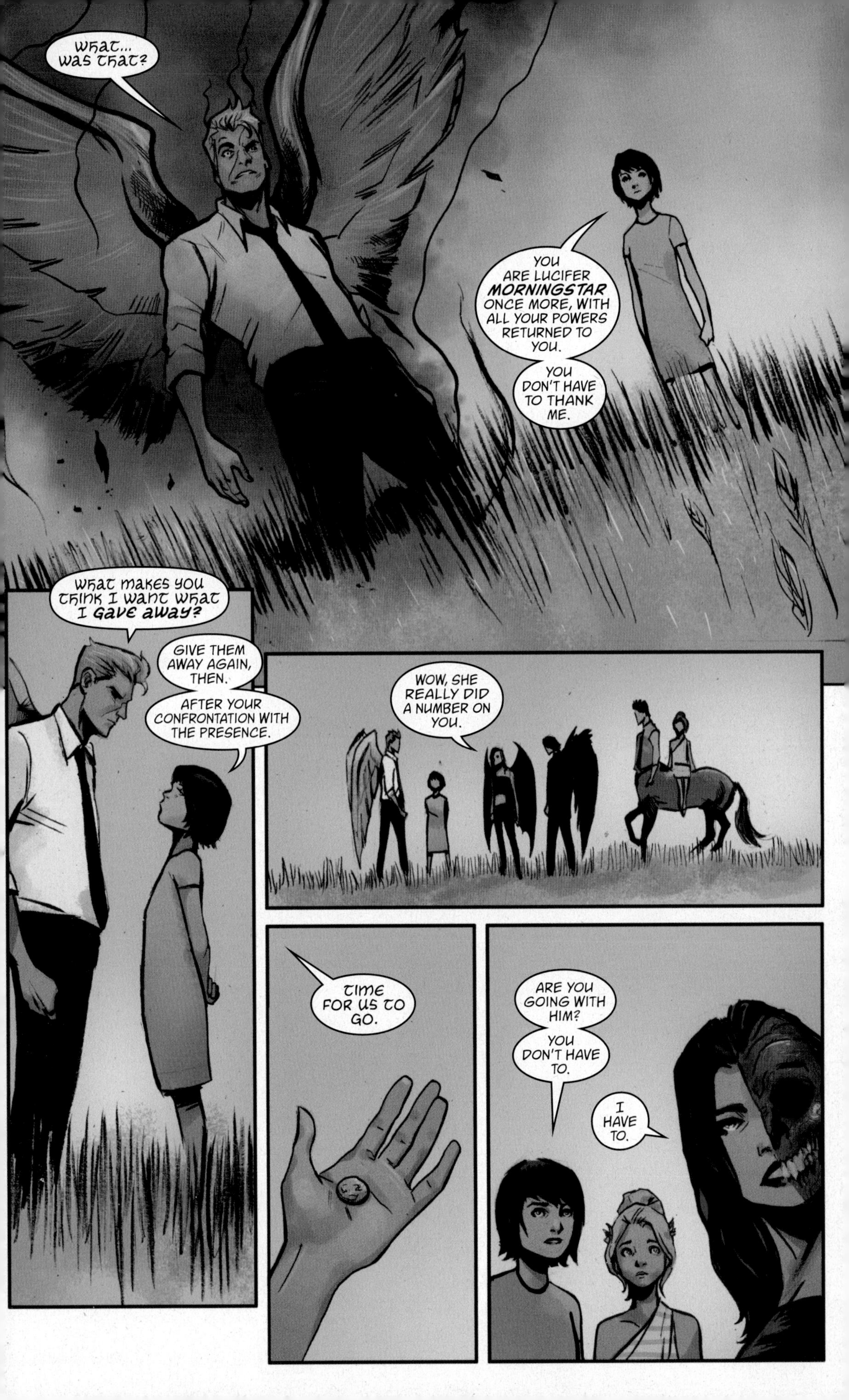
WHAT... WAS THAT?
YOU ARE LUCIFER MORNINGSTAR ONCE MORE, WITH ALL YOUR POWERS RETURNED TO YOU.
YOU DON'T HAVE TO THANK ME.
WHAT MAKES YOU THINK I WANT WHAT I GAVE AWAY?
GIVE THEM AWAY AGAIN, THEN.
AFTER YOUR CONFRONTATION WITH THE PRESENCE.
WOW, SHE REALLY DID A NUMBER ON YOU.
TIME FOR US TO GO.
ARE YOU GOING WITH HIM?
YOU DON'T HAVE TO.
I HAVE TO.

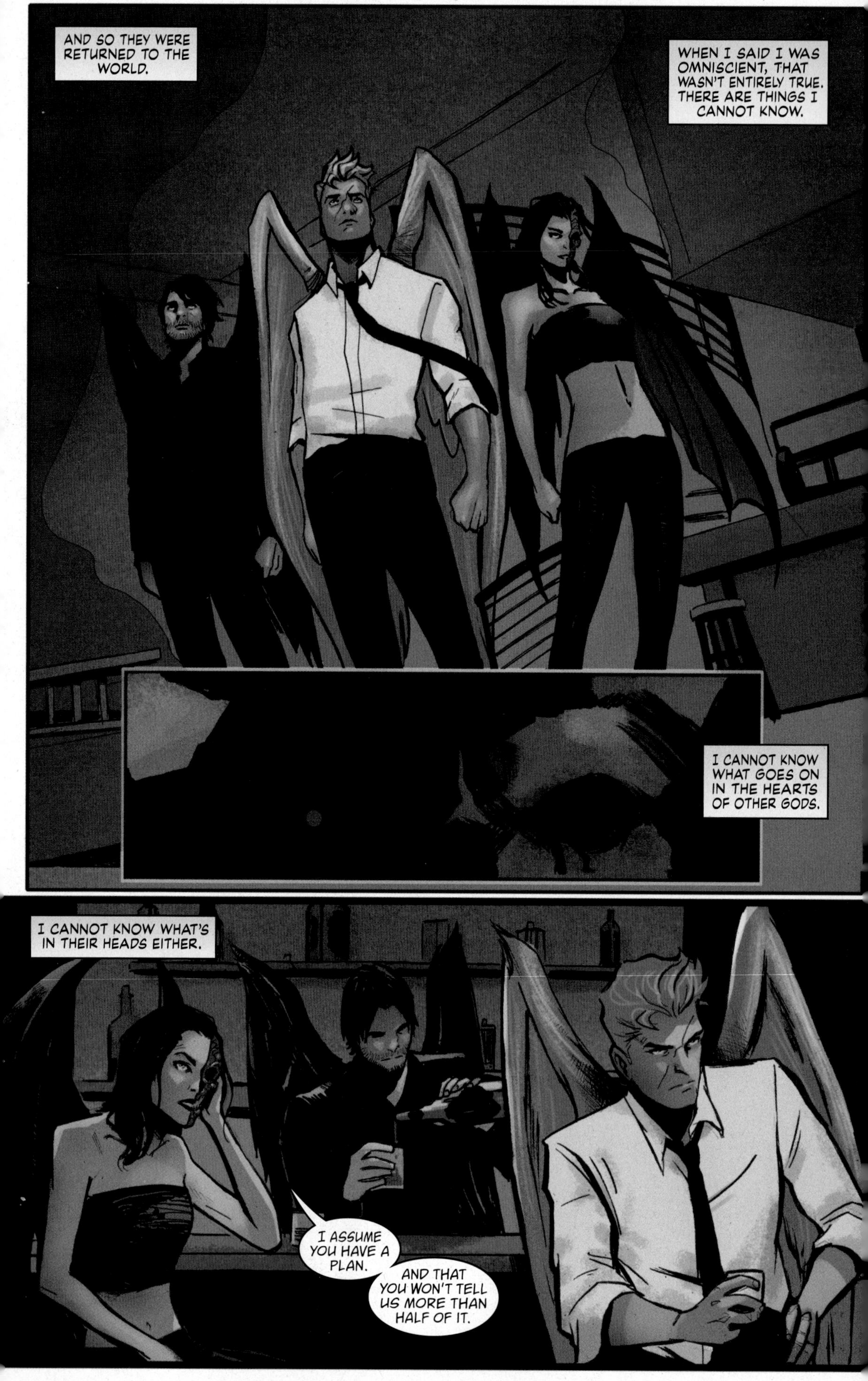
AND SO THEY WERE RETURNED TO THE WORLD.
WHEN I SAID I WAS OMNISCIENT, THAT WASN'T ENTIRELY TRUE. THERE ARE THINGS I CANNOT KNOW.
I CANNOT KNOW WHAT GOES ON IN THE HEARTS OF OTHER GODS.
I CANNOT KNOW WHAT'S IN THEIR HEADS EITHER.
I ASSUME YOU HAVE A PLAN.
AND THAT YOU WON'T TELL US MORE THAN HALF OF IT.

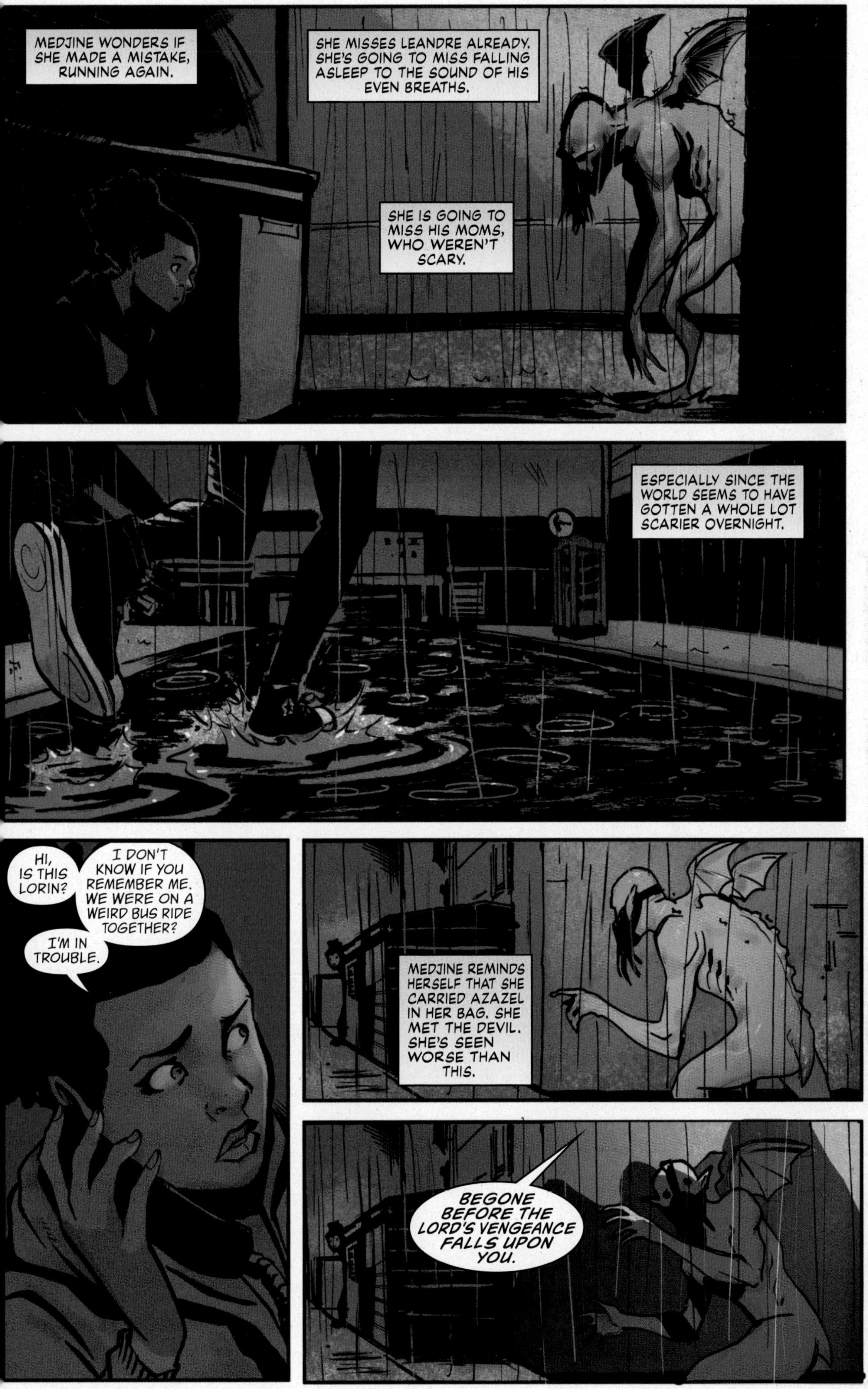

MEDJINE WONDERS IF SHE MADE A MISTAKE, RUNNING AGAIN.
SHE MISSES LEANDRE ALREADY. SHE'S GOING TO MISS FALLING ASLEEP TO THE SOUND OF HIS EVEN BREATHS.
SHE IS GOING TO MISS HIS MOMS, WHO WEREN'T SCARY.
ESPECIALLY SINCE THE WORLD SEEMS TO HAVE GOTTEN A WHOLE LOT SCARIER OVERNIGHT.
HI, IS THIS LORIN?
I DON'T KNOW IF YOU REMEMBER ME. WE WERE ON A WEIRD BUS RIDE TOGETHER?
I'M IN TROUBLE.
MEDJINE REMINDS HERSELF THAT SHE CARRIED AZAZEL IN HER BAG. SHE MET THE DEVIL. SHE'S SEEN WORSE THAN THIS.
BEGONE BEFORE THE LORD'S VENGEANCE FALLS UPON YOU.

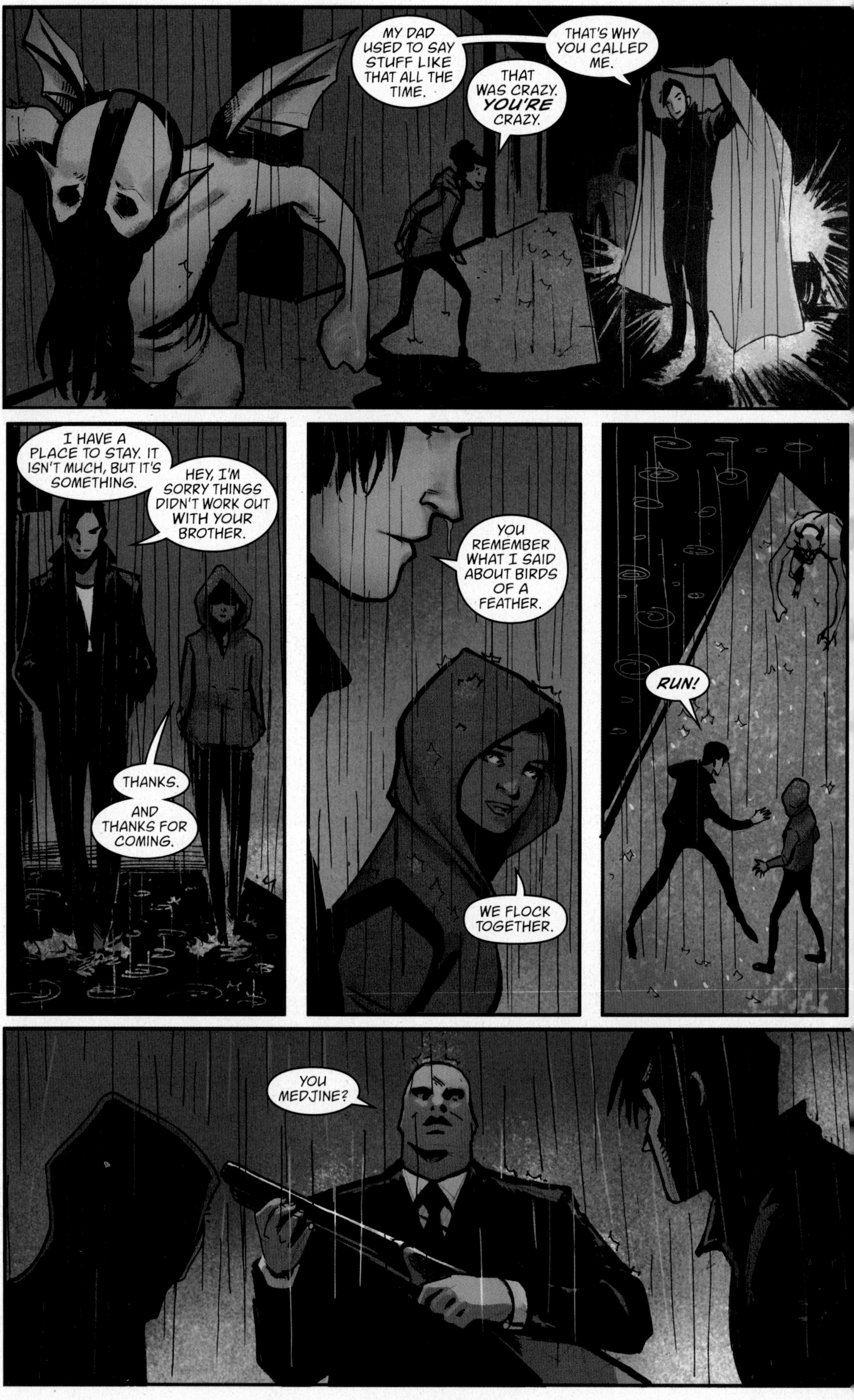
MY DAD USED TO SAY STUFF LIKE THAT ALL THE TIME.
THAT'S WHY YOU CALLED ME.
THAT WAS CRAZY. YOU'RE CRAZY.
I HAVE A PLACE TO STAY. IT ISN'T MUCH, BUT IT'S SOMETHING.
HEY, I'M SORRY THINGS DIDN'T WORK OUT WITH YOUR BROTHER.
THANKS.
AND THANKS FOR COMING.
YOU REMEMBER WHAT I SAID ABOUT BIRDS OF A FEATHER.
WE FLOCK TOGETHER.
RUN!
YOU MEDJINE?

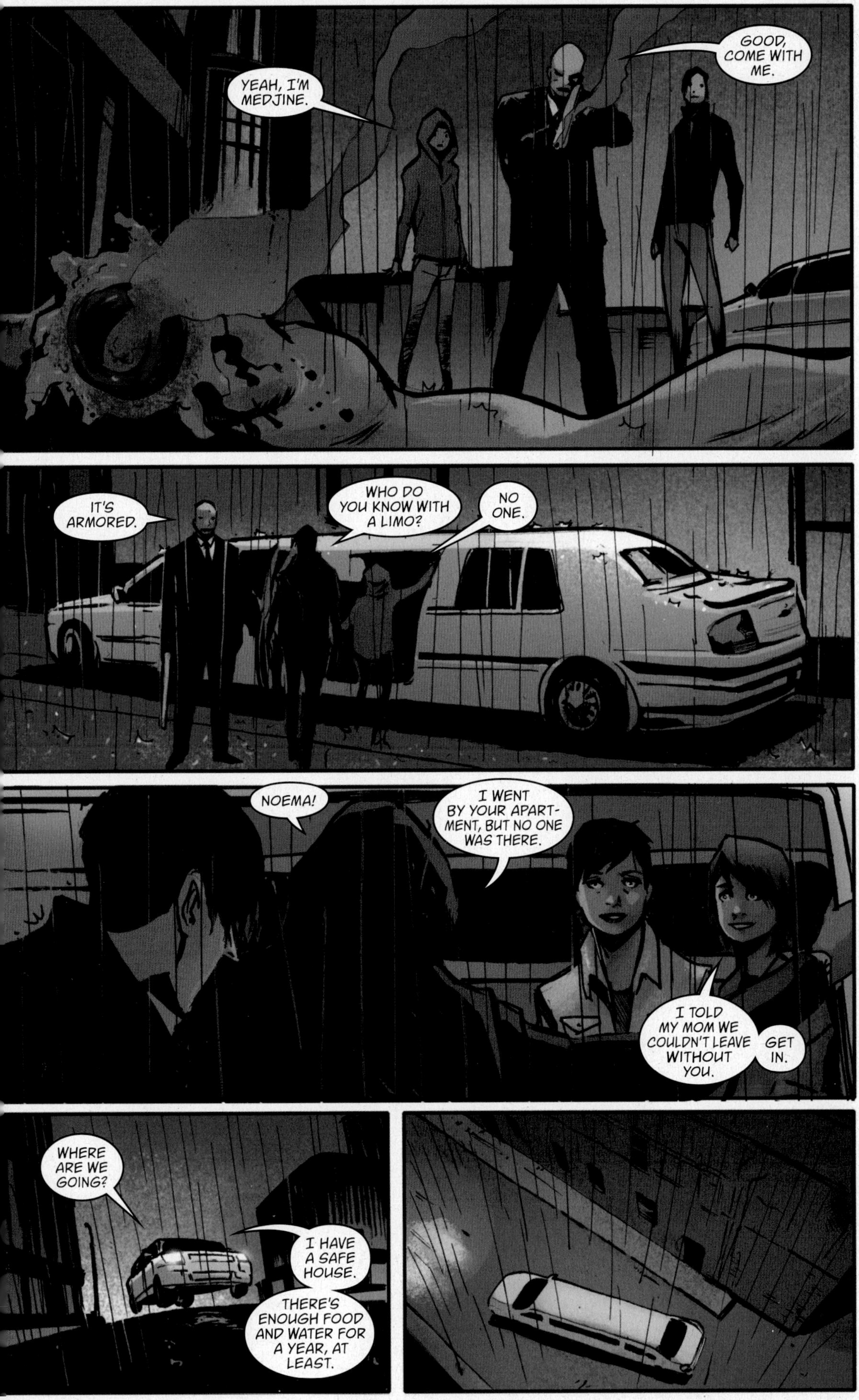
YEAH, I'M MEDJINE.
GOOD, COME WITH ME.
IT'S ARMORED.
WHO DO YOU KNOW WITH A LIMO?
NO ONE.
NOEMA!
I WENT BY YOUR APARTMENT, BUT NO ONE WAS THERE.
I TOLD MY MOM WE COULDN'T LEAVE WITHOUT YOU.
GET IN.
WHERE ARE WE GOING?
I HAVE A SAFE HOUSE.
THERE'S ENOUGH FOOD AND WATER FOR A YEAR, AT LEAST.

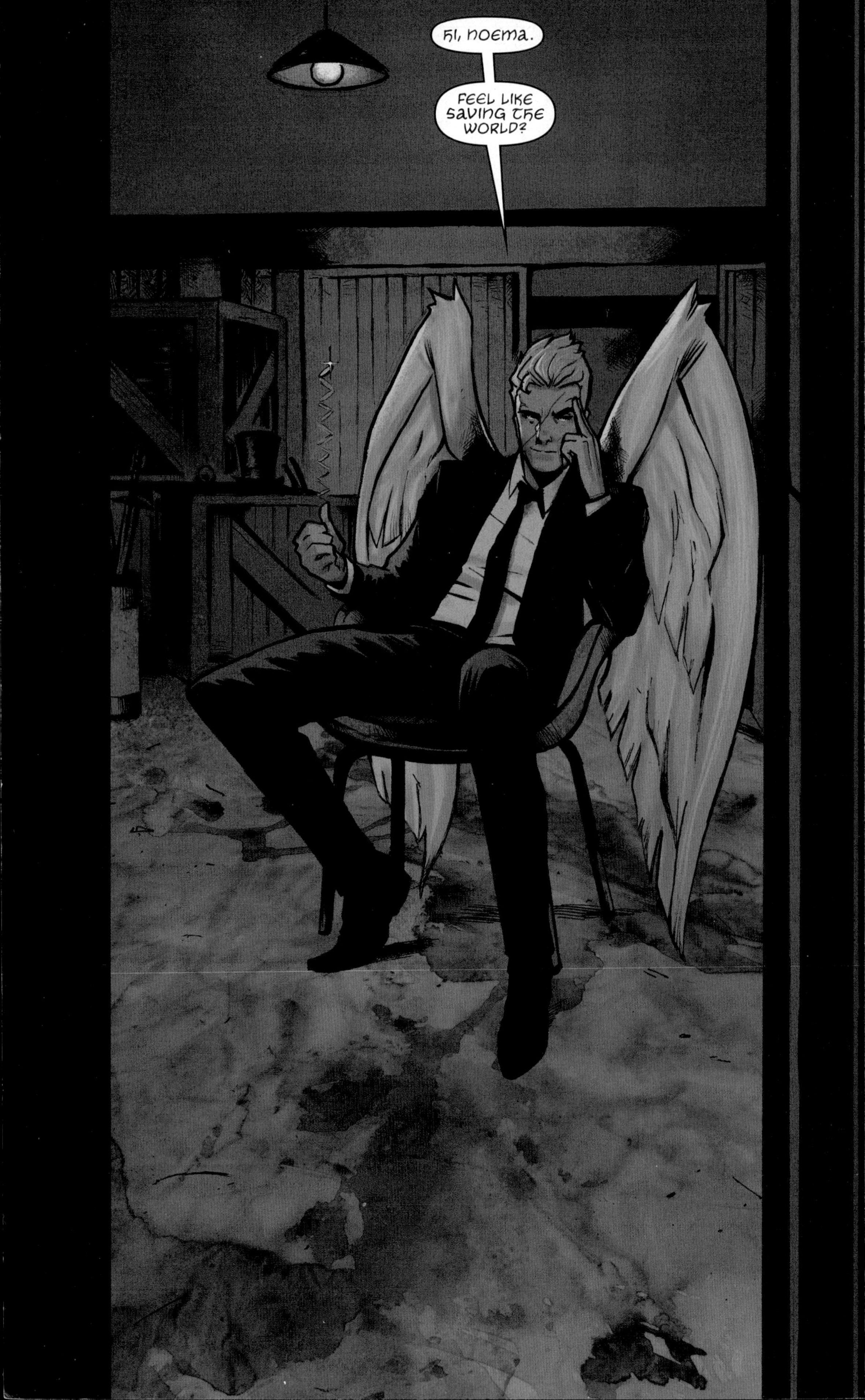
HI, NOEMA.
FEEL LIKE SAVING THE WORLD?

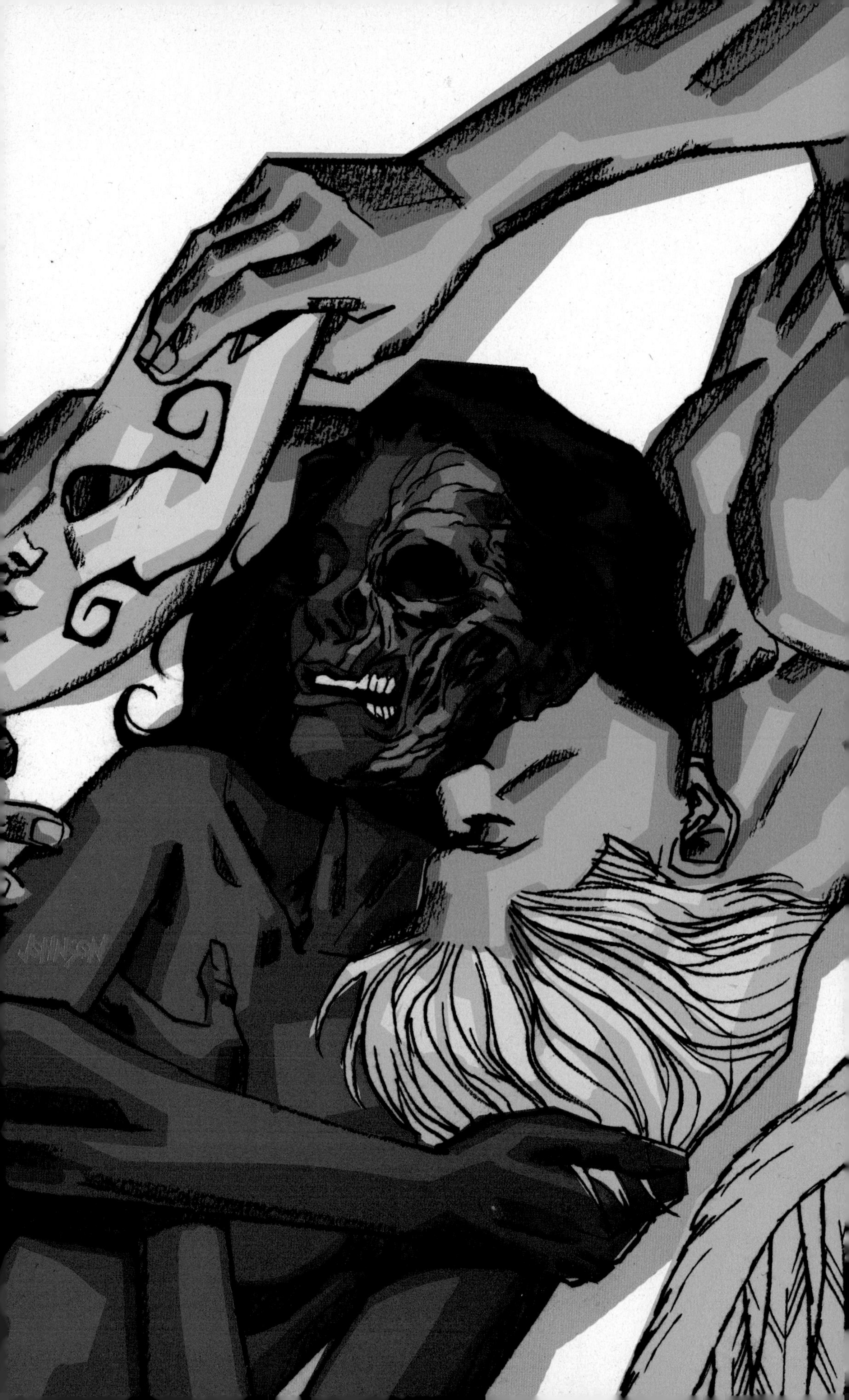

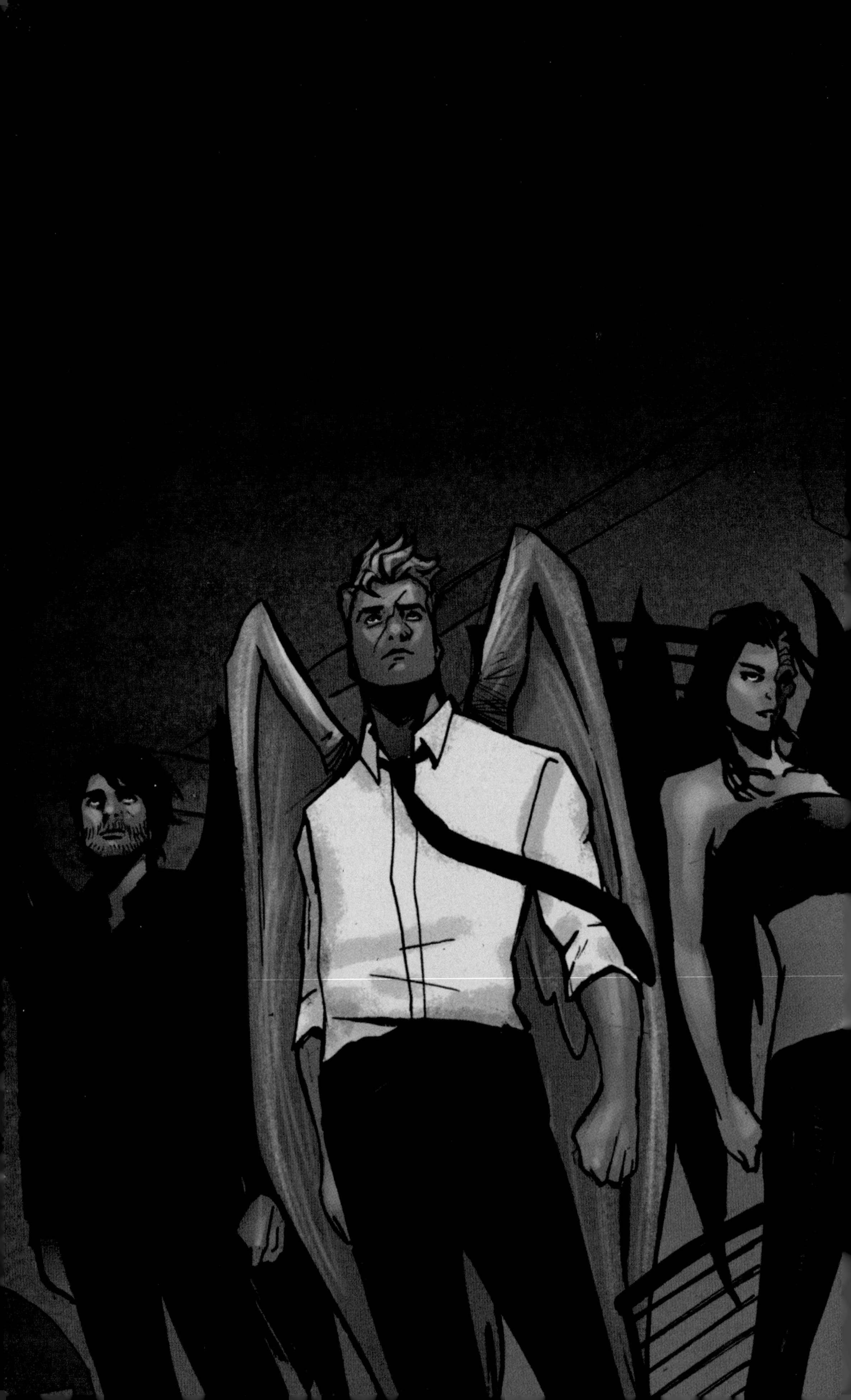

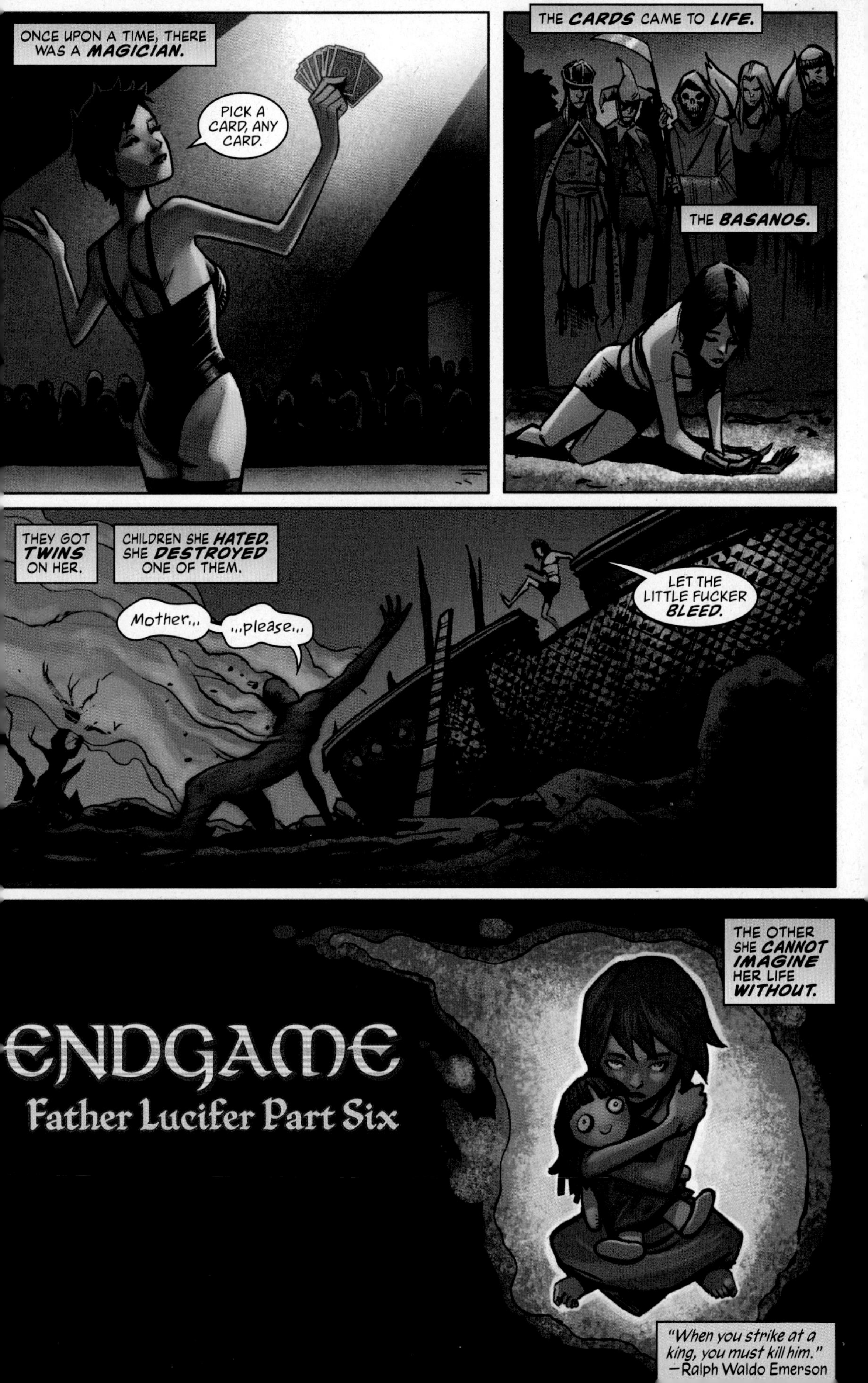

ONCE UPON A TIME, THERE WAS A MAGICIAN.
PICK A CARD, ANY CARD.
THE CARDS CAME TO LIFE.
THE BASANOS.
THEY GOT TWINS ON HER.
CHILDREN SHE HATED. SHE DESTROYED ONE OF THEM.
Mother...
...please...
LET THE LITTLE FUCKER BLEED.
THE OTHER SHE CANNOT IMAGINE HER LIFE WITHOUT.
ENDGAME
Father Lucifer Part Six
"When you strike at a king, you must kill him."
—Ralph Waldo Emerson

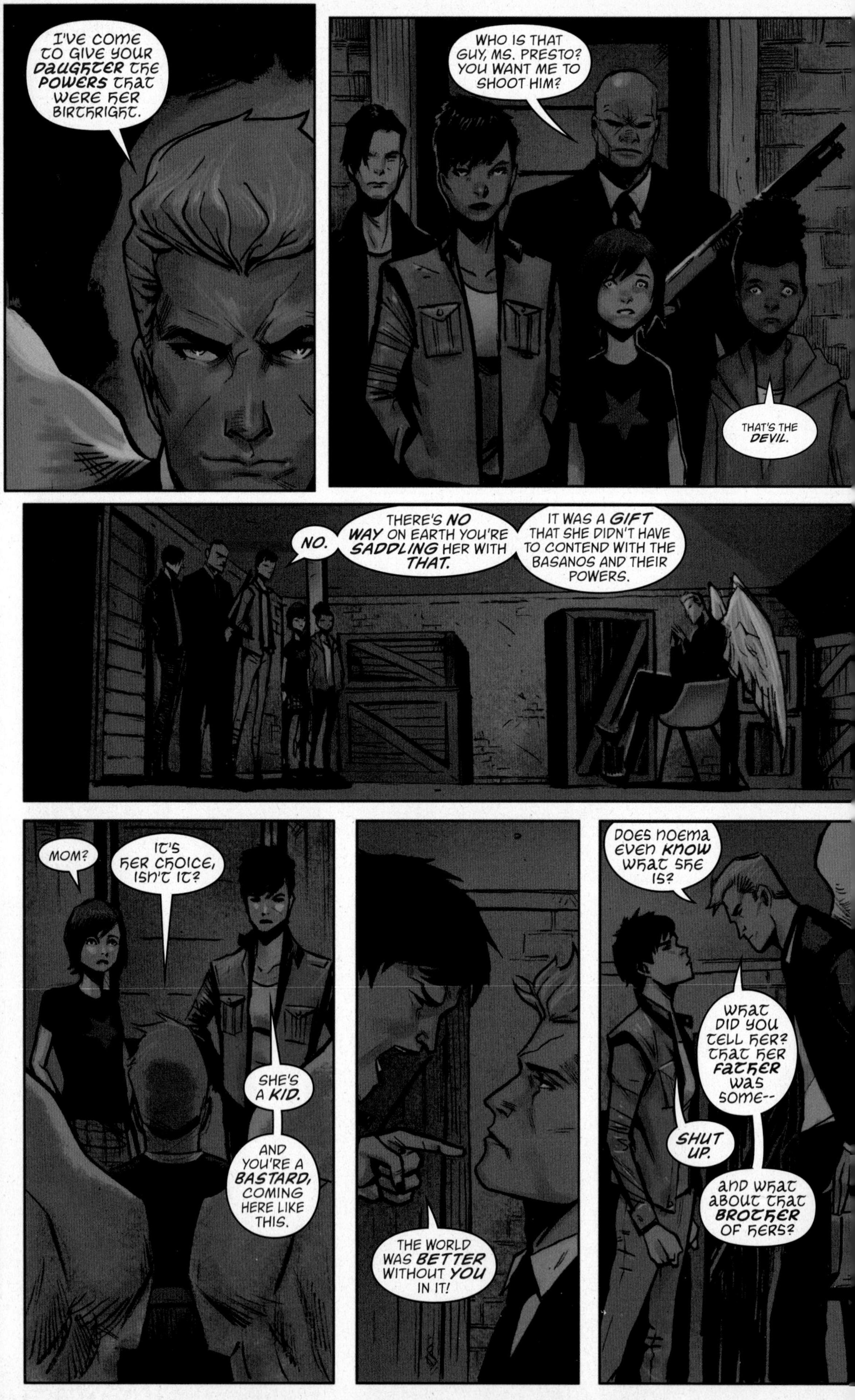
I'VE COME TO GIVE YOUR DAUGHTER THE POWERS THAT WERE HER BIRTHRIGHT.
WHO IS THAT GUY, MS. PRESTO? YOU WANT ME TO SHOOT HIM?
THAT'S THE DEVIL.
NO.
THERE'S NO WAY ON EARTH YOU'RE SADDLING HER WITH THAT.
IT WAS A GIFT THAT SHE DIDN'T HAVE TO CONTEND WITH THE BASANOS AND THEIR POWERS.
MOM?
IT'S HER CHOICE, ISN'T IT?
SHE'S A KID.
AND YOU'RE A BASTARD, COMING HERE LIKE THIS.
THE WORLD WAS BETTER WITHOUT YOU IN IT!
DOES NOEMA EVEN KNOW WHAT SHE IS?
WHAT DID YOU TELL HER? THAT HER FATHER WAS SOME--
SHUT UP.
AND WHAT ABOUT THAT BROTHER OF HERS?

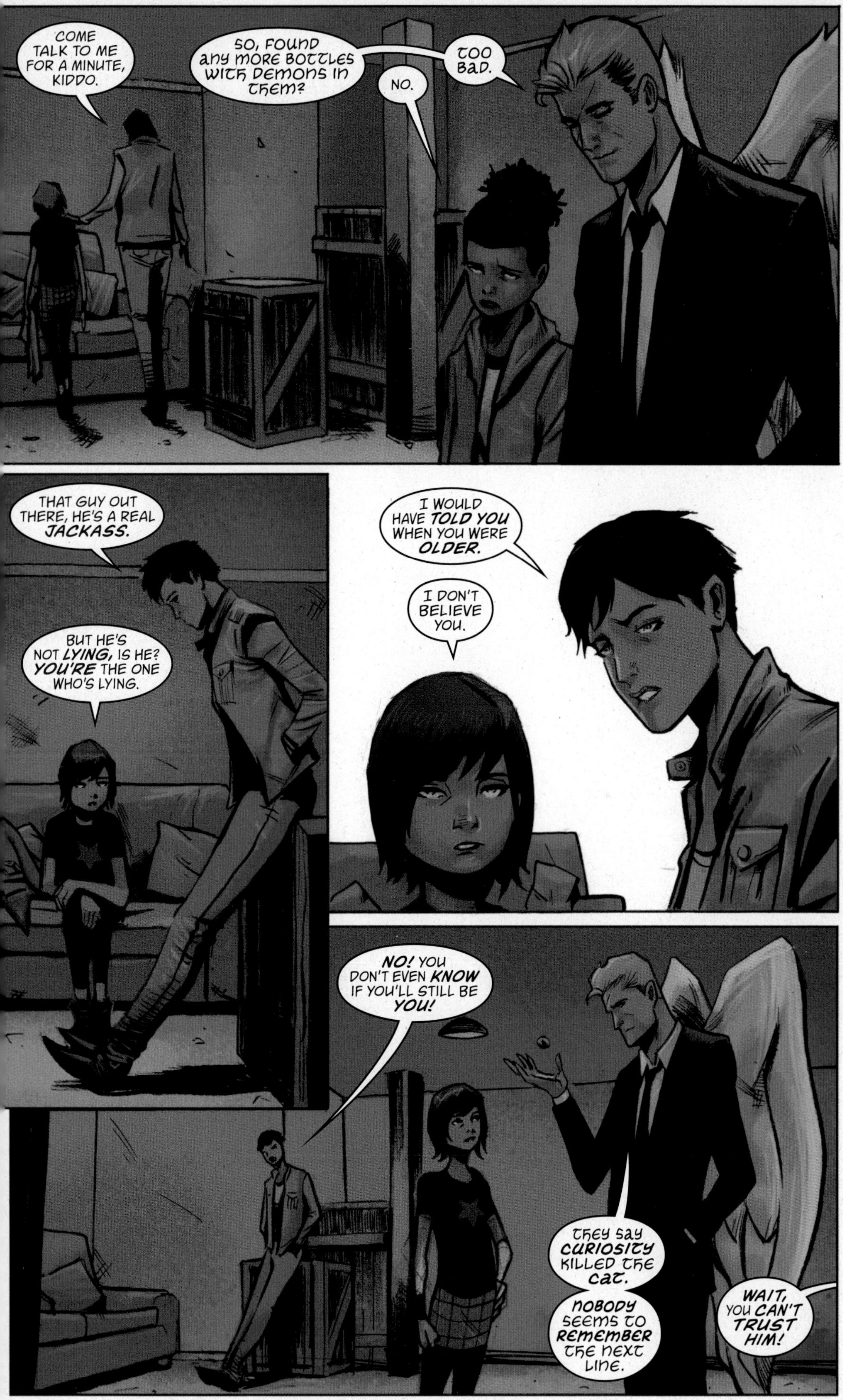
COME TALK TO ME FOR A MINUTE, KIDDO.
SO, FOUND ANY MORE BOTTLES WITH DEMONS IN THEM?
NO.
TOO BAD.
THAT GUY OUT THERE, HE'S A REAL JACKASS.
BUT HE'S NOT LYING, IS HE? YOU'RE THE ONE WHO'S LYING.
I WOULD HAVE TOLD YOU WHEN YOU WERE OLDER.
I DON'T BELIEVE YOU.
NO! YOU DON'T EVEN KNOW IF YOU'LL STILL BE YOU!
THEY SAY CURIOSITY KILLED THE CAT.
NOBODY SEEMS TO REMEMBER THE NEXT LINE.
WAIT, YOU CAN'T TRUST HIM!

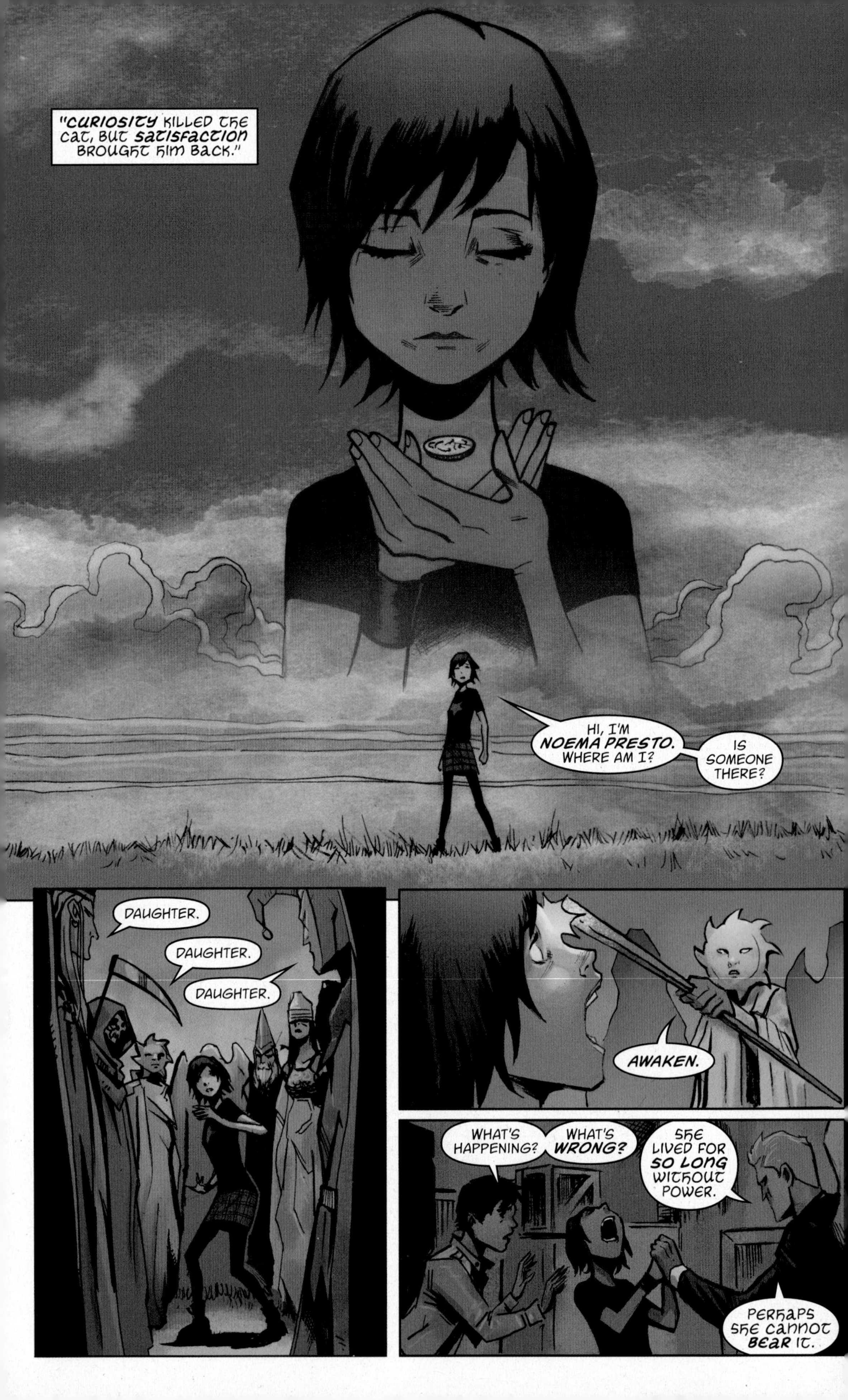
"CURIOSITY KILLED THE CAT, BUT SATISFACTION BROUGHT HIM BACK."
HI, I'M NOEMA PRESTO. WHERE AM I?
IS SOMEONE THERE?
DAUGHTER.
DAUGHTER.
DAUGHTER.
AWAKEN.
WHAT'S HAPPENING?
WHAT'S WRONG?
SHE LIVED FOR SO LONG WITHOUT POWER.
PERHAPS SHE CANNOT BEAR IT.

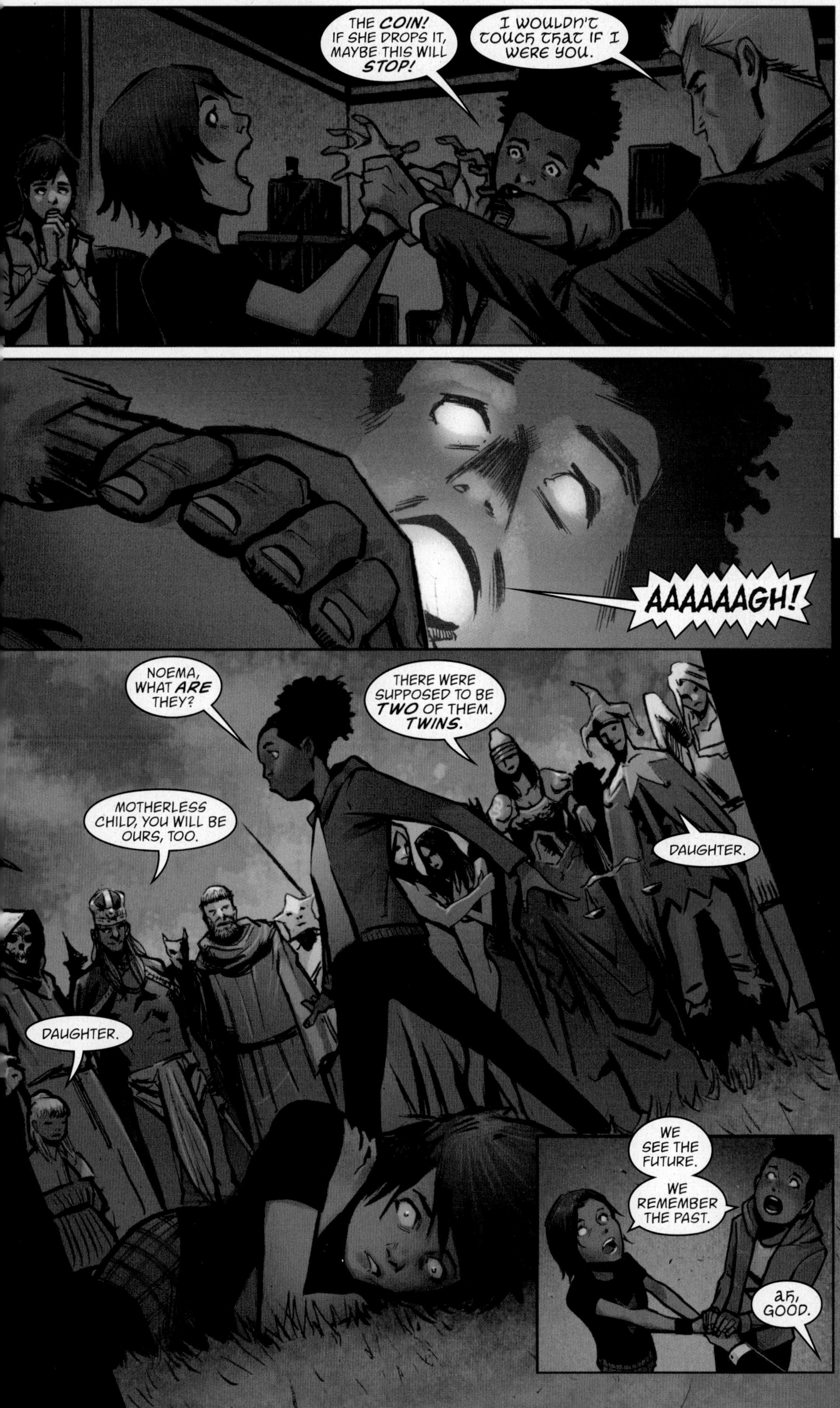
THE COIN! IF SHE DROPS IT, MAYBE THIS WILL STOP!
I WOULDN'T TOUCH THAT IF I WERE YOU.
AAAAAAGH!
NOEMA, WHAT ARE THEY?
THERE WERE SUPPOSED TO BE TWO OF THEM. TWINS.
MOTHERLESS CHILD, YOU WILL BE OURS, TOO.
DAUGHTER.
DAUGHTER.
WE SEE THE FUTURE.
WE REMEMBER THE PAST.
AH, GOOD.

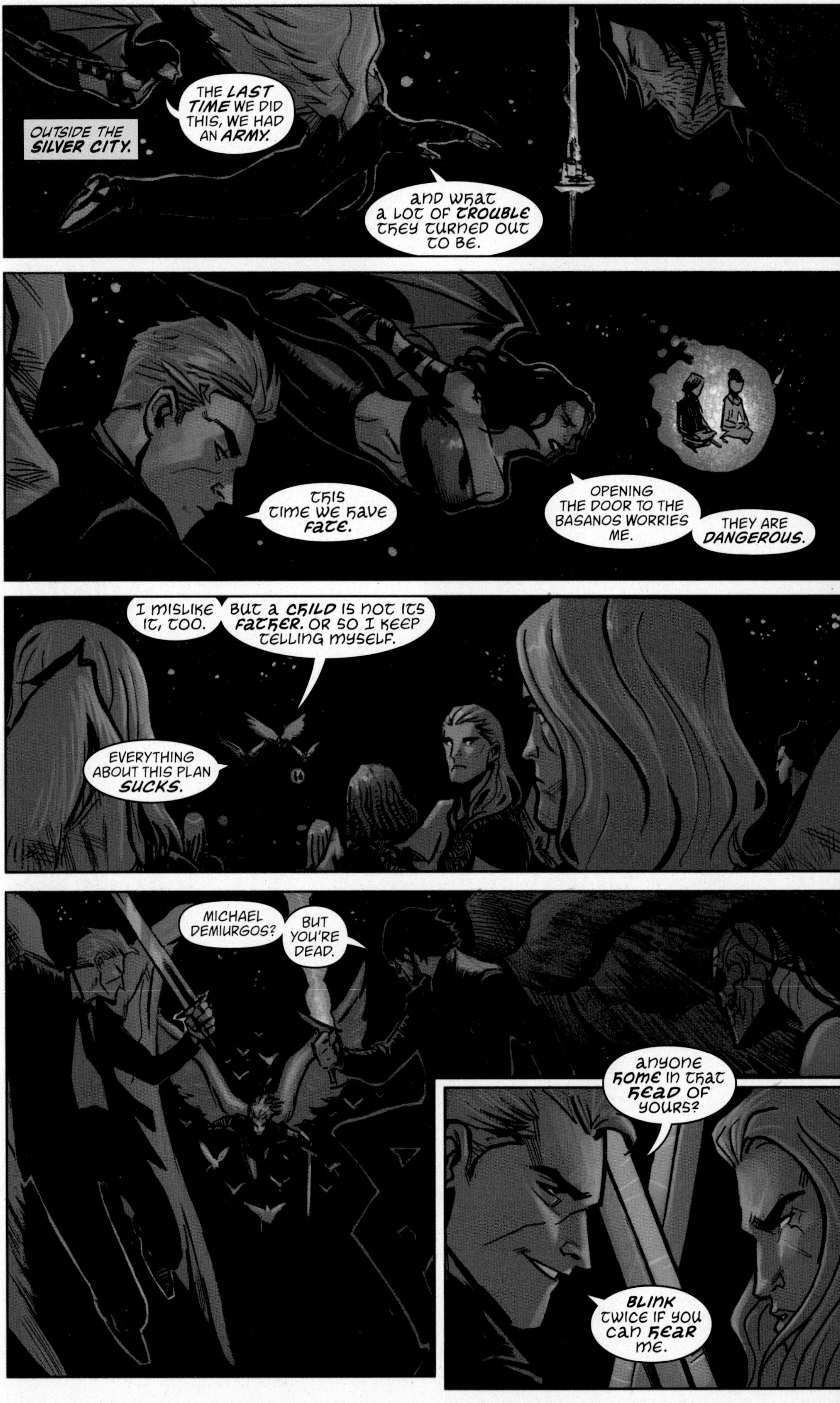

OUTSIDE THE SILVER CITY.
THE LAST TIME WE DID THIS, WE HAD AN ARMY.
AND WHAT A LOT OF TROUBLE THEY TURNED OUT TO BE.
THIS TIME WE HAVE FATE.
OPENING THE DOOR TO THE BASANOS WORRIES ME.
THEY ARE DANGEROUS.
I MISLIKE IT, TOO.
BUT A CHILD IS NOT ITS FATHER. OR SO I KEEP TELLING MYSELF.
EVERYTHING ABOUT THIS PLAN SUCKS.
MICHAEL DEMIURGOS?
BUT YOU'RE DEAD.
ANYONE HOME IN THAT HEAD OF YOURS?
BLINK TWICE IF YOU CAN HEAR ME.

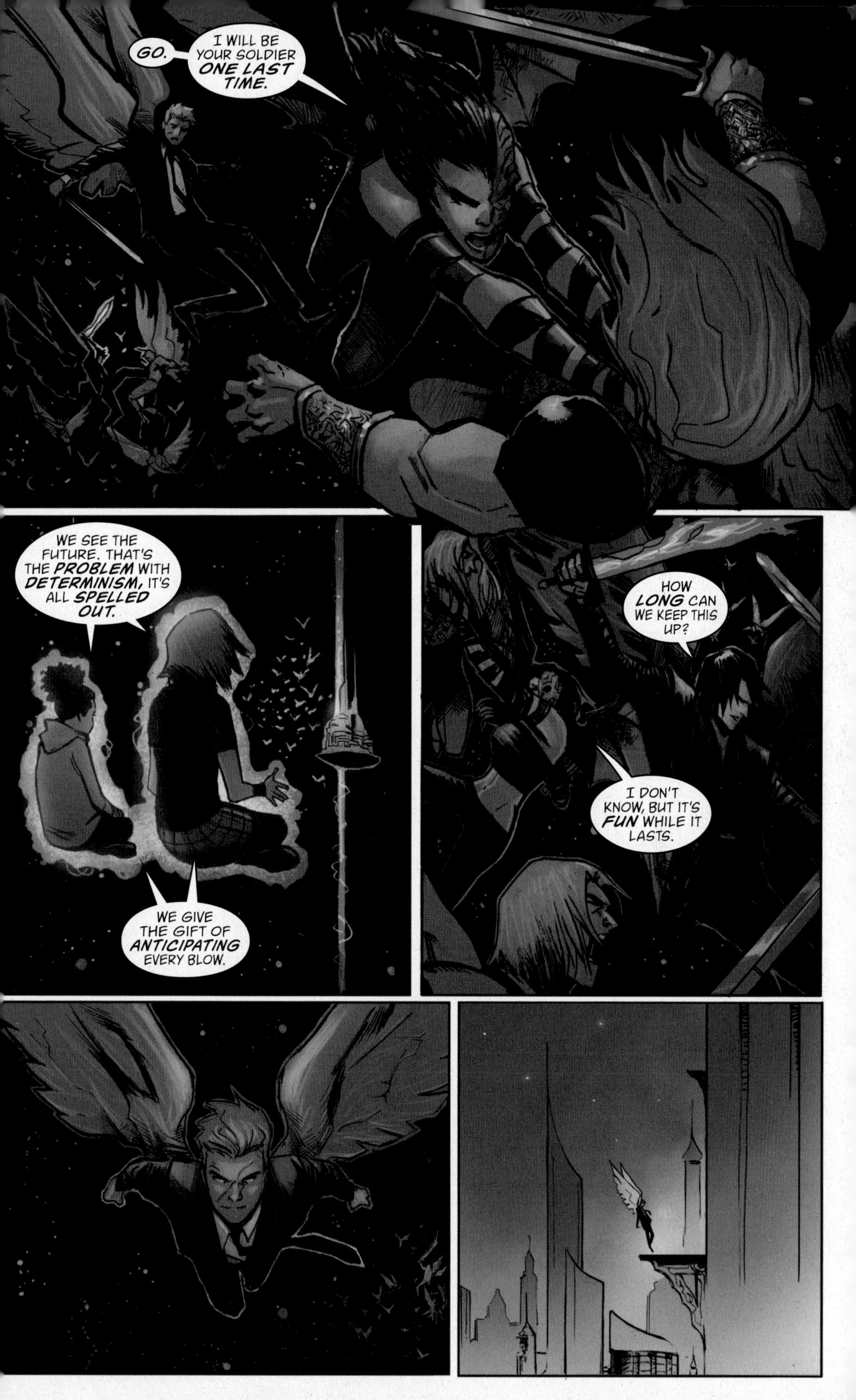
GO.
I WILL BE YOUR SOLDIER ONE LAST TIME.
WE SEE THE FUTURE. THAT'S THE PROBLEM WITH DETERMINISM, IT'S ALL SPELLED OUT.
WE GIVE THE GIFT OF ANTICIPATING EVERY BLOW.
HOW LONG CAN WE KEEP THIS UP?
I DON'T KNOW, BUT IT'S FUN WHILE IT LASTS.

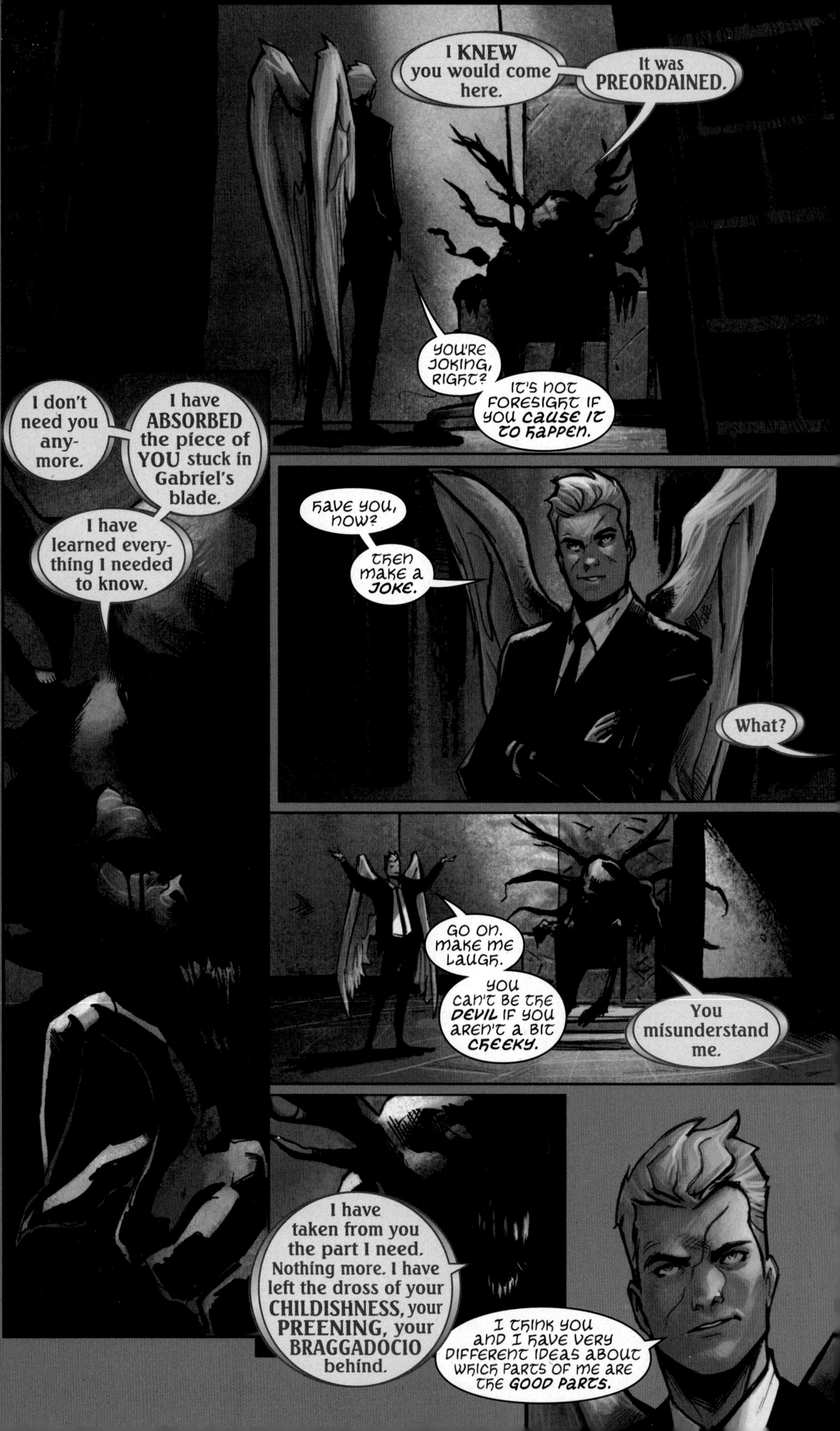
I KNEW you would come here.
It was PREORDAINED.
YOU'RE JOKING, RIGHT?
IT'S NOT FORESIGHT IF YOU CAUSE IT TO HAPPEN.
I don't need you any-more.
I have ABSORBED the piece of YOU stuck in Gabriel's blade.
I have learned every-thing I needed to know.
HAVE YOU, NOW?
THEN MAKE A JOKE.
What?
GO ON. MAKE ME LAUGH.
YOU CAN'T BE THE DEVIL IF YOU AREN'T A BIT CHEEKY.
You misunderstand me.
I have taken from you the part I need. Nothing more. I have left the dross of your CHILDISHNESS, your PREENING, your BRAGGADOCIO behind.
I THINK YOU AND I HAVE VERY DIFFERENT IDEAS ABOUT WHICH PARTS OF ME ARE THE GOOD PARTS.

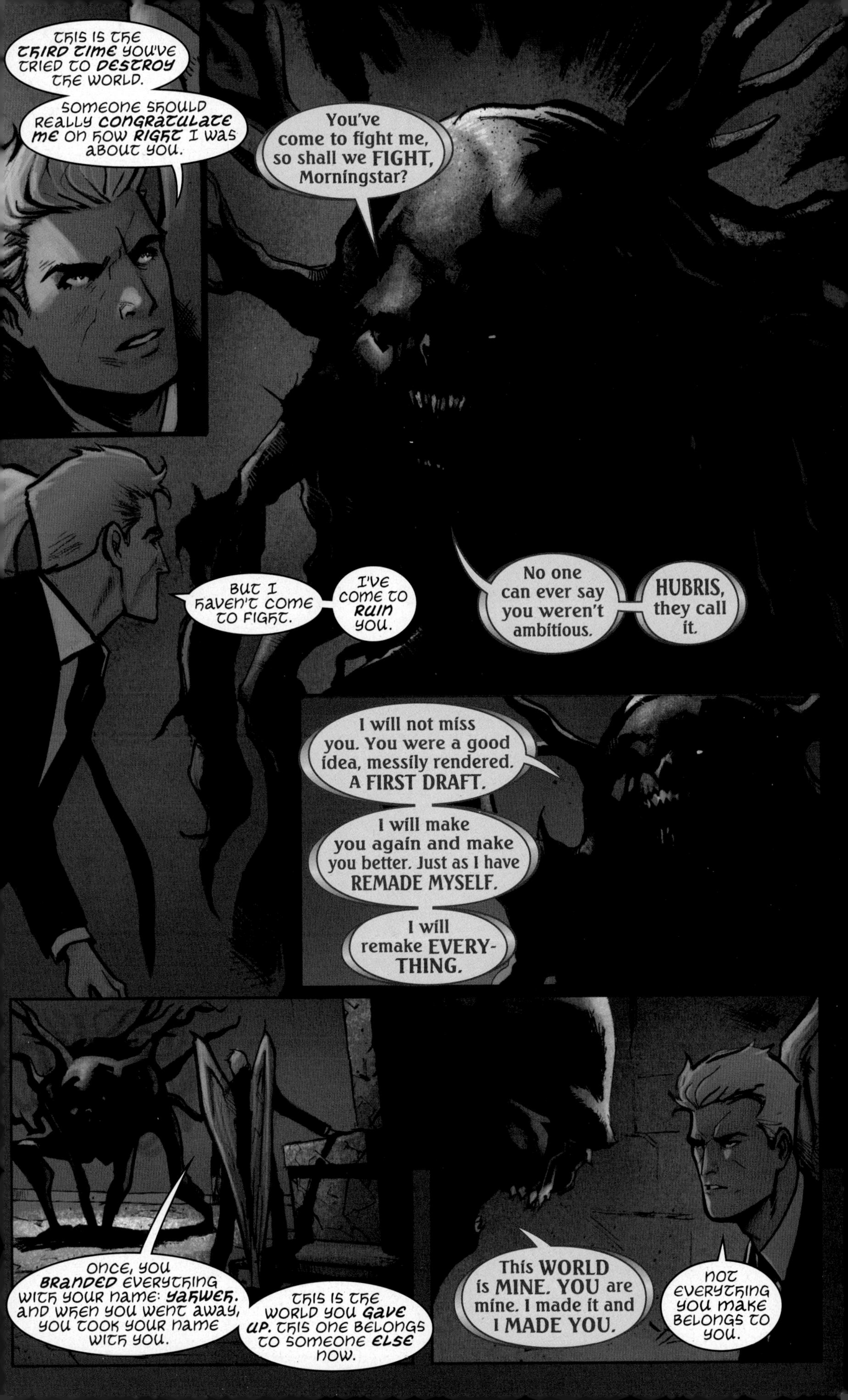
THIS IS THE THIRD TIME YOU'VE TRIED TO DESTROY THE WORLD.
SOMEONE SHOULD REALLY CONGRATULATE ME ON HOW RIGHT I WAS ABOUT YOU.
You've come to fight me, so shall we FIGHT, Morningstar?
BUT I HAVEN'T COME TO FIGHT.
I'VE COME TO RUIN YOU.
No one can ever say you weren't ambitious.
HUBRIS, they call it.
I will not miss you. You were a good idea, messily rendered. A FIRST DRAFT.
I will make you again and make you better. Just as I have REMADE MYSELF.
I will remake EVERY-THING.
ONCE, YOU BRANDED EVERYTHING WITH YOUR NAME: YAHWEH. AND WHEN YOU WENT AWAY, YOU TOOK YOUR NAME WITH YOU.
THIS IS THE WORLD YOU GAVE UP. THIS ONE BELONGS TO SOMEONE ELSE NOW.
This WORLD is MINE. YOU are mine. I made it and I MADE YOU.
NOT EVERYTHING YOU MAKE BELONGS TO YOU.

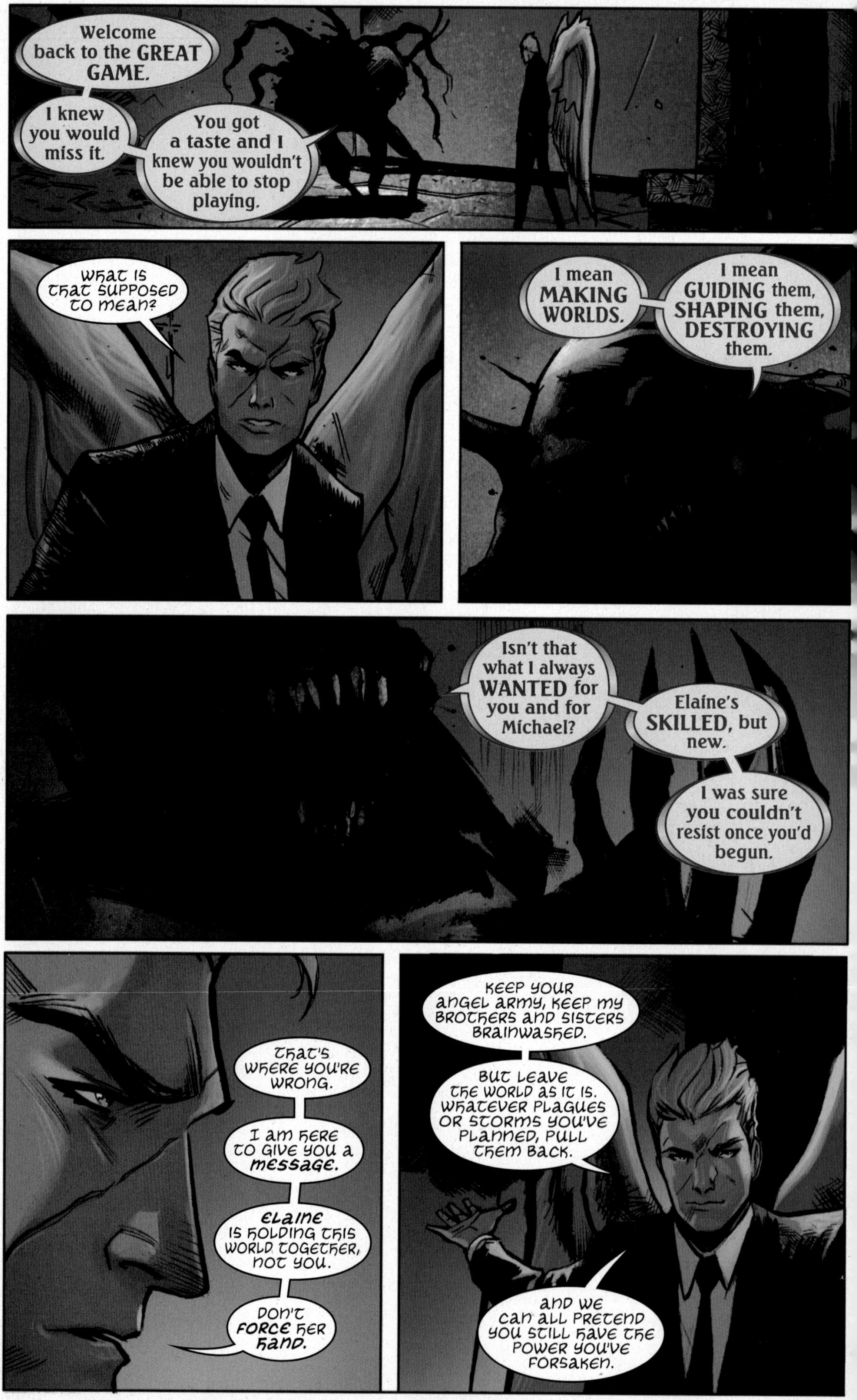
Welcome back to the GREAT GAME.
I knew you would miss it.
You got a taste and I knew you wouldn't be able to stop playing.
WHAT IS THAT SUPPOSED TO MEAN?
I mean MAKING WORLDS.
I mean GUIDING them, SHAPING them, DESTROYING them.
Isn't that what I always WANTED for you and for Michael?
Elaine's SKILLED, but new.
I was sure you couldn't resist once you'd begun.
THAT'S WHERE YOU'RE WRONG.
I AM HERE TO GIVE YOU A MESSAGE.
ELAINE IS HOLDING THIS WORLD TOGETHER, NOT YOU.
DON'T FORCE HER HAND.
KEEP YOUR ANGEL ARMY, KEEP MY BROTHERS AND SISTERS BRAINWASHED.
BUT LEAVE THE WORLD AS IT IS. WHATEVER PLAGUES OR STORMS YOU'VE PLANNED, PULL THEM BACK.
AND WE CAN ALL PRETEND YOU STILL HAVE THE POWER YOU'VE FORSAKEN.

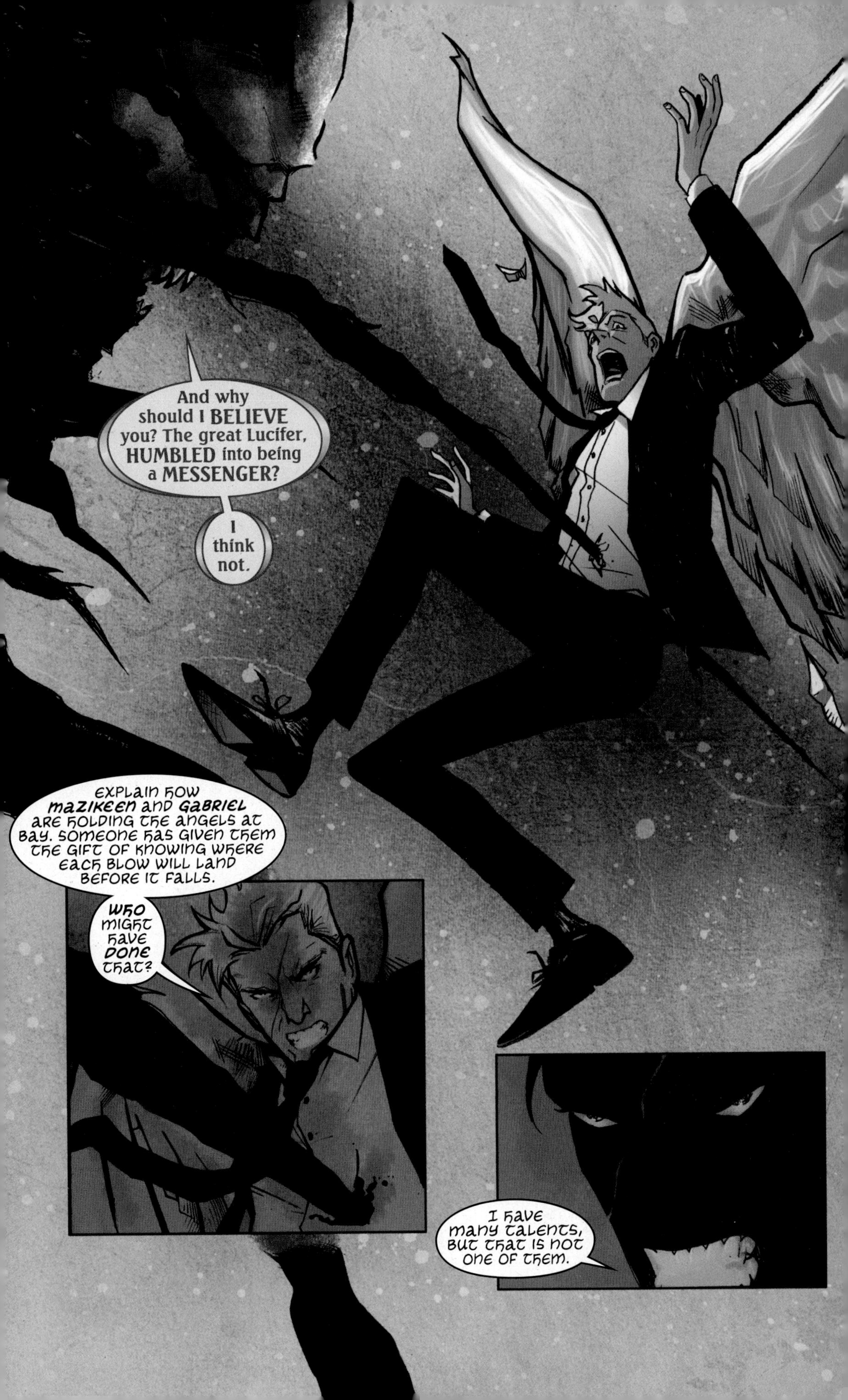
And why should I BELIEVE you? The great Lucifer, HUMBLED into being a MESSENGER?
I think not.
EXPLAIN HOW MAZIKEEN AND GABRIEL ARE HOLDING THE ANGELS AT BAY. SOMEONE HAS GIVEN THEM THE GIFT OF KNOWING WHERE EACH BLOW WILL LAND BEFORE IT FALLS.
WHO MIGHT HAVE DONE THAT?
I HAVE MANY TALENTS, BUT THAT IS NOT ONE OF THEM.

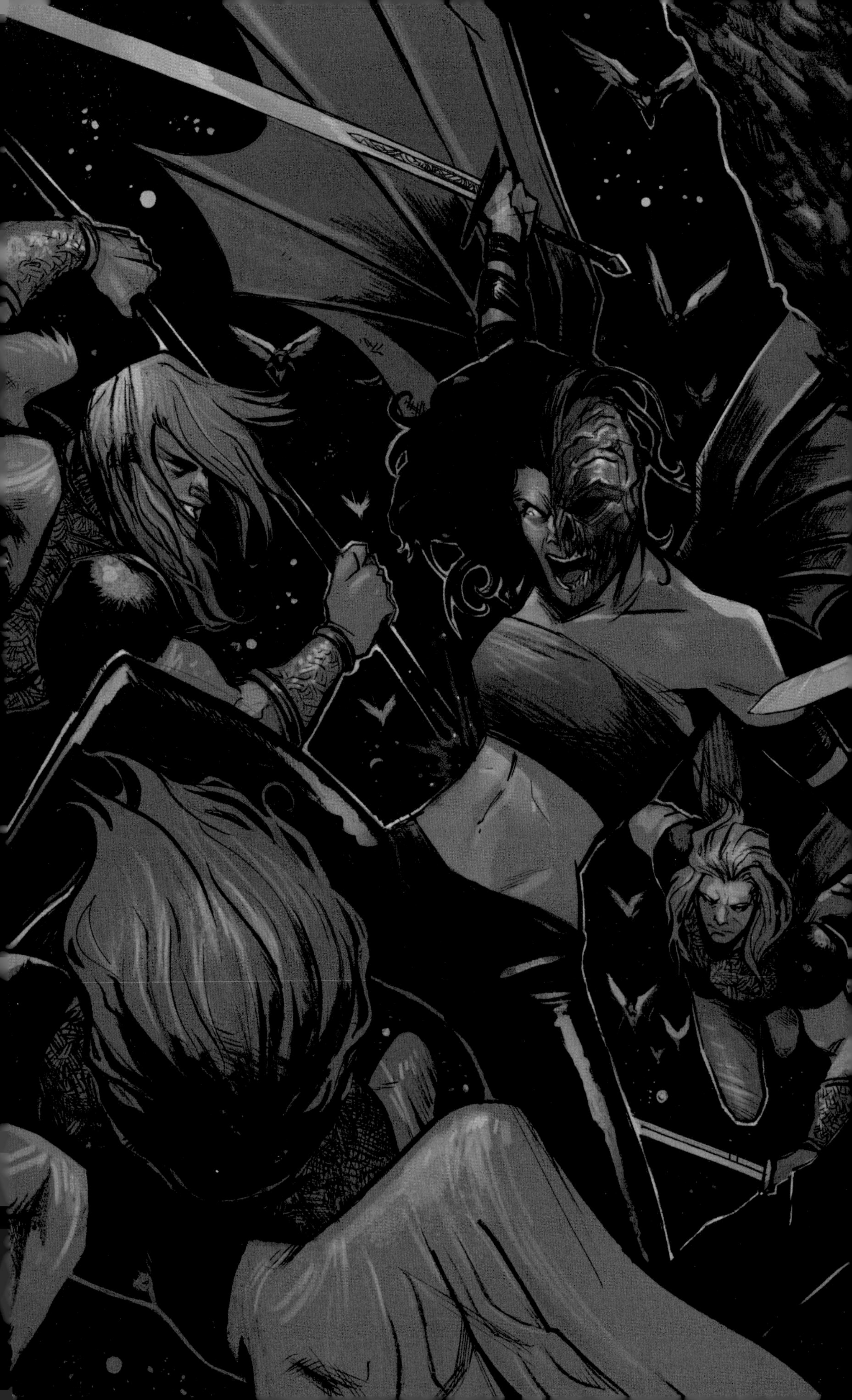

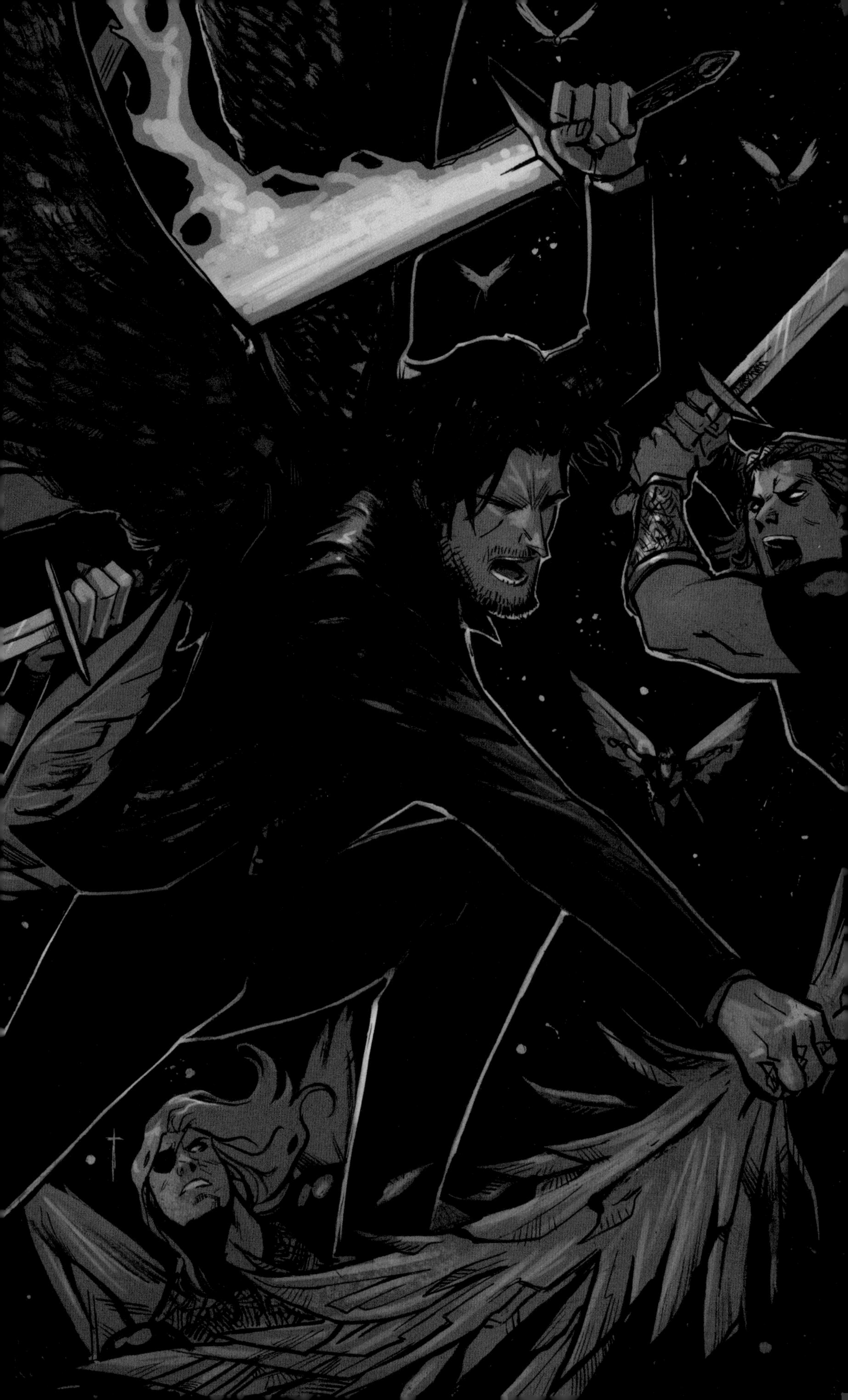

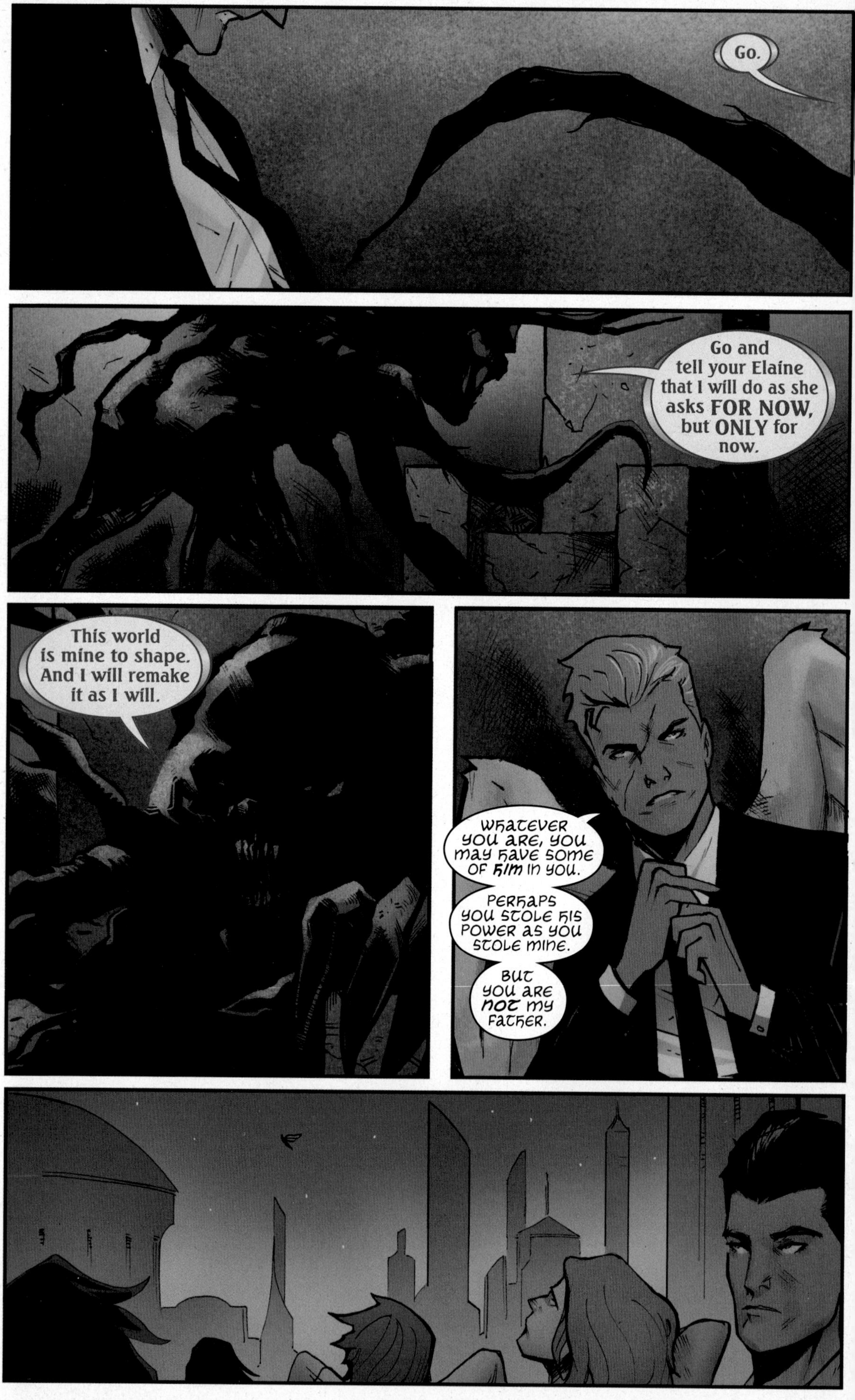
Go.
Go and tell your Elaine that I will do as she asks FOR NOW, but ONLY for now.
This world is mine to shape. And I will remake it as I will.
WHATEVER YOU ARE, YOU MAY HAVE SOME OF HIM IN YOU.
PERHAPS YOU STOLE HIS POWER AS YOU STOLE MINE.
BUT YOU ARE NOT MY FATHER.

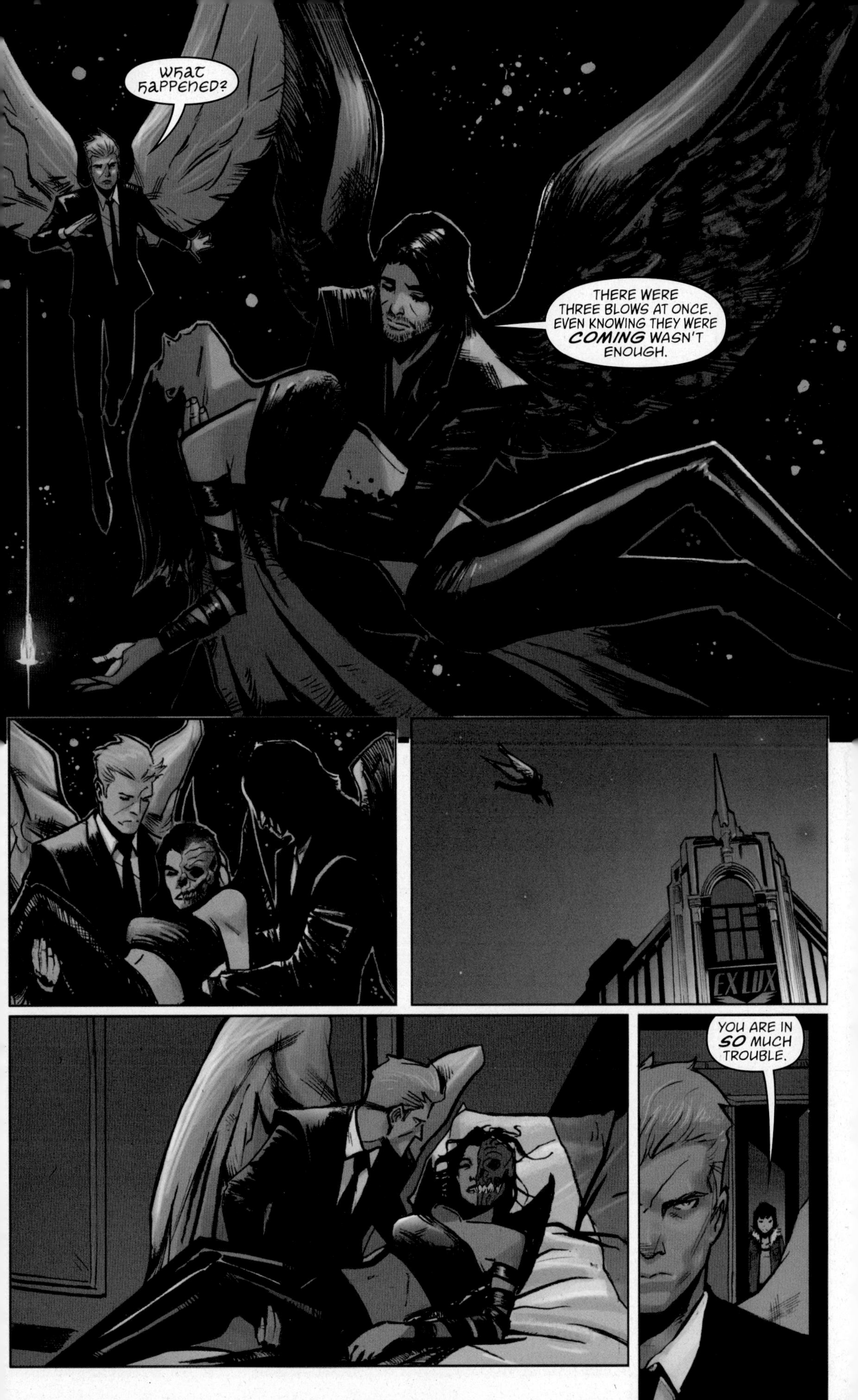
WHAT HAPPENED?
THERE WERE THREE BLOWS AT ONCE. EVEN KNOWING THEY WERE COMING WASN'T ENOUGH.
EX LUX
YOU ARE IN SO MUCH TROUBLE.

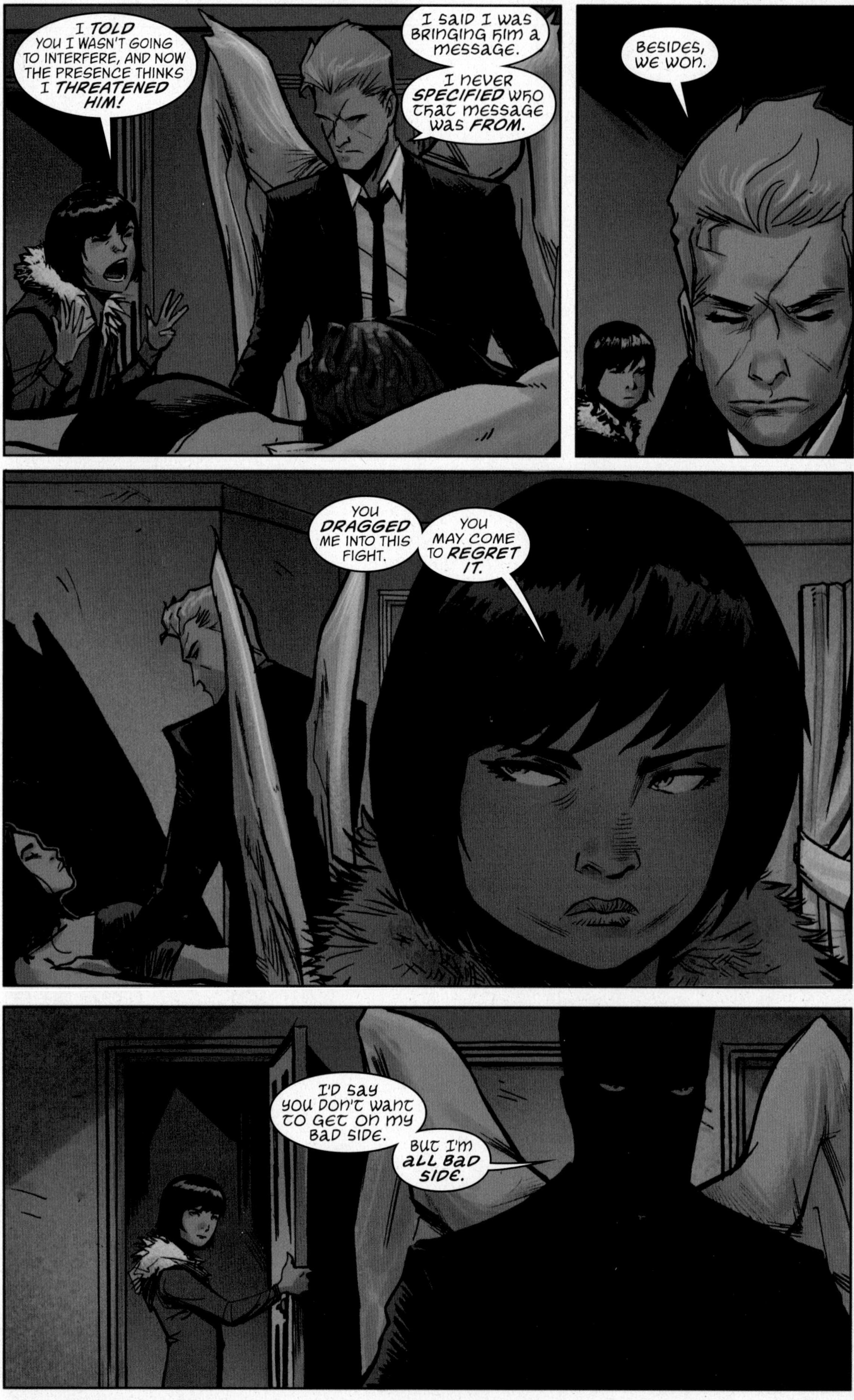
I TOLD YOU I WASN'T GOING TO INTERFERE, AND NOW THE PRESENCE THINKS I THREATENED HIM!
I SAID I WAS BRINGING HIM A MESSAGE.
I NEVER SPECIFIED WHO THAT MESSAGE WAS FROM.
BESIDES, WE WON.
YOU DRAGGED ME INTO THIS FIGHT.
YOU MAY COME TO REGRET IT.
I'D SAY YOU DON'T WANT TO GET ON MY BAD SIDE.
BUT I'M ALL BAD SIDE.

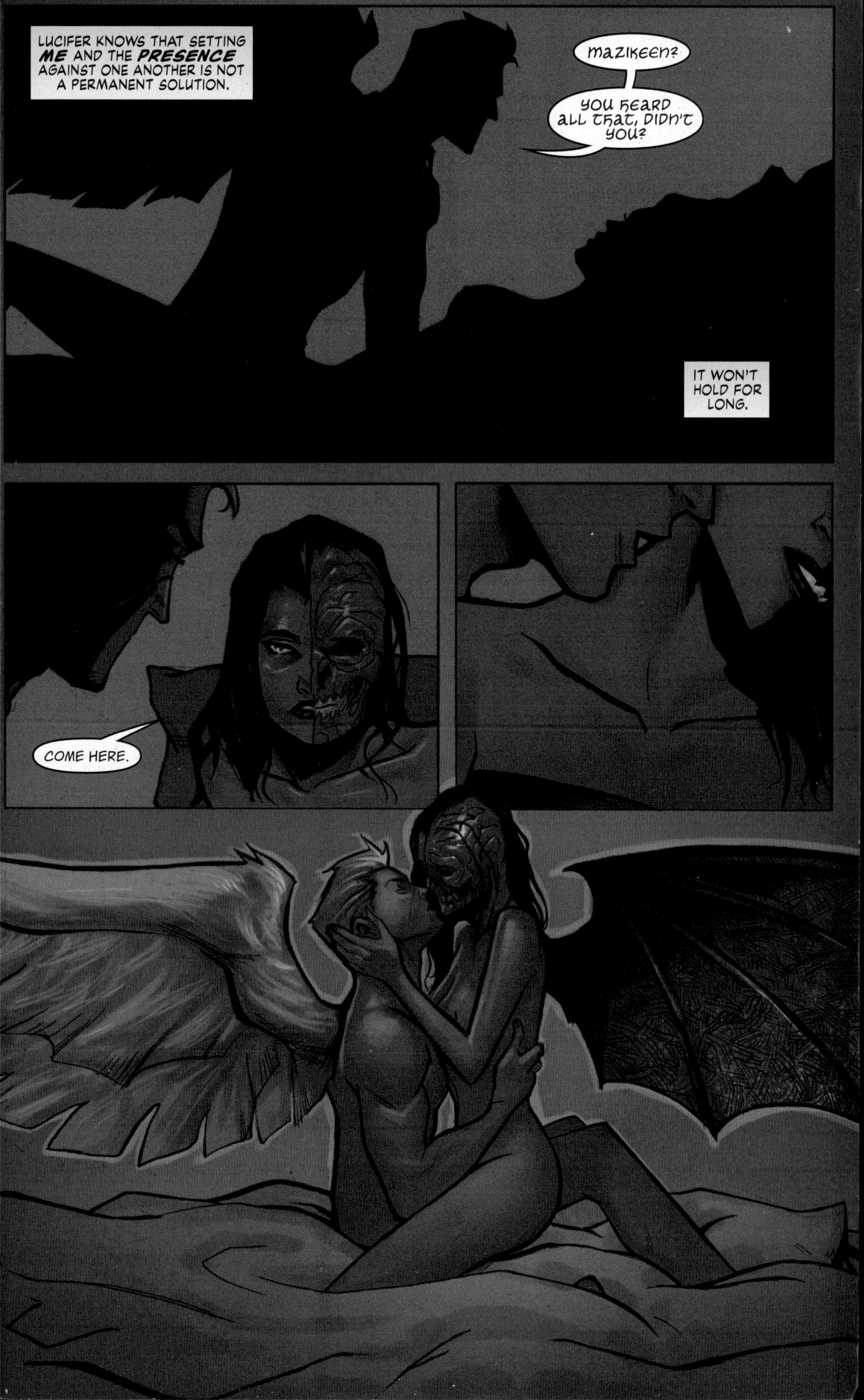
LUCIFER KNOWS THAT SETTING ME AND THE PRESENCE AGAINST ONE ANOTHER IS NOT A PERMANENT SOLUTION.
MAZIKEEN?
YOU HEARD ALL THAT, DIDN'T YOU?
IT WON'T HOLD FOR LONG.
COME HERE.

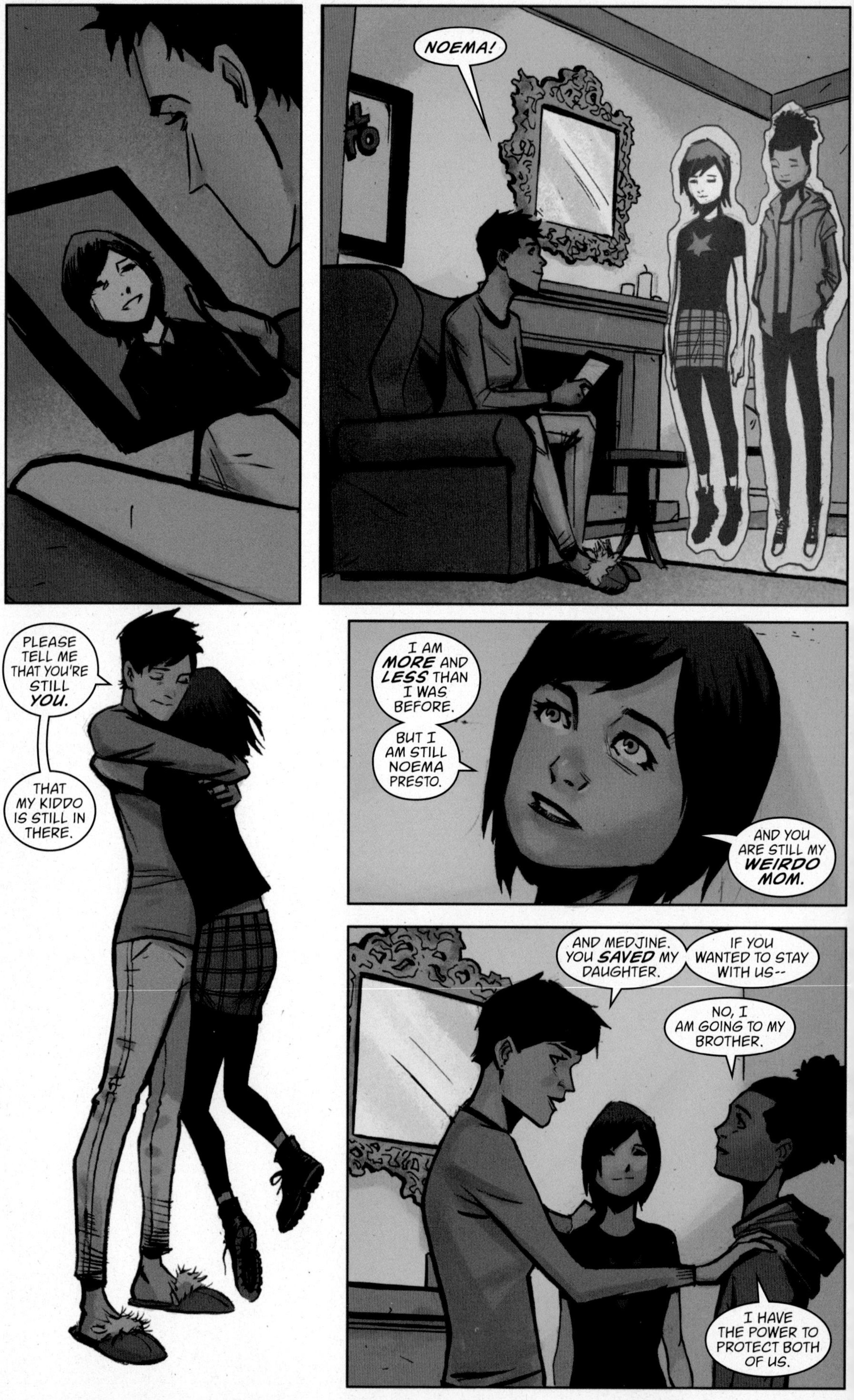
NOEMA!
PLEASE TELL ME THAT YOU'RE STILL YOU.
THAT MY KIDDO IS STILL IN THERE.
I AM MORE AND LESS THAN I WAS BEFORE.
BUT I AM STILL NOEMA PRESTO.
AND YOU ARE STILL MY WEIRDO MOM.
AND MEDJINE. YOU SAVED MY DAUGHTER.
IF YOU WANTED TO STAY WITH US--
NO, I AM GOING TO MY BROTHER.
I HAVE THE POWER TO PROTECT BOTH OF US.

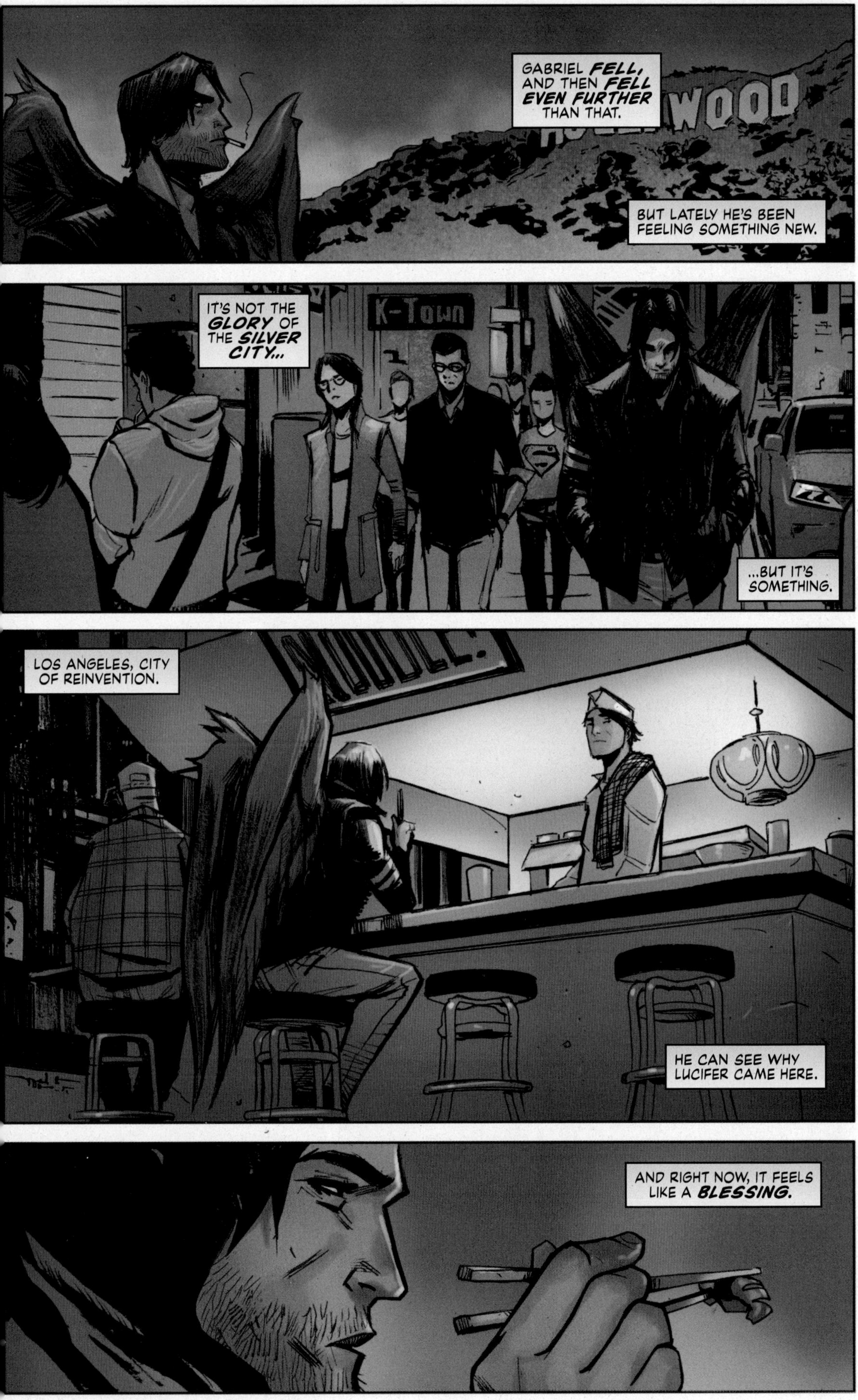
GABRIEL **FELL,** AND THEN **FELL EVEN FURTHER** THAN THAT.
WOOD
BUT LATELY HE'S BEEN FEELING SOMETHING NEW.
IT'S NOT THE **GLORY** OF THE **SILVER CITY...**
K-Town
...BUT IT'S SOMETHING.
LOS ANGELES, CITY OF REINVENTION.
HE CAN SEE WHY LUCIFER CAME HERE.
AND RIGHT NOW, IT FEELS LIKE A **BLESSING.**

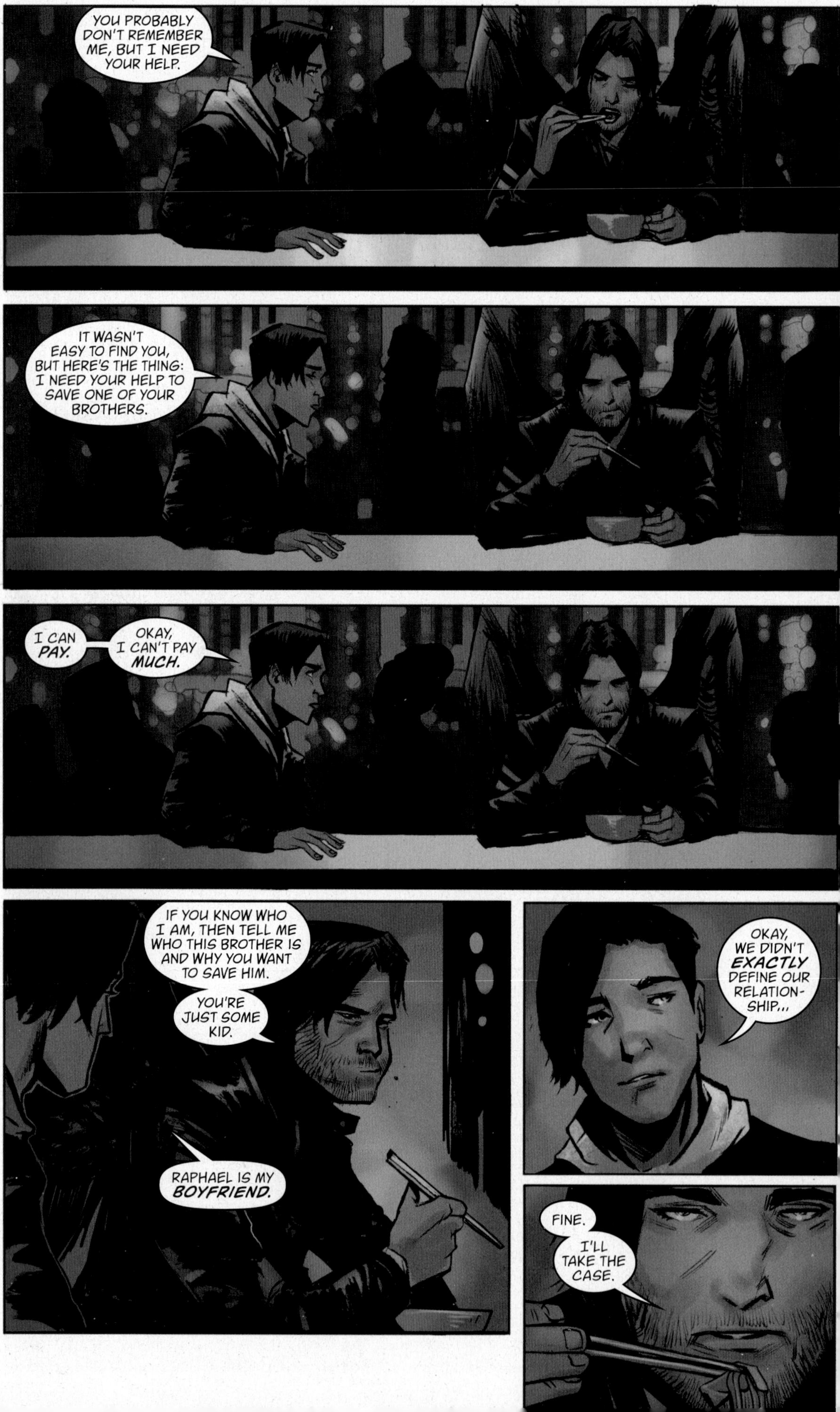
YOU PROBABLY DON'T REMEMBER ME, BUT I NEED YOUR HELP.
IT WASN'T EASY TO FIND YOU, BUT HERE'S THE THING: I NEED YOUR HELP TO SAVE ONE OF YOUR BROTHERS.
I CAN *PAY.*
OKAY, I CAN'T PAY *MUCH.*
IF YOU KNOW WHO I AM, THEN TELL ME WHO THIS BROTHER IS AND WHY YOU WANT TO SAVE HIM.
YOU'RE JUST SOME KID.
RAPHAEL IS MY *BOYFRIEND.*
OKAY, WE DIDN'T *EXACTLY* DEFINE OUR RELATION-SHIP...
FINE.
I'LL TAKE THE CASE.

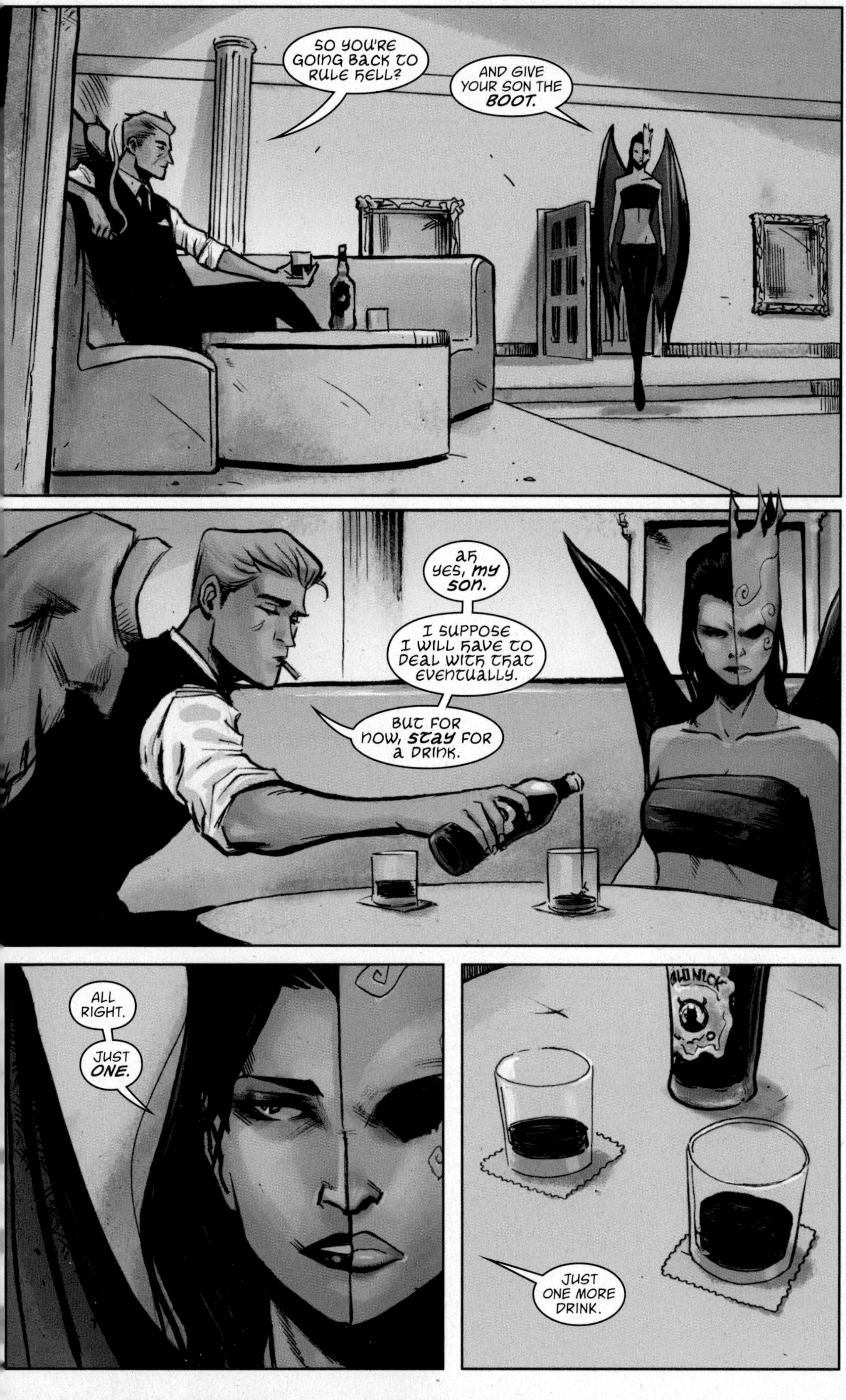
SO YOU'RE GOING BACK TO RULE HELL?
AND GIVE YOUR SON THE BOOT.
AH YES, MY SON.
I SUPPOSE I WILL HAVE TO DEAL WITH THAT EVENTUALLY.
BUT FOR NOW, STAY FOR A DRINK.
ALL RIGHT.
JUST ONE.
JUST ONE MORE DRINK.

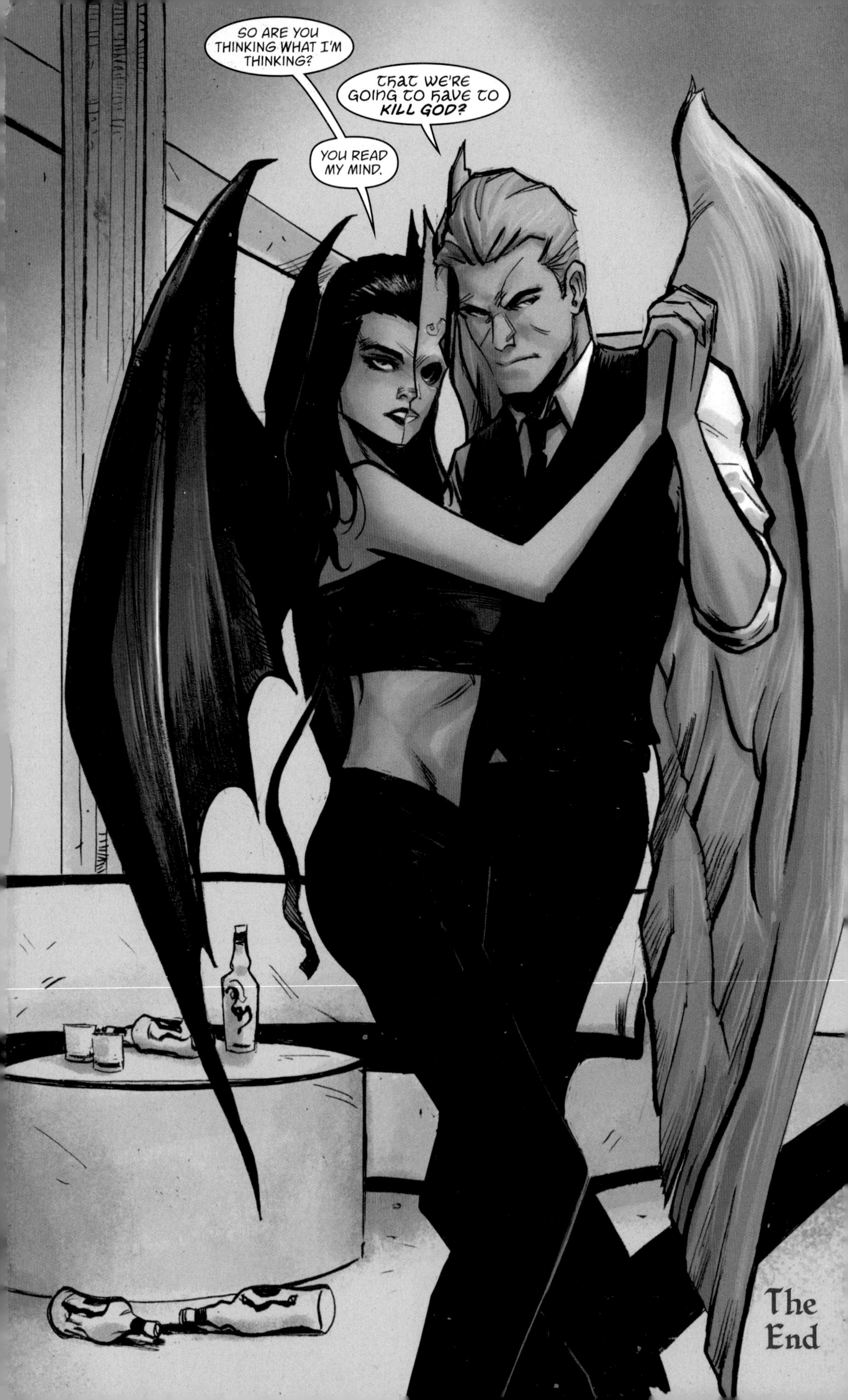
SO ARE YOU THINKING WHAT I'M THINKING?
THAT WE'RE GOING TO HAVE TO KILL GOD?
YOU READ MY MIND.
The End